Circular Economy

Circular Economy

Gabriel Cox
Paisley Kennedy

Kruger Brentt
Publishers
2026

Kruger Brentt Publishers UK. LTD.
Company Number 9728962

Regd. Office: 68 St Margarets Road, Edgware, Middlesex HA8 9UU

ISBN: 978-1-78715-606-7

For information on all our publications visit our website at http://krugerbrentt.com/

Preface

Circular Economy explores a transformative approach to economic development that prioritizes sustainability, resource efficiency, and the reduction of waste. Unlike the traditional linear economy, which follows a "take-make-dispose" model, the circular economy aims to design out waste, keep products and materials in use for as long as possible, and regenerate natural systems. This concept is increasingly recognized as a critical strategy for addressing global challenges such as climate change, resource depletion, and environmental degradation.

This book is intended for students, researchers, policymakers, and professionals across business, engineering, environmental science, and public policy who wish to understand and implement circular economy principles. It provides both theoretical foundations and practical frameworks for applying circularity in diverse sectors, from manufacturing and energy to agriculture, textiles, and urban development.

The text begins by introducing the concepts and principles of the circular economy, including product life-cycle thinking, the 3Rs (reduce, reuse, recycle), and systems level design. It then explores key strategies for implementation, such as eco-design, sustainable supply chains, resource recovery, and business model innovation. Real-world examples and case studies are included to illustrate successful circular practices, challenges faced, and lessons learned from companies and communities worldwide.

Special attention is given to the role of policy, governance, and technological innovation in enabling circular systems. The book also addresses measurement and assessment tools for evaluating circularity, such as life cycle assessment, material flow analysis, and environmental impact metrics. Emerging trends, including the integration of digital technologies, circular cities, and circular business ecosystems, are discussed to provide readers with a forward-looking perspective.

We hope that Circular Economy will serve as a valuable resource for learners, practitioners, and decision-makers seeking to create sustainable, resilient, and economically viable systems. By fostering an understanding of circular principles and their applications, this book aims to inspire innovation, responsible consumption, and a more sustainable future for society and the planet.

Gabriel Cox

Paisley Kennedy

Contents

CHAPTER

Introduction to Circular Economy

1

1.1 DEFINING CIRCULAR ECONOMY

1.1.1 Principles of Circular Economy

The circular economy is an economic model designed to minimize waste and make the most of available resources. Unlike the traditional linear economy, which follows a "take, make, dispose" approach, the circular economy emphasizes sustainability by designing products and systems that reduce environmental impact and enhance efficiency. This model revolves around three main principles: designing out waste and pollution, keeping products and materials in use, and regenerating natural systems. By shifting to a circular economy, businesses and societies can reduce resource consumption, lower carbon emissions, and foster long-term sustainability.

The circular economy presents a transformative approach to economic growth and sustainability. By designing out waste, keeping products and materials in use, and regenerating natural systems, this model promotes a more efficient and environmentally responsible way of managing resources. Although challenges exist, the benefits of a circular economy far outweigh the obstacles, offering economic opportunities, environmental protection, and a path towards a more sustainable future. With continued innovation, consumer engagement, and policy support, the circular economy can become a mainstream economic model that ensures long-term prosperity for both people and the planet.

Designing out Waste and Pollution

One of the fundamental principles of the circular economy is eliminating waste and pollution from the outset. Conventional production methods often lead to significant waste generation, which harms the environment and depletes natural resources. In a circular system, products and processes are designed to reduce waste at every stage. This approach involves using sustainable materials, adopting efficient production techniques, and integrating waste reduction strategies into design principles. For example, manufacturers can utilize biodegradable materials or develop modular products that can be easily repaired and upgraded, thereby extending their lifespan and minimizing waste. By designing out waste and pollution, businesses can create more efficient supply chains and contribute to a cleaner environment.

Keeping Products and Materials in Use

Another key principle of the circular economy is maintaining the use of products and materials for as long as possible. Instead of discarding items after a single use, circular systems promote reuse, refurbishment, remanufacturing, and recycling. This strategy reduces the demand for virgin raw materials, conserves energy, and decreases environmental impact. Businesses can adopt product-as-a-service models, where consumers lease or rent products instead of owning them outright, ensuring that items remain in circulation for extended periods. Additionally, recycling and remanufacturing allow materials to be recovered and repurposed, preventing them from ending up in landfills. By fostering a culture of reuse and extending product lifecycles, industries can contribute to a more resource-efficient economy.

Regenerating Natural Systems

A circular economy aims not only to minimize environmental harm but also to restore and regenerate natural ecosystems. Conventional economic practices often lead to resource depletion and environmental degradation, whereas circular systems focus on replenishing what has been extracted. This principle emphasizes sustainable agriculture, responsible forestry, and the restoration of biodiversity. Practices such as composting organic waste, using regenerative farming techniques, and investing in renewable energy sources help rebuild natural capital. By ensuring that resources are used in a way that benefits the environment, circular economies create a sustainable balance between human activities and nature.

Shifting from Linear to Circular Business Models

For companies and industries to transition successfully to a circular economy, they must move away from traditional linear business models. This shift requires businesses to rethink product design, production processes, and supply chain management. Companies can adopt circular strategies such as leasing, sharing, and take-back programs, which encourage continuous product circulation. Businesses that integrate circular principles can reduce costs, improve resource efficiency, and enhance brand reputation by demonstrating a commitment to sustainability. Additionally, governments and policymakers play a crucial role in incentivizing circular practices through regulations, tax benefits, and funding initiatives that support sustainable development.

Innovation and Technological Advancements

Technological advancements play a critical role in the successful implementation of circular economy principles. Innovations such as artificial intelligence, blockchain, and the Internet of Things (IoT) enable better resource management, enhance supply chain transparency, and facilitate waste reduction. For example, smart sensors can track product lifecycles, ensuring timely maintenance and refurbishment. Blockchain technology can provide traceability, allowing businesses to verify sustainable sourcing and ethical production. Additionally, advances in material science have led to the development of biodegradable packaging and recyclable components, reducing environmental impact. By leveraging technology, industries can accelerate the transition to a more circular and efficient economic system.

Consumer Awareness and Behavioral Change

The success of the circular economy also depends on consumer awareness and behavioral changes. Educating individuals about sustainable consumption and waste reduction can drive demand for circular products and services. Consumers can contribute by choosing durable products, supporting companies with sustainable practices, and participating in recycling programs. Governments and organizations can promote circular economy principles through public campaigns, incentives, and educational initiatives that encourage responsible consumption. When consumers actively engage in sustainable practices, businesses are incentivized to adopt circular strategies, creating a positive feedback loop that reinforces circularity.

Challenges in Implementing a Circular Economy

Despite its numerous benefits, the transition to a circular economy presents several challenges. One major obstacle is the resistance to change from businesses and consumers accustomed to linear models. Many industries rely on established production and distribution systems, making it difficult to shift towards circular practices. Additionally, inadequate infrastructure for recycling and waste management limits the effectiveness of circular systems. Financial barriers, such as the initial investment required for sustainable technologies and processes, also hinder widespread adoption. Addressing these challenges requires collaboration among governments, businesses, and consumers to develop policies, incentives, and solutions that facilitate the transition to a circular economy.

Economic and Environmental Benefits

A well-implemented circular economy offers significant economic and environmental benefits. From an economic perspective, it reduces production costs by maximizing resource efficiency and minimizing waste disposal expenses. Businesses that embrace circular models can develop new revenue streams through leasing, refurbishment, and recycling initiatives. Job creation in sectors such as repair, remanufacturing, and waste management also contributes to economic growth. Environmentally, a circular economy reduces greenhouse gas emissions, lowers pollution levels, and conserves natural resources. By prioritizing sustainability, industries can help mitigate climate change and protect ecosystems while ensuring long-term economic stability.

Future Prospects of the Circular Economy

The future of the circular economy depends on continued innovation, policy support, and collaboration across industries. As awareness of environmental issues grows, businesses and governments are increasingly investing in circular solutions. Advances in sustainable materials, digital technologies, and waste management practices will further enhance circularity. Policymakers are expected to introduce stricter regulations and incentives to promote resource efficiency and reduce environmental impact. If successfully implemented on a global scale, the circular economy has the potential to reshape industries, create sustainable growth, and improve quality of life while preserving the planet's resources for future generations.

1.1.2 The Shift from Linear to Circular Models

The transition from linear to circular economic models represents a fundamental shift in how resources are used, managed, and conserved. The traditional linear economy follows a "take, make, dispose" model, where raw materials are extracted, transformed into products, and discarded after use. This approach results in significant environmental degradation, resource depletion, and waste accumulation. In contrast, a circular economy seeks to extend the lifespan of products, promote reuse, and regenerate natural systems. By focusing on sustainability, efficiency, and innovation, the shift from linear to circular models aims to create long-term economic and environmental benefits.

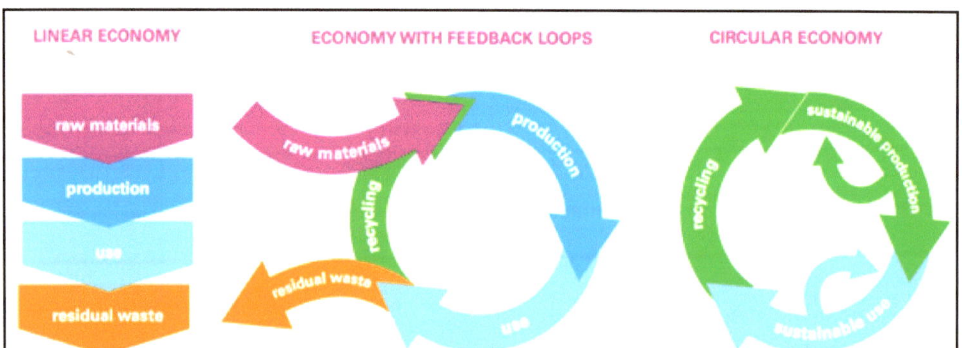

Fig: The Transition from Linear to Circular Business Models

The shift from linear to circular models is a necessary evolution in response to environmental, economic, and social challenges. By embracing circular principles, industries can reduce waste, optimize resource use, and contribute to a more sustainable future. While challenges exist, technological advancements, consumer engagement, and supportive policies provide opportunities for successful implementation. As more businesses and individuals recognize the value of circularity, the transition will accelerate, ultimately leading to a more efficient and regenerative economic system. The continued commitment to circular models will play a crucial role in shaping a sustainable world for future generations.

Understanding the Linear Economy and Its Challenges

The linear economic model has been the dominant system for centuries, driving industrialization and economic growth. This model relies on a continuous cycle of production and consumption, where resources are extracted, processed, and eventually discarded as waste. While it has contributed to economic development, the linear economy has several drawbacks. It leads to excessive resource consumption, environmental pollution, and an unsustainable reliance on finite materials. The increasing demand for raw materials has resulted in deforestation, loss of biodiversity, and rising carbon emissions. Additionally, waste management has become a growing challenge, with landfills and oceans filled with discarded products. As global populations and consumption patterns increase, the limitations of the linear model become more evident, necessitating a shift towards a more sustainable approach.

Principles of the Circular Economy

A circular economy is built on three core principles: designing out waste and pollution, keeping products and materials in use, and regenerating natural systems. Instead of discarding materials after a single use, this model promotes recycling, reuse, and remanufacturing. By rethinking product design, companies can develop items that last longer, require fewer raw materials, and generate less waste. The circular model also encourages businesses to adopt sustainable practices, such as leasing and product-as-a-service models, to extend the lifespan of goods. Additionally, natural resources are managed in a way that supports regeneration rather than depletion, ensuring long-term sustainability.

Key Drivers of the Shift to Circular Models

Several factors are driving the transition from linear to circular models. Environmental concerns, including climate change and pollution, have led to growing awareness of the need for sustainable practices. Consumers and businesses are increasingly prioritizing eco-friendly solutions, prompting industries to adopt circular strategies. Advances in technology have also played a crucial role, enabling more efficient recycling, resource tracking, and waste management. Government policies and regulations are further accelerating the shift by imposing restrictions on single-use plastics, encouraging extended producer responsibility, and providing incentives for sustainable innovations. Economic benefits, such as cost savings through resource efficiency and new business opportunities, are additional motivators for companies to embrace circular models.

Business Strategies for Circular Transformation

For companies to successfully transition to circular models, they must rethink their business strategies. One approach is to adopt circular design principles, where products are developed with durability, repairability, and recyclability in mind. Companies can also implement closed-loop supply chains, where materials from end-of-life products are recovered and reintegrated into new production processes. Collaborative consumption models, such as sharing and leasing, reduce resource demand while providing consumers with flexible access to goods. Digital technologies, including artificial intelligence and blockchain, enhance transparency and efficiency in resource management. By embedding circularity into their business models, companies can improve profitability while contributing to environmental sustainability.

The Role of Consumers in the Circular Economy

Consumers play a critical role in the shift from linear to circular models. Their purchasing decisions and behavior directly influence market demand for sustainable products and services. By choosing durable, repairable, and recyclable goods, consumers encourage businesses to prioritize circular design. Additionally, participation in recycling programs, product take-back initiatives, and sustainable consumption practices helps reduce waste and extend the lifespan of materials. Awareness campaigns and educational initiatives can further empower individuals to make informed choices that support circular economies. As consumer preferences continue to evolve, businesses must adapt to meet the growing demand for environmentally responsible solutions.

Technological Innovations Supporting Circularity

Advancements in technology are playing a significant role in facilitating the shift to circular models. Innovations in material science have led to the development of biodegradable packaging, recyclable composites, and sustainable alternatives to traditional materials. Digital platforms enable product tracking, allowing businesses to monitor resource flows and optimize supply chains. The Internet of Things (IoT) and smart sensors improve waste management by providing real-time data on material usage and product conditions. 3D printing technology enables on-demand manufacturing, reducing excess production and waste. These technological breakthroughs support circular practices by enhancing efficiency, reducing environmental impact, and creating new opportunities for sustainable development.

Policy and Regulatory Frameworks

Government policies and regulations play a crucial role in supporting the transition from linear to circular models. Many countries have introduced legislation to promote sustainable practices, including bans on single-use plastics, tax incentives for green businesses, and extended producer responsibility programs. Circular economy strategies are increasingly integrated into national and international policy frameworks, encouraging industries to adopt environmentally friendly practices. Public-private partnerships further drive innovation and investment in circular solutions. By establishing clear regulatory guidelines and financial support mechanisms, governments can accelerate the adoption of circular economy principles across various sectors.

Economic and Environmental Benefits of Circular Models

The adoption of circular models offers numerous economic and environmental advantages. From an economic perspective, circular practices reduce costs associated with raw material extraction, waste disposal, and energy consumption. Companies that embrace circularity can unlock new revenue streams through product refurbishment, remanufacturing, and leasing models. Job creation in areas such as recycling, repair services, and sustainable production further contributes to economic growth. Environmentally, circular models reduce greenhouse gas emissions, minimize pollution, and conserve natural resources. By decreasing reliance on finite materials and optimizing resource use, circular economies promote long-term ecological balance and sustainability.

Challenges in Transitioning to Circular Models

Despite the benefits, the shift to circular models presents several challenges. Many industries rely on established linear processes, making it difficult to transition without significant investment in new technologies and infrastructure. Resistance to change, both at the corporate and consumer levels, can slow adoption rates. Inadequate recycling systems and lack of standardized regulations further complicate the implementation of circular practices. Additionally, businesses must navigate supply chain complexities to ensure circularity at every stage of production. Overcoming these challenges requires collaboration among governments, industries, and consumers to develop solutions that facilitate a smooth transition to circular models.

The Future of Circular Economies

The future of the circular economy depends on continued innovation, collaboration, and policy support. As industries increasingly recognize the economic and environmental benefits of circular models, investment in sustainable solutions is expected to grow. Companies will continue to integrate circular design principles, develop eco-friendly materials, and adopt new business models that prioritize resource efficiency. Consumer awareness and demand for sustainable products will further drive market transformations. Governments will play a key role in shaping regulatory frameworks that support circular economies, ensuring long-term viability and global adoption. With ongoing efforts, the transition from linear to circular models has the potential to create a more sustainable and resilient economy for future generations.

1.2 THE IMPORTANCE OF CIRCULAR ECONOMY FOR SUSTAINABLE DEVELOPMENT

1.2.1 Environmental Impacts and Resource Efficiency

Sustainable development has become a central focus for governments, businesses, and societies as environmental concerns and resource depletion continue to escalate. The traditional linear economic model, characterized by excessive resource consumption and waste generation, poses significant challenges to environmental sustainability. The circular economy, by contrast, offers a promising alternative that minimizes waste, conserves resources, and promotes long-term ecological balance. By integrating principles of resource efficiency, waste reduction, and regenerative practices, the circular economy plays a crucial role in addressing environmental issues while supporting economic growth.

The circular economy presents a viable solution to the environmental challenges posed by the linear economic model. By prioritizing resource efficiency, waste reduction, and sustainability, this approach minimizes environmental impact while supporting economic growth. The transition to circularity requires collaboration among businesses, consumers, and policymakers to implement innovative solutions and drive meaningful change. Although challenges exist, the long-term benefits of a circular economy far outweigh the obstacles, offering a pathway towards sustainable development. By embracing circular principles, societies can ensure a more sustainable and prosperous future for generations to come.

Environmental Impacts of the Linear Economy

The linear economy, based on the "take, make, dispose" model, has contributed to widespread environmental degradation. Large-scale extraction of raw materials depletes natural resources, leading to deforestation, habitat destruction, and loss of biodiversity. Industrial activities release significant amounts of greenhouse gases, exacerbating climate change and increasing global temperatures. The accumulation of waste, particularly plastic pollution, contaminates ecosystems and threatens wildlife. Water and air pollution caused by industrial and consumer waste further deteriorate environmental quality. The unsustainable nature of the linear economy highlights the urgent need for a more circular approach that prioritizes environmental conservation and resource efficiency.

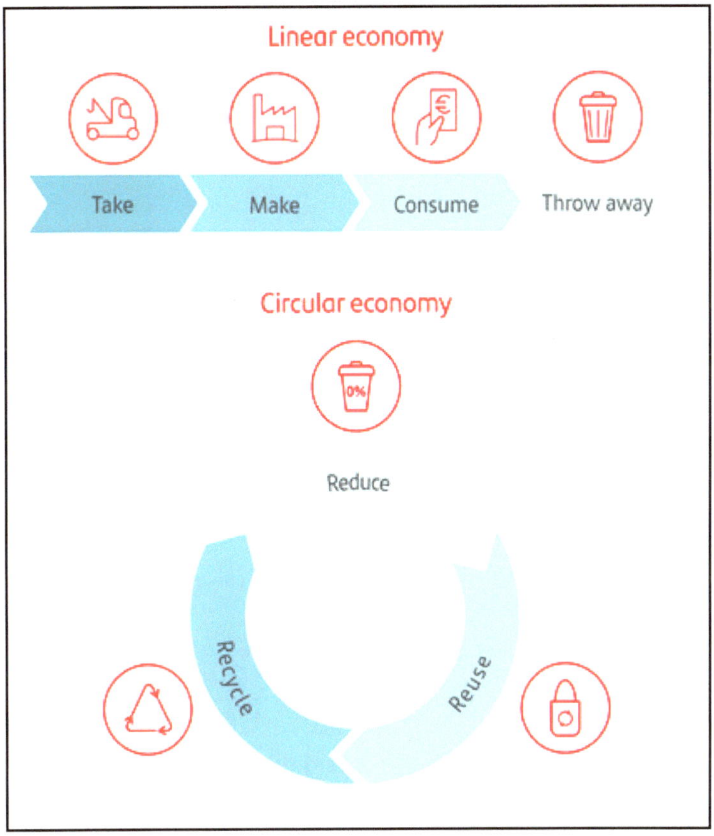

Fig: The Environmental Impact of Linear Economy

Principles of Resource Efficiency in the Circular Economy

Resource efficiency is a fundamental aspect of the circular economy, aiming to maximize the value of materials while minimizing waste. This approach involves optimizing product design, enhancing manufacturing processes, and encouraging the reuse and recycling of materials. Efficient resource management reduces dependency on finite raw materials, lowering the environmental footprint of production and consumption. By prioritizing energy-efficient technologies and sustainable material sourcing, industries can significantly cut down on emissions and waste. Resource efficiency also involves developing closed-loop systems where materials are continuously cycled through various stages of use, ensuring minimal resource loss.

Reducing Waste through Circular Economy Practices

One of the key advantages of the circular economy is its ability to reduce waste generation. Unlike the linear model, which discards products after use, circular systems encourage repair, refurbishment, and recycling. Designing products for longevity, modularity, and disassembly enables easier maintenance and resource recovery. By implementing extended producer responsibility programs, businesses can take accountability for the entire lifecycle of their products, promoting sustainable disposal and recycling practices. Waste-to-energy initiatives further enhance resource efficiency by converting non-recyclable waste into energy, reducing landfill reliance and decreasing environmental pollution.

Conserving Natural Resources and Biodiversity

The circular economy promotes the sustainable use of natural resources by minimizing extraction and maximizing reuse. Overexploitation of natural resources has led to severe environmental consequences, including soil degradation, water scarcity, and deforestation. Circular strategies such as sustainable agriculture, responsible forestry, and regenerative farming help restore ecosystems and maintain biodiversity. By reducing reliance on virgin materials, the circular economy alleviates pressure on natural habitats, preserving wildlife and promoting ecological stability. Conservation efforts within circular systems support a balance between human activities and nature, ensuring long-term resource availability for future generations.

Lowering Carbon Emissions and Combating Climate Change

A significant environmental benefit of the circular economy is its potential to reduce carbon emissions. The production and disposal of goods in a linear economy contribute to high levels of CO2 emissions, exacerbating climate change. Circular practices such as energy-efficient production, renewable energy integration, and material reuse lower the carbon footprint of industrial activities.

Sustainable transportation systems, including electric vehicles and shared mobility services, further contribute to emissions reduction. By shifting towards a circular model, businesses and governments can play a critical role in mitigating climate change and meeting international climate targets.

Sustainable Production and Consumption Patterns

The transition to a circular economy requires a fundamental change in production and consumption patterns. Industries must adopt sustainable manufacturing techniques that minimize waste and energy consumption.

Consumers, on the other hand, play an essential role by choosing eco-friendly products, reducing excessive consumption, and participating in recycling programs. Awareness campaigns and policy incentives can further encourage sustainable behavior, promoting a shift towards responsible consumption. Businesses that align their operations with circular economy principles not only reduce their environmental impact but also gain a competitive advantage in an increasingly sustainability-conscious market.

Economic and Social Benefits of Circularity

Beyond its environmental advantages, the circular economy offers significant economic and social benefits. Resource efficiency leads to cost savings for businesses by reducing material and energy expenses. Circular business models, such as leasing and product-as-a-service, provide new revenue opportunities while promoting sustainability. Job creation in sectors like recycling, refurbishment, and sustainable manufacturing further boosts economic growth. Social benefits include improved public health due to reduced pollution and enhanced community engagement in sustainability initiatives. By fostering economic resilience and social well-being, the circular economy contributes to holistic sustainable development.

The Role of Policy and Regulation in Circular Economy Implementation

Governments and policymakers play a crucial role in facilitating the transition to a circular economy. Regulations promoting sustainable practices, such as bans on single-use plastics, extended producer responsibility laws, and tax incentives for green businesses, drive industry-wide adoption of circular strategies. International agreements and collaborative initiatives further strengthen global efforts towards sustainability. Investment in research and development supports the creation of innovative circular solutions, accelerating the shift away from the linear model. By implementing robust policies and regulatory frameworks, governments can create an enabling environment for circular economy practices to thrive.

Challenges and Barriers to Circular Economy Adoption

Despite its many benefits, the transition to a circular economy faces several challenges. One major barrier is the resistance to change from industries and consumers accustomed to linear systems. The lack of infrastructure for recycling and waste management limits the effectiveness of circular practices. Financial constraints, particularly for small and medium-sized enterprises, hinder the adoption of sustainable technologies. Additionally, the complexity of global supply chains makes it difficult to implement closed-loop systems. Overcoming these challenges requires collaborative efforts from businesses, governments, and consumers to develop scalable and practical solutions for circular economy integration.

Future Prospects of the Circular Economy for Sustainable Development

As the world moves towards a more sustainable future, the circular economy will play an increasingly vital role in global development. Continued innovation in sustainable materials, digital technologies, and waste management will enhance circularity across industries. Businesses will continue to explore new models that balance profitability with environmental responsibility. Governments will strengthen policy frameworks to support circular practices and drive large-scale adoption. Increased consumer awareness and engagement in sustainable living will further reinforce circular economy principles. The successful implementation of circular strategies will lead to a more resilient, resource-efficient, and environmentally friendly global economy.

1.2.2 Economic Benefits: Cost Savings, Job Creation, and Innovation

Cost Savings

Fig: **Cost Savings**

Cost savings play a fundamental role in enhancing economic efficiency and business sustainability. Reducing expenses while maintaining or improving productivity allows businesses and economies to allocate resources effectively, maximize profitability, and sustain long-term growth. Companies that implement cost-saving strategies gain a competitive advantage by optimizing operations, improving financial stability, and investing in innovation. On a larger scale, cost savings contribute to economic development by fostering business expansion, job creation, and increased consumer purchasing power.

The economic benefits of cost savings extend across industries, businesses, and global economies, creating a foundation for financial stability, growth, and competitiveness. By enhancing profitability, improving operational efficiency, and reducing production costs, businesses strengthen their market position and drive economic expansion. Cost savings facilitate business growth, job creation, consumer affordability, and technological advancements, fostering sustainable development. On a broader scale, economic resilience, global trade, and public sector efficiency benefit from cost-saving strategies, ensuring long-term financial stability. As businesses and policymakers continue to prioritize cost efficiency, economies will experience sustained growth, innovation, and prosperity in an increasingly competitive global landscape.

Enhancing Business Profitability

One of the most direct economic benefits of cost savings is the enhancement of business profitability. When companies reduce operational costs, they can allocate more resources to revenue-generating activities, research and development, and workforce expansion. Lower expenses translate into higher profit margins, allowing businesses to invest in innovation and market expansion. Businesses that consistently practice cost-saving measures maintain financial stability, ensuring long-term success even during economic downturns. By minimizing waste, improving efficiency, and reducing unnecessary expenditures, organizations strengthen their bottom line and create sustainable growth opportunities.

Improving Operational Efficiency

Cost-saving strategies contribute to operational efficiency by optimizing resource utilization and streamlining workflows. Companies that embrace lean management practices, automation, and digital transformation eliminate redundancies, reduce production costs, and improve service delivery. Efficient resource allocation minimizes waste and ensures that businesses can produce goods and services at a lower cost while maintaining quality standards. Enhanced efficiency not only increases productivity but also enables organizations to respond swiftly to market demands and consumer needs. In a competitive business environment, operational efficiency driven by cost savings is essential for long-term economic success.

Reducing Production Costs and Increasing Competitiveness

Lower production costs give businesses a competitive edge in domestic and international markets. Companies that effectively reduce material expenses, labor costs, and energy consumption can offer products at competitive prices while maintaining profitability. Cost-efficient production methods, such as just-in-time manufacturing and process optimization, enhance product affordability, making businesses more attractive to consumers. Reduced costs also enable companies to invest in branding, marketing, and customer engagement, further strengthening their market position. The ability to maintain high-quality standards at lower costs fosters industry growth and enhances economic resilience.

Encouraging Business Growth and Expansion

Cost savings provide businesses with the financial flexibility needed for expansion and diversification. By reducing expenses, companies can reinvest savings into new product lines, market penetration strategies, and infrastructure development. Expansion into new regions and sectors stimulates economic growth by creating employment opportunities and increasing trade activities. Businesses that allocate cost savings toward innovation and technological advancements enhance their capacity for long-term sustainability. Economic benefits extend beyond individual businesses, as industry-wide cost-saving measures contribute to broader economic development and stability.

Promoting Job Creation and Workforce Development

Contrary to the misconception that cost savings result in job cuts, effective cost management often leads to job creation and workforce development. Businesses that optimize expenses without compromising productivity can allocate savings to employee training programs, wage increases, and new hiring initiatives. Skilled workforce development enhances employee performance, innovation, and job satisfaction, contributing to overall economic progress. When businesses achieve financial stability through cost savings, they can offer better working conditions, invest in career development programs, and improve job security, ultimately fostering economic growth.

Increasing Consumer Purchasing Power

Cost savings at the business level often lead to lower consumer prices, increasing purchasing power and overall economic activity. Companies that reduce production and operational costs can pass on savings to consumers by offering more affordable goods and services. Lower costs encourage higher consumer spending, stimulating demand across various industries. Increased affordability allows consumers to allocate resources efficiently, supporting economic circulation and growth. A stable economic environment driven by cost savings benefits businesses, consumers, and policymakers alike, ensuring sustained economic expansion.

Encouraging Sustainable Practices and Environmental Responsibility

Cost savings and sustainability often go hand in hand, as resource efficiency reduces waste and minimizes environmental impact. Businesses that implement energy-efficient technologies, waste reduction strategies, and sustainable sourcing benefit from both financial savings and improved environmental stewardship. Green business practices, such as circular economy models and renewable energy integration, lower operating costs while promoting ecological responsibility. Reduced utility expenses, optimized supply chains, and eco-friendly production methods contribute to long-term economic stability by mitigating environmental risks and regulatory costs. Sustainable cost-saving initiatives support economic development while preserving natural resources for future generations.

Enhancing Economic Resilience and Stability

Cost-saving measures improve economic resilience by equipping businesses with the financial flexibility needed to withstand economic fluctuations and uncertainties. Companies that maintain lean operations and efficient resource allocation can navigate financial crises, supply chain disruptions, and market volatility with greater stability. Economic downturns often highlight the importance of cost efficiency, as organizations with well-managed expenses can sustain operations and recover more quickly. Cost savings enable businesses to adapt to changing market conditions, reinforcing economic stability and preventing large-scale financial disruptions.

Fostering Innovation and Technological Advancements

Financial savings generated through cost optimization allow businesses to invest in innovation and technological advancements. Research and development initiatives benefit from cost reductions, driving the creation of new products, services, and digital solutions. Businesses that leverage cost savings for technological improvements enhance productivity, competitiveness, and market relevance. Innovations such as artificial intelligence, automation, and data analytics improve efficiency while reducing labor and operational costs. The integration of cost-effective technological solutions accelerates economic growth by increasing industry-wide productivity and expanding digital transformation.

Strengthening Global Trade and Investment

Cost-saving strategies improve global trade dynamics by enhancing the competitiveness of businesses in international markets. Countries that prioritize cost efficiency in manufacturing, logistics, and infrastructure development attract foreign direct investment and trade partnerships. Competitive pricing enabled by cost savings increases export potential, boosting national economic performance. International businesses seeking cost-effective supply chain solutions invest in economies that offer efficient production capabilities, creating economic opportunities and fostering cross-border trade. By strengthening global trade networks, cost savings contribute to economic integration and financial growth on an international scale.

Improving Public Sector Efficiency and Economic Policy

Governments and public sector institutions benefit from cost-saving strategies by improving budget allocation and financial management. Efficient use of public funds allows governments to invest in infrastructure, healthcare, education, and social programs without increasing fiscal burdens. Cost savings in government operations, procurement, and administration enhance service delivery while reducing taxpayer expenses. Economic policies that promote cost efficiency in public spending contribute to financial stability, national development, and sustainable growth. Well-managed public sector cost savings improve economic resilience and ensure long-term prosperity for citizens and businesses alike.

Job Creation

Job creation is one of the most significant drivers of economic growth and development. A robust labor market fuels consumer spending, increases productivity, and strengthens overall economic stability. Employment opportunities contribute to poverty reduction, improved living standards, and the development of a skilled workforce. Governments and businesses play a vital role in job creation by fostering entrepreneurship, supporting industrial expansion, and investing in innovation. Understanding the economic benefits of job creation helps policymakers and organizations develop strategies that promote sustainable employment and economic resilience.

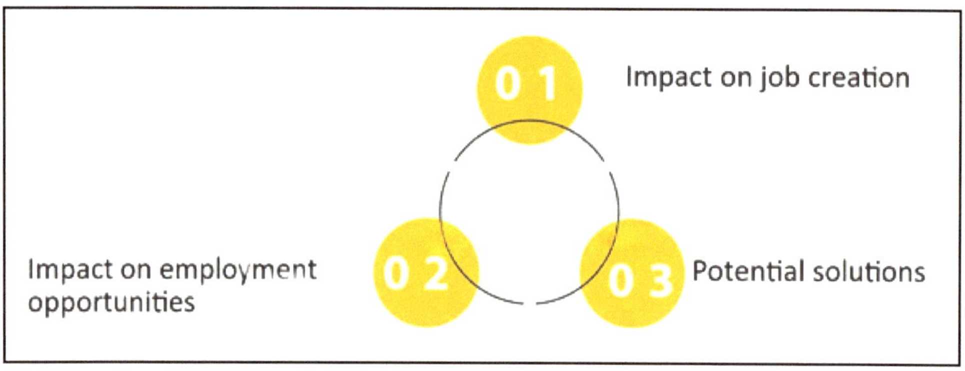

Fig: Job creation

The economic benefits of job creation extend across multiple dimensions, shaping businesses, industries, and national economies. Employment opportunities drive consumer spending, poverty reduction, business growth, and economic resilience. A skilled and engaged workforce enhances productivity, innovation, and global competitiveness. By fostering entrepreneurship, workforce development, and inclusive labor markets, governments and businesses create sustainable employment ecosystems. Job creation strengthens public revenues, reduces economic inequalities, and supports long-term economic stability. As global economies continue to evolve, prioritizing job creation remains a key strategy for ensuring prosperity, resilience, and sustainable development.

Boosting Consumer Spending and Economic Growth

Employment provides individuals with income, increasing their purchasing power and contributing to overall economic activity. When more people have jobs, consumer spending rises, driving demand for goods and services. Increased consumption stimulates production and business expansion, creating a cycle of economic growth.

Higher employment rates lead to greater economic stability, reducing reliance on government assistance programs and increasing tax revenues. As businesses thrive, they reinvest in the economy by hiring more employees, expanding operations, and innovating new products and services. A strong job market supports economic momentum, ensuring sustainable long-term development.

Reducing Poverty and Enhancing Living Standards

Job creation plays a critical role in poverty alleviation by providing individuals and families with financial stability. Access to stable employment allows people to meet their basic needs, invest in education, and improve their overall quality of life. As employment rates rise, the number of individuals living in poverty decreases, reducing social inequalities and economic disparities. Stable incomes enable households to afford better healthcare, housing, and education, leading to long-term social and economic improvements. Sustainable job opportunities empower communities, creating a more equitable society and fostering national economic progress.

Strengthening Business Performance and Productivity

A well-employed workforce contributes to increased business productivity and profitability. Employees bring skills, expertise, and innovation that drive efficiency and competitiveness. Companies with access to a diverse and skilled labor pool experience higher levels of performance, innovation, and market adaptability. When businesses expand their workforce, they can enhance production capabilities, improve service delivery, and invest in research and development. Job creation leads to a motivated and engaged workforce, fostering a culture of continuous improvement and industry advancement. Strong labor markets contribute to business success, reinforcing economic stability and growth.

Encouraging Entrepreneurship and Small Business Growth

Entrepreneurship is a major source of job creation, as new businesses generate employment opportunities across various industries. Startups and small businesses play a crucial role in economic development by introducing innovative products and services, fostering competition, and driving regional growth. Governments and financial institutions that support entrepreneurship through funding, training, and policy incentives create an environment conducive to business expansion and job creation. When small businesses succeed, they contribute to economic diversification and local job markets, strengthening overall economic resilience. Entrepreneurial ventures drive industry transformation, ensuring continuous job opportunities and market evolution.

Enhancing Workforce Skills and Economic Competitiveness

Job creation contributes to workforce development by equipping individuals with skills necessary for economic advancement. Employment opportunities provide workers with on-the-job training, professional development, and career growth prospects. As industries evolve, workers gain experience in new technologies, business strategies, and market trends, increasing their employability and adaptability. A skilled workforce enhances a country's economic competitiveness, attracting investment and fostering innovation. Governments and businesses that prioritize education and vocational training create a dynamic labor market capable of meeting the demands of a rapidly changing economy. Investing in workforce development strengthens economic sustainability and global market positioning.

Reducing Economic Inequality and Social Disparities

Job creation contributes to reducing income inequality by providing equal employment opportunities for diverse demographics. Inclusive labor markets ensure that individuals from different backgrounds have access to stable income sources, reducing economic disparities and fostering social cohesion. Gender equality in employment, support for marginalized communities, and fair wages contribute to a more balanced economic landscape. When employment opportunities are distributed equitably, economic growth becomes more inclusive, benefiting society as a whole. Governments that implement policies promoting job accessibility and fair wages contribute to a stronger and more unified economy.

Generating Government Revenue and Strengthening Public Services

A thriving job market increases government revenues through taxation, enabling investments in public infrastructure, healthcare, and education. Employed individuals contribute to income tax, while businesses pay corporate taxes and social security contributions. Increased tax revenue allows governments to fund essential services, social programs, and economic development initiatives. Sustainable job creation reduces dependency on welfare programs, freeing up public funds for infrastructure improvements, technological advancements, and industry support. A well-functioning labor market strengthens national economies by ensuring a balanced approach to fiscal policies and public investments.

Fostering Economic Resilience and Stability

A strong employment sector enhances economic resilience by reducing vulnerability to financial crises and market fluctuations. Countries with stable job markets can withstand economic downturns more effectively, as employed populations maintain consumer spending and business activity. Diversified employment opportunities across industries provide economies with flexibility, ensuring stability during periods of economic uncertainty. Governments that prioritize job creation through infrastructure projects, industry incentives, and workforce training build resilient economies capable of adapting to global challenges. Sustainable employment policies contribute to long-term economic strength and national stability.

Attracting Foreign Investment and Strengthening Global Trade

A well-developed labor market attracts foreign investment by providing businesses with a skilled and productive workforce. Multinational corporations seek locations with stable employment environments, access to talent, and economic growth potential. Countries that prioritize job creation through business-friendly policies, infrastructure development, and education initiatives become attractive destinations for global investors. Increased foreign direct investment boosts economic growth, generates employment, and enhances trade opportunities. Strong labor markets contribute to a country's economic credibility, reinforcing its position in international markets and global supply chains.

Supporting Sustainable Economic Development and Innovation

Job creation fosters long-term economic sustainability by driving innovation, industry diversification, and technological advancements. A well-employed workforce supports research and development initiatives, leading to groundbreaking solutions and market advancements. Innovation-driven employment sectors, such as technology, renewable energy, and healthcare, contribute to economic modernization and global competitiveness. Governments and businesses that invest in emerging industries create new job opportunities, ensuring future economic stability. Sustainable job creation strategies align with environmental and social development goals, balancing economic progress with ecological responsibility and inclusive growth.

Innovation

Innovation is a driving force behind economic growth and prosperity. It fosters the development of new products, services, and business models that improve efficiency, productivity, and competitiveness. The integration of innovative technologies and processes enhances economic resilience by creating jobs, generating wealth, and optimizing resource utilization. In a rapidly evolving global economy, innovation plays a crucial role in shaping industries, attracting investment, and ensuring sustainable progress. From technological advancements to strategic business transformations, the economic benefits of innovation are profound and far-reaching.

Innovation is a catalyst for economic advancement, offering numerous benefits that extend across industries and societies. From enhancing productivity and job creation to fostering sustainability and global competitiveness, the economic advantages of innovation are undeniable. Businesses that embrace innovative practices gain a competitive edge, attract investment, and ensure long-term profitability. Governments that prioritize research and development create environments conducive to economic growth and technological progress. As the world continues to evolve, innovation remains a fundamental pillar of economic success, shaping the future of industries and driving sustainable development. By embracing innovation, economies can unlock their full potential, ensuring prosperity and resilience in an ever-changing global landscape.

Fig: Innovation Economics

Boosting Productivity and Efficiency

One of the primary economic benefits of innovation is its ability to enhance productivity and efficiency across industries. By introducing advanced technologies such as automation, artificial intelligence, and data analytics, businesses can streamline operations and reduce costs. Improved processes enable companies to produce goods and services faster, with higher quality and fewer resources. Enhanced productivity leads to increased output, allowing businesses to meet growing consumer demands while maintaining competitive pricing. In turn, these advancements drive economic expansion by fostering higher levels of economic activity, increasing revenues, and promoting sustainable development.

Job Creation and Employment Growth

Innovation contributes significantly to job creation by introducing new industries and expanding existing ones. As businesses adopt innovative practices, they require a skilled workforce to develop, implement, and manage technological advancements. This demand creates employment opportunities in various sectors, ranging from research and development to manufacturing and digital services. Additionally, innovation supports entrepreneurship by providing a platform for startups to introduce disruptive solutions that challenge traditional business models. The expansion of innovative industries not only generates jobs but also enhances workforce capabilities, driving long-term economic growth.

Encouraging Entrepreneurship and Business Expansion

Entrepreneurship thrives in an environment driven by innovation. The development of new ideas and technologies enables entrepreneurs to establish businesses that address market gaps and consumer needs. Startups that leverage innovation often introduce groundbreaking products and services, gaining a competitive edge in the market. As these businesses grow, they contribute to economic development by attracting investment, creating employment, and driving industry transformation. Furthermore, large corporations that prioritize innovation expand their market presence through diversification and strategic partnerships. By fostering a culture of innovation, economies encourage business expansion and competitiveness in global markets.

Enhancing Global Competitiveness

Innovation plays a vital role in positioning businesses and economies on the global stage. Countries that invest in research and development gain a competitive advantage by developing cutting-edge technologies and solutions. Businesses that prioritize innovation are more adaptable to market changes, ensuring long-term sustainability and profitability. By adopting innovative practices, industries can enhance product differentiation, improve customer experiences, and capture new markets. The ability to remain competitive in a rapidly evolving landscape strengthens economic resilience, ensuring continued growth and development.

Attracting Investment and Capital Growth

Investment flows toward economies and businesses that demonstrate a commitment to innovation. Investors seek opportunities in industries that drive technological advancements and offer high growth potential. By fostering innovation-friendly environments, governments and organizations attract foreign direct investment, venture capital, and private equity funding.

These financial inflows support business expansion, infrastructure development, and technological research, further stimulating economic progress. Additionally, innovative enterprises generate high returns, reinforcing investor confidence and promoting capital growth within the economy.

Developing Sustainable Solutions for Long-Term Growth

Sustainability has become a critical focus for modern economies, and innovation plays a key role in developing sustainable solutions. Green technologies, renewable energy, and circular economy initiatives drive resource efficiency while minimizing environmental impact.

Companies that invest in sustainable innovations reduce operational costs, improve regulatory compliance, and appeal to environmentally conscious consumers. By integrating sustainable practices, businesses enhance their long-term viability while contributing to economic and environmental well-being. Innovation-driven sustainability ensures that economic progress aligns with ecological preservation, fostering a balanced and resilient economy.

Increasing Consumer Benefits and Market Expansion

Innovation leads to the development of products and services that improve consumer experiences and enhance quality of life. Technological advancements introduce convenience, efficiency, and customization, meeting the evolving needs of consumers. As businesses innovate, they create diverse product offerings that expand market reach and increase consumer engagement. The rise of digital platforms, e-commerce, and artificial intelligence-driven services has transformed industries, enabling companies to cater to a global audience. By driving consumer satisfaction and market expansion, innovation contributes to economic prosperity and business success.

Fostering Technological Advancements and Industry Transformation

Technological innovation accelerates industry transformation by revolutionizing traditional business models. Industries such as healthcare, finance, transportation, and manufacturing have undergone significant advancements through the adoption of digital technologies. The implementation of artificial intelligence, blockchain, and the Internet of Things has optimized efficiency, security, and decision-making processes. These technological shifts create new economic opportunities, stimulate investment, and redefine industry standards. The continuous evolution of technology ensures that economies remain dynamic, adaptable, and prepared for future challenges.

Reducing Costs and Increasing Profitability

Businesses that incorporate innovation into their operations benefit from cost reduction and increased profitability. Process optimization, automation, and data-driven decision-making enhance efficiency, reducing wastage and operational expenses. The adoption of smart technologies, cloud computing, and machine learning enables businesses to streamline workflows, minimize errors, and maximize productivity. Cost savings allow companies to reinvest in research and development, further fueling innovation and business growth. By improving profitability through innovation, businesses strengthen their financial stability and contribute to overall economic expansion.

Encouraging Collaboration and Knowledge Sharing

Innovation fosters collaboration between businesses, research institutions, and government agencies. Partnerships and knowledge-sharing initiatives accelerate technological advancements and drive industry-wide improvements. Collaborative efforts in innovation lead to the development of groundbreaking solutions that address global challenges such as climate change, healthcare accessibility, and digital transformation. By promoting open innovation and cross-sector cooperation, economies benefit from shared expertise, increased research capabilities, and enhanced problem-solving approaches. The integration of diverse perspectives fuels creativity, ensuring continuous economic progress.

Building Economic Resilience and Adaptability

Economic resilience is crucial in navigating uncertainties and disruptions. Innovation enhances economic adaptability by equipping businesses and industries with the tools to respond effectively to challenges. Whether facing financial crises, supply chain disruptions, or technological shifts, innovation-driven economies can adjust strategies and maintain stability. Digital transformation, automation, and predictive analytics empower businesses to make data-informed decisions, mitigating risks and ensuring long-term sustainability. By fostering an innovation-oriented economy, nations strengthen their ability to withstand economic fluctuations and drive consistent growth.

1.2.3 Social and Ethical Dimensions of Circularity

The concept of circularity extends beyond economic and environmental benefits to encompass social and ethical dimensions. A circular economy aims to minimize waste, optimize resource use, and promote sustainability. However, for a circular economy to be truly effective, it must also address social equity, human rights, labor conditions, and ethical considerations. The transition from a linear to a circular model has profound implications for workers, communities, and global supply chains. Ensuring fair access to resources, creating equitable economic opportunities, and fostering responsible production practices are critical aspects of a socially just and ethically sound circular economy.

The circular economy is not just an environmental and economic concept—it is also deeply intertwined with social and ethical considerations. Ensuring social equity, ethical labor practices, and inclusive participation is essential for building a circular system that benefits all members of society. Ethical circularity promotes fair access to resources, sustainable business practices, and responsible consumption. Governments, businesses, and individuals must work collaboratively to integrate social justice into circular economy strategies. By addressing ethical challenges and prioritizing human well-being, the circular economy can become a transformative force for sustainability and social progress. A truly circular future is one that values people as much as it values the planet.

Social Equity and Inclusivity in Circular Economy Practices

A circular economy must be inclusive, ensuring that all individuals and communities have equal access to its benefits. Economic transitions can often result in disparities, with marginalized communities experiencing the greatest challenges. Historically, lower-income populations have faced limited access to sustainable resources, green technologies, and employment opportunities in emerging industries. To prevent the circular economy from becoming an exclusive model that benefits only certain segments of society, policymakers must design strategies that ensure fair distribution of opportunities. Educational programs, vocational training, and access to financing for sustainable businesses should be prioritized to ensure broad participation in circular economic activities. By focusing on inclusivity, a circular economy can uplift communities and provide opportunities for economic empowerment.

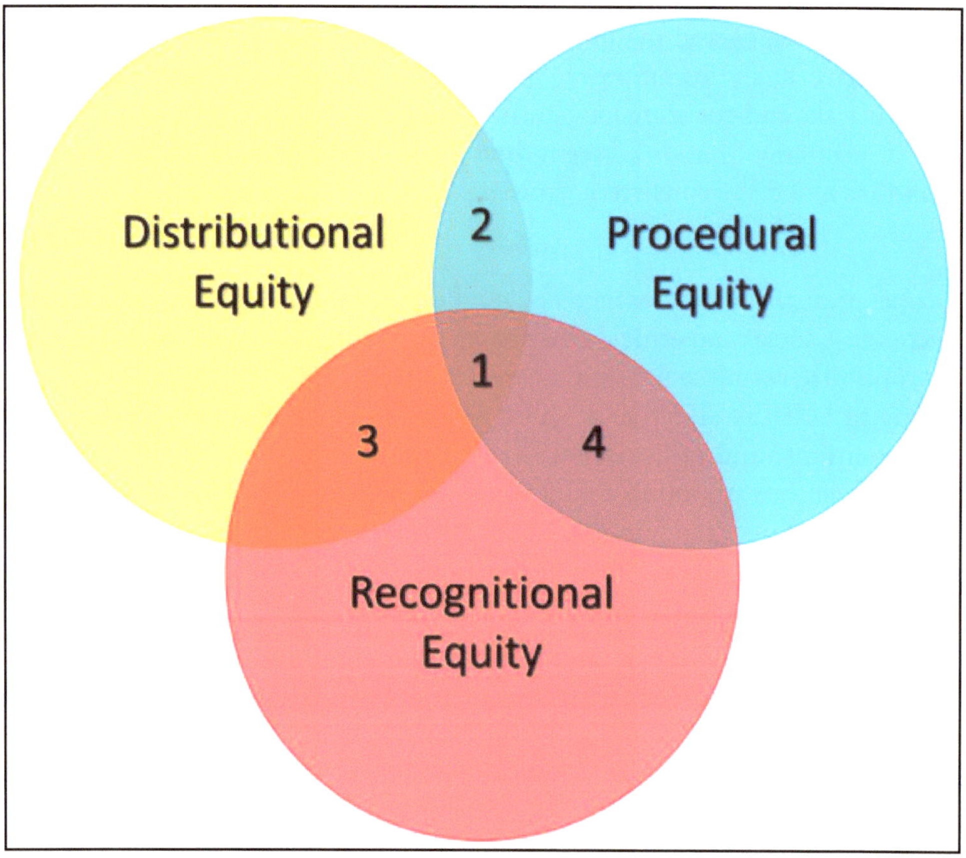

Fig: Promoting Social Equity and Building Resilience through Value-Inclusive Design

Fair Labor Practices and Ethical Supply Chains

As industries shift towards circular business models, ensuring fair labor practices becomes increasingly important. Many supply chains, particularly in industries such as textiles, electronics, and agriculture, have historically been linked to exploitative labor practices, including low wages, poor working conditions, and child labor. Ethical circularity demands transparency and accountability in production processes to ensure that workers are treated fairly. Companies embracing circular principles must also adhere to ethical labor standards, providing safe working conditions and fair wages. This can be achieved through regulatory frameworks, corporate social responsibility initiatives, and consumer-driven demand for ethically produced goods. Sustainable supply chains should integrate circular principles without compromising human rights and labor rights, ensuring that economic gains do not come at the expense of worker welfare.

Consumer Awareness and Ethical Consumption

Consumers play a vital role in driving the transition towards a circular economy. Ethical consumption involves making purchasing decisions that consider environmental sustainability, labor conditions, and social impact. Increasing awareness about the benefits of circularity empowers consumers to choose products that align with ethical and sustainable principles. Brands and corporations have a responsibility to provide transparency regarding their sourcing, production methods, and sustainability commitments. Certification labels, ethical sourcing initiatives, and corporate accountability measures help consumers make informed choices. Public awareness campaigns and educational initiatives can further enhance consumer participation in ethical circular practices, fostering a culture of responsibility and sustainability.

The Role of Businesses in Promoting Socially Responsible Circularity

Businesses play a crucial role in embedding social and ethical values into circular economy practices. Corporate responsibility should extend beyond profit-making to include environmental stewardship and social impact. Companies should adopt sustainable production methods that minimize waste, reduce environmental harm, and prioritize human well-being. Business models such as product-as-a-service, remanufacturing, and material recovery can be designed to support both economic growth and social progress. Engaging in partnerships with local communities, supporting small and medium-sized enterprises, and investing in workforce training programs contribute to a more equitable transition to circularity. Ethical leadership within corporations ensures that circular economy initiatives align with human rights and social justice principles.

Reducing Waste and Addressing the Social Impact of Pollution

The linear economy's wastefulness has led to severe social and environmental consequences, disproportionately affecting vulnerable communities. Pollution from industrial activities, improper waste disposal, and non-biodegradable materials has significant health implications, particularly in low-income regions where waste management infrastructure is inadequate. Circular solutions, such as recycling, upcycling, and composting, help mitigate these negative impacts by reducing landfill waste and lowering pollution levels. Ethical circularity prioritizes waste reduction strategies that safeguard public health, particularly in communities most affected by environmental degradation. Sustainable waste management policies, community engagement in recycling initiatives, and corporate accountability in pollution reduction are key elements of a socially responsible circular economy.

The Ethical Use of Resources and Indigenous Knowledge

Ethical circularity also involves respecting the rights of indigenous communities and traditional knowledge systems. Many indigenous cultures have long practiced sustainable resource management, emphasizing balance and regeneration. Integrating indigenous wisdom into circular economy models can provide valuable insights into conservation, biodiversity, and sustainable land use. Ethical considerations must also address land rights, ensuring that circular economy initiatives do not lead to displacement or exploitation of indigenous populations. Collaboration between governments, businesses, and indigenous communities can foster a holistic approach to circularity that respects cultural heritage while promoting sustainability.

Education and Skill Development for an Inclusive Circular Economy

The transition to a circular economy requires a workforce equipped with relevant skills and knowledge. Investing in education and training programs ensures that workers can adapt to changing industries and participate in sustainable economic activities. Circular economy principles should be integrated into school curricula, vocational training programs, and higher education institutions. Skill development programs focused on sustainable design, waste management, and green technologies enable individuals to contribute to circular initiatives while securing stable employment. Governments and private institutions must work together to provide accessible training opportunities, particularly for communities vulnerable to economic shifts. By prioritizing education, a circular economy can be a driver of social mobility and long-term economic security.

Government Policies and Regulatory Frameworks for Ethical Circularity

Governments play a critical role in shaping the ethical dimensions of circularity through policies and regulations. Strong regulatory frameworks ensure that businesses comply with environmental and labor standards, preventing exploitative practices and greenwashing. Policies that incentivize circular business models, such as tax benefits for sustainable enterprises and penalties for unsustainable practices, encourage ethical decision-making. Public investment in sustainable infrastructure, such as renewable energy and waste management systems, further supports the transition to a circular economy. Governments should also facilitate multi-stakeholder collaboration, bringing together businesses, non-governmental organizations, and civil society to create comprehensive circular economy strategies.

The Ethical Dilemmas in Circularity and the Need for Balanced Solutions

While the circular economy presents numerous benefits, ethical dilemmas also arise in its implementation. Some industries may experience job losses as a result of automation and efficiency-driven circular solutions. Addressing these challenges requires careful planning to ensure that economic shifts do not lead to increased unemployment or social displacement. Ethical circularity must balance technological advancements with human-centered policies, ensuring that workers are reskilled and redeployed into new sectors. Additionally, the challenge of ensuring fair global trade in circular materials must be addressed to prevent exploitation of developing economies. Ethical considerations must guide circular economy policies to ensure that they promote fairness, inclusivity, and long-term social well-being.

1.3 CIRCULAR ECONOMY VS. TRADITIONAL ECONOMY: KEY DIFFERENCES

The concept of a circular economy is increasingly gaining attention as a sustainable alternative to the traditional linear economic model. The traditional economy, often referred to as the linear economy, follows a 'take-make-dispose' approach, where raw materials are extracted, processed into products, and eventually discarded as waste. This model has driven industrial and economic growth for centuries but has also led to resource depletion, environmental degradation, and increasing waste generation. In contrast, the circular economy seeks to minimize waste and maximize resource efficiency by designing products for reuse, repair, and recycling. This shift presents significant differences in terms of production, consumption, sustainability, and economic impact.

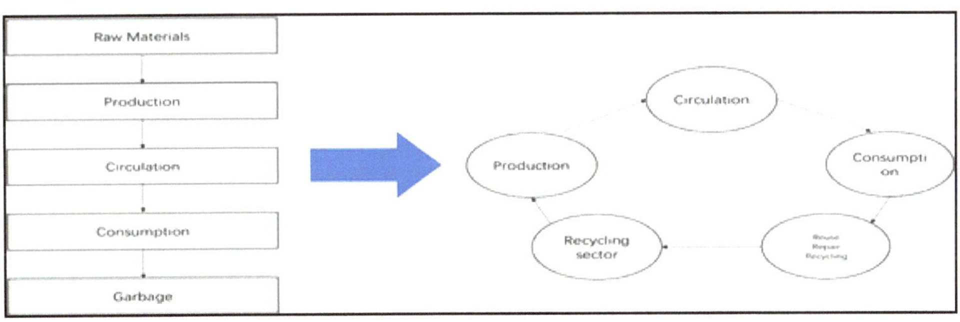

Fig: Comparison between Traditional and Circular Economy

The key differences between the circular economy and the traditional economy highlight the need for a fundamental shift in how resources are used, products are designed, and waste is managed. While the traditional economy prioritizes linear consumption and short-term profitability, the circular economy emphasizes sustainability, efficiency, and long-term value creation. The transition towards circularity requires collaborative efforts from businesses, consumers, policymakers, and innovators to drive systemic change. By adopting circular principles, economies can reduce environmental impact, enhance economic resilience, and create new opportunities for sustainable development. As awareness of resource limitations and environmental concerns continues to grow, embracing the circular economy becomes not only a necessity but also an opportunity for a more sustainable and prosperous future.

1.3.1 Resource Utilization and Waste Management

One of the fundamental differences between the circular economy and the traditional economy is how resources are utilized and waste is managed. In a linear economy, raw materials are extracted and processed into products with little consideration for the long-term consequences of resource depletion. Once products reach the end of their lifecycle, they are typically discarded, contributing to growing landfill waste and pollution. The circular economy, on the other hand, prioritizes resource efficiency by ensuring that materials are kept in circulation for as long as possible. It promotes practices such as recycling, remanufacturing, and upcycling to minimize the need for virgin materials and reduce waste. By designing products with durability, reusability, and recyclability in mind, the circular economy reduces dependence on finite resources and mitigates environmental damage.

1.3.2 Environmental Impact and Sustainability

The traditional economy is characterized by a high environmental footprint due to excessive resource extraction, energy consumption, and waste generation. This model contributes significantly to deforestation, water scarcity, greenhouse gas emissions, and pollution. The circular economy, in contrast, is rooted in sustainability principles that aim to minimize environmental harm. By reducing reliance on raw materials, promoting renewable energy sources, and implementing sustainable production processes, the circular economy lowers carbon emissions and lessens the strain on natural ecosystems. Furthermore, circular practices such as composting organic waste and adopting biodegradable materials contribute to ecosystem restoration and biodiversity conservation. As the world faces climate change challenges, transitioning to a circular economy is essential for achieving long-term environmental sustainability.

1.3.3 Economic Efficiency and Business Models

The traditional economy emphasizes mass production and rapid consumption, with businesses prioritizing short-term profits over long-term sustainability. This approach often results in inefficiencies, such as excess inventory, supply chain disruptions, and increased disposal costs. The circular economy, however, introduces innovative business models that enhance economic efficiency and create long-term value. Circular business models include product-as-a-service, where customers pay for usage rather than ownership, thereby extending product lifespans. Additionally, businesses embracing remanufacturing, leasing, and sharing economy principles benefit from cost savings and increased customer engagement. By shifting from a disposable culture to a regenerative system, businesses can reduce operational costs, secure material supply chains, and strengthen resilience against market fluctuations.

1.3.4 Consumer Behavior and Participation

In the traditional economy, consumer behavior is largely driven by convenience and affordability, often at the expense of sustainability. The linear model encourages overconsumption, planned obsolescence, and throwaway culture, resulting in increased waste and pollution. The circular economy, however, fosters responsible consumer behavior by promoting mindful consumption, product longevity, and waste reduction. Consumers are encouraged to repair rather than replace products, choose sustainable alternatives, and participate in recycling and reuse initiatives. Additionally, businesses are increasingly offering take-back programs, second-hand marketplaces, and eco-friendly packaging options to facilitate consumer engagement in circular practices. As awareness grows about the environmental and social impact of consumption, the shift towards circular consumer habits is gaining momentum.

1.3.5 Technological Innovation and Industrial Transformation

Technological advancements play a crucial role in differentiating the circular economy from the traditional economy. In the linear model, industrial processes prioritize efficiency and cost-cutting without necessarily considering sustainability. However, the circular economy leverages cutting-edge technologies such as artificial intelligence, blockchain, and 3D printing to optimize resource use and enhance waste management. Smart manufacturing, predictive maintenance, and digital platforms for sharing and remanufacturing enable industries to operate more sustainably. Innovations in material science, such as biodegradable plastics and renewable energy storage solutions, further support circular economy goals. As industries continue to adopt technology-driven circular strategies, the economic and environmental benefits of these innovations become increasingly evident.

1.3.6 Employment and Economic Opportunities

The transition from a traditional economy to a circular economy has significant implications for job creation and economic growth. In the linear model, employment is often concentrated in resource extraction, manufacturing, and waste disposal sectors, many of which face automation and declining demand due to sustainability concerns. The circular economy, however, creates diverse job opportunities in recycling, refurbishment, green technology, and sustainable design. As businesses invest in circular practices, new skill sets are required, leading to workforce upskilling and training programs. Additionally, the growth of circular industries such as renewable energy, repair services, and sustainable agriculture contributes to economic diversification and resilience. Governments and businesses that support circular workforce development can enhance economic security while promoting environmental sustainability.

1.3.7 Global Supply Chains and Economic Resilience

Global supply chains in the traditional economy are often characterized by long, complex networks that are vulnerable to resource scarcity, price volatility, and geopolitical instability. The reliance on finite raw materials and fossil fuels increases economic risks, particularly for industries dependent on international trade. In contrast, the circular economy emphasizes localized supply chains, material recovery, and resource efficiency, reducing dependence on unpredictable global markets. By prioritizing regional production, closed-loop systems, and circular procurement, businesses can mitigate supply chain disruptions and enhance economic resilience. Additionally, circular trade policies that promote sustainable sourcing and fair labor practices contribute to more stable and ethical global supply chains.

1.3.8 Regulatory Frameworks and Policy Support

Governments and policymakers play a critical role in shaping the economic landscape by implementing regulations that support sustainability and resource efficiency. The traditional economy has long been supported by policies that incentivize extraction, industrial expansion, and consumer-driven growth without adequate consideration for environmental impact. However, as concerns about climate change and resource depletion rise, governments are increasingly introducing circular economy policies. These include extended producer responsibility (EPR) regulations, waste reduction targets, and incentives for sustainable business practices. Tax benefits for companies that adopt circular strategies, bans on single-use plastics, and investment in green infrastructure further support the transition towards circularity. Strong regulatory frameworks ensure that businesses and consumers are aligned with sustainability goals, accelerating the shift from a linear to a circular economy.

1.4 HISTORICAL EVOLUTION OF CIRCULAR ECONOMY CONCEPTS

1.4.1 Early Circular Economy Thinking

The concept of a circular economy has gained significant attention in recent years as a sustainable alternative to the traditional linear economic model. However, the origins of circular economy thinking date back centuries, with early civilizations and economic theorists recognizing the value of resource efficiency, waste reduction, and sustainable systems. The shift from a wasteful, consumption-driven economy to a regenerative model is not a recent phenomenon but rather a continuation of age-old practices that emphasized reuse, repair, and resource conservation.

The early thinking behind the circular economy reflects a long history of resource efficiency, sustainability, and innovative economic models. From ancient practices of material reuse to modern industrial ecology and circular design, the principles of circularity have evolved in response to environmental and economic challenges. Visionaries such as Kenneth Boulding, Walter Stahel, and William McDonough laid the intellectual foundation for today's circular economy initiatives. As businesses, governments, and consumers embrace circular strategies, the early lessons of circular economy thinking remain relevant in guiding the transition toward a more sustainable and regenerative future. Understanding the historical roots of circularity helps to appreciate its significance and reinforces the need for continued efforts in building a circular world.

Early Practices of Resource Efficiency

Long before the industrial revolution and mass production, societies practiced resource efficiency out of necessity. In ancient civilizations, such as those in Mesopotamia, Egypt, and Rome, materials were reused and repurposed due to the high cost and difficulty of obtaining new resources. Metals, textiles, and construction materials were salvaged and repurposed to extend their lifespan. For example, ancient Romans recycled glass, and medieval blacksmiths often reforged metal tools and weapons. Indigenous communities around the world also practiced sustainable resource management by following ecological cycles, using every part of an animal or plant, and avoiding unnecessary waste. These early practices laid the foundation for circular economy thinking, emphasizing the need to maximize the utility of resources.

Industrial Revolution and the Rise of Linear Economy

The advent of the Industrial Revolution in the 18th and 19th centuries marked a significant shift from localized, resource-efficient practices to large-scale production and consumption. The introduction of steam power, mechanized manufacturing, and global trade led to an increase in material extraction and waste generation. The traditional linear economic model—based on the 'take-make-dispose' approach—became dominant, with industries focusing on rapid production and consumer-driven growth. While this model contributed to economic expansion and technological advancements, it also led to resource depletion, pollution, and environmental degradation. Despite this shift, some industries continued to practice recycling and reuse. For instance, during periods of economic hardship or war, societies returned to resource conservation strategies, such as metal and paper recycling during World War II.

The Emergence of Ecological and Economic Theories

The 20th century saw the emergence of ecological and economic theories that challenged the unsustainable nature of the linear economy. One of the earliest thinkers to introduce the idea of circularity in economic systems was Kenneth Boulding, an economist and systems theorist. In his 1966 essay, The Economics of the Coming Spaceship Earth, Boulding argued that Earth should be viewed as a closed system, similar to a spaceship, where resources must be managed efficiently and waste must be minimized. His work laid the intellectual groundwork for later discussions on sustainable development and circular economy principles.

Another key contributor to early circular economy thinking was Walter Stahel, an architect and economist, who introduced the concept of a "closed-loop economy" in the 1970s. Stahel emphasized the economic and environmental benefits of extending product lifecycles through maintenance, reuse, remanufacturing, and recycling. He later co-founded the Product-Life Institute, which advocated for circular business models and strategies to reduce waste and resource consumption. His work directly influenced modern circular economy frameworks and policies adopted by governments and businesses worldwide.

The Role of Industrial Ecology

Industrial ecology, a discipline that emerged in the 1980s, further contributed to the development of circular economy principles. Industrial ecologists studied the flow of materials and energy within industrial systems, emphasizing the need to design processes that mimic natural ecosystems. In nature, waste from one organism serves as a resource for another, creating a balanced and regenerative cycle. Applying this concept to industrial production led to the idea of "industrial symbiosis," where industries collaborate to share resources, byproducts, and waste streams. The Kalundborg Eco-Industrial Park in Denmark became a pioneering example of industrial symbiosis, where businesses exchange excess heat, water, and materials to reduce waste and improve efficiency. This approach demonstrated the economic and environmental advantages of circular thinking in industrial settings.

Regulatory and Policy Developments

As concerns about resource depletion, pollution, and climate change grew in the late 20th century, governments and international organizations began exploring policy measures to promote sustainable economic practices. The European Union played a leading role in advancing circular economy policies by implementing waste reduction targets, recycling mandates, and extended producer responsibility regulations. In the early 2000s, the concept of the circular economy gained traction in China, where policymakers introduced legislation to promote resource efficiency and industrial sustainability. These regulatory efforts helped shape the global discourse on circular economy strategies and their integration into economic planning and environmental management.

The Influence of Biomimicry and Cradle-to-Cradle Design

Another significant influence on early circular economy thinking was the concept of biomimicry, which draws inspiration from nature to design sustainable systems. Biologist Janine Benyus popularized biomimicry in the 1990s, advocating for solutions that emulate natural processes to create resilient and regenerative technologies. Around the same time, the Cradle-to-Cradle design philosophy, developed by architect William McDonough and chemist Michael Braungart, introduced a framework for designing products with a focus on recyclability, biodegradability, and non-toxic materials. Cradle-to-Cradle principles emphasized the importance of designing products that could be continuously cycled through biological and technical loops, eliminating the concept of waste altogether.

The Transition to Modern Circular Economy Models

By the early 21st century, the circular economy had evolved from a theoretical concept into a practical framework adopted by businesses, policymakers, and environmental organizations. The Ellen MacArthur Foundation, established in 2010, became a key driver in promoting circular economy principles globally. Through research, advocacy, and collaboration with industries, the foundation helped mainstream the concept, emphasizing the economic benefits of circularity alongside its environmental advantages. Companies across various sectors, from fashion and technology to construction and agriculture, began integrating circular strategies such as product leasing, material recovery, and closed-loop supply chains into their operations.

Challenges and Opportunities in Circular Economy Adoption

Despite the progress made in advancing circular economy thinking, challenges remain in achieving widespread adoption. One of the primary obstacles is the deeply entrenched linear economic model, which continues to prioritize short-term profitability over long-term sustainability. Transitioning to a circular economy requires significant investment in infrastructure, innovation, and policy reform. Additionally, consumer behavior and cultural attitudes toward consumption and waste must shift to support circular practices. However, the opportunities presented by the circular economy, including job creation, resource security, and climate resilience, outweigh these challenges. With continued research, technological advancements, and collaborative efforts, the principles of early circular economy thinking can be fully realized in modern economic systems.

1.4.2 Circular Economy in Practice: Global Adoption and Trends

The global adoption of the circular economy is advancing at varying speeds across different regions, driven by policy measures, corporate initiatives, and consumer awareness. Europe has established itself as a leader in circular policies, while China has integrated circular principles into its industrial strategies. North America is seeing significant corporate innovation, Latin America is addressing waste challenges, Africa is exploring circular solutions for economic growth, and the Asia-Pacific region is leveraging circular business models for sustainable development. While challenges remain, such as regulatory barriers and infrastructure gaps, the momentum behind the circular economy continues to grow. As new technologies, business models, and policy frameworks emerge, the transition towards a global circular economy is becoming increasingly viable. By embracing circularity on a larger scale, societies can achieve long-term sustainability, economic resilience, and environmental conservation, creating a regenerative and prosperous future for all.

Europe: A Leader in Circular Economy Policies

Europe has been at the forefront of circular economy adoption, driven by ambitious policy frameworks and strong environmental regulations. The European Union (EU) has played a key role in advancing circular strategies through initiatives such as the Circular Economy Action Plan, which was introduced in 2015 and later updated in 2020. This plan focuses on sustainable product design, waste reduction, and the development of circular business models across various industries. The EU has also implemented extended producer responsibility (EPR) regulations, requiring manufacturers to take responsibility for the end-of-life management of their products. Countries such as the Netherlands, Sweden, and Germany have set ambitious targets to transition toward fully circular economies by 2050, investing in circular infrastructure, innovation, and education. European companies in sectors like fashion, automotive, and electronics have embraced circular practices such as remanufacturing, repair services, and closed-loop supply chains to reduce their environmental footprint and enhance sustainability.

China: Integrating Circular Economy into Industrial Policy

China has recognized the importance of the circular economy as a strategy to address environmental pollution, resource scarcity, and economic resilience. The country has incorporated circular principles into its national policies, particularly through its Circular Economy Promotion Law enacted in 2009. China's approach emphasizes industrial symbiosis, where industries collaborate to reuse waste materials and optimize resource efficiency. The development of eco-industrial parks, such as the Suzhou Industrial Park, serves as a model for integrating circular economy principles into large-scale manufacturing. Additionally, China has taken significant steps in electronic waste recycling, implementing policies to recover valuable materials from discarded electronics. The shift towards a circular economy is also evident in China's Belt and Road Initiative, which includes sustainable infrastructure and green investment projects aimed at fostering circular development across multiple regions.

North America: Corporate Innovation and Consumer Awareness

In North America, the adoption of circular economy principles has been driven primarily by corporate initiatives and growing consumer awareness of sustainability. The United States and Canada have seen an increase in businesses incorporating circular strategies into their operations, particularly in the technology, retail, and food industries. Companies such as Apple, Patagonia, and Loop Industries have pioneered circular business models by focusing on product longevity, material recovery, and circular supply chains. Apple, for instance, has invested in robotic disassembly systems to recover rare metals from used devices, reducing reliance on virgin materials. Circular economy initiatives in North America also include zero-waste packaging solutions, food waste reduction programs, and increased recycling infrastructure. However, policy support for circularity in the U.S. has been less comprehensive than in Europe, with efforts often led by state and local governments rather than federal mandates. Despite this, the private sector's commitment to circular economy practices continues to drive progress in the region.

Latin America: Addressing Waste and Promoting Circular Solutions

Latin America faces significant challenges related to waste management, resource efficiency, and environmental conservation, making the circular economy an essential strategy for sustainable development. Several countries in the region, including Brazil, Chile, and Colombia, have introduced circular economy initiatives to improve waste management and promote sustainable production. Brazil has implemented waste-picking cooperatives that integrate informal waste collectors into the recycling economy, providing economic opportunities while enhancing recycling rates. Chile has adopted extended producer responsibility laws to ensure manufacturers take responsibility for product disposal and material recovery. Additionally, circular agriculture practices are gaining traction in Latin America, with regenerative farming techniques and organic waste composting being used to improve soil health and reduce reliance on chemical fertilizers. While challenges such as regulatory enforcement and infrastructure limitations remain, the circular economy is gradually becoming a key component of sustainable development strategies in the region.

Africa: Circular Economy for Economic Growth and Sustainability

In Africa, circular economy initiatives are being explored as solutions to address waste management, job creation, and resource efficiency. Many African countries struggle with inadequate waste disposal systems and high levels of environmental pollution, particularly from plastic waste. However, innovative solutions are emerging to tackle these challenges. Countries like Kenya and Rwanda have implemented plastic bans and encouraged the development of alternative biodegradable packaging materials. Circular entrepreneurship is also growing in Africa, with businesses focusing on upcycling waste materials into valuable products. For example, companies in Ghana and Nigeria have developed programs to recycle electronic waste, turning discarded electronics into reusable components. Additionally, circular agriculture and water conservation initiatives are being promoted to enhance food security and resilience to climate change. While the circular economy in Africa is still in its early stages, the potential for sustainable economic growth through circular practices is becoming increasingly recognized.

Asia-Pacific: Circular Business Models and Sustainable Innovation

The Asia-Pacific region is experiencing rapid economic growth, accompanied by significant environmental challenges such as pollution, deforestation, and resource depletion. Many countries in the region, including Japan, South Korea, and Australia, have embraced circular economy principles to address these issues. Japan has long been a leader in circular economy thinking, implementing strict recycling regulations and promoting the development of resource-efficient industries. South Korea has adopted circular policies such as landfill bans on food waste and incentives for companies that implement circular strategies. Australia has introduced initiatives to promote a circular plastics economy, investing in research and infrastructure for recycling and material recovery. Additionally, circular fashion and sustainable packaging innovations are gaining momentum in the region, with brands focusing on eco-friendly materials and closed-loop production processes. The Asia-Pacific region's commitment to circularity is driven by both policy measures and corporate sustainability goals, positioning it as a key player in the global circular economy movement.

Emerging Trends in the Circular Economy

As the circular economy continues to evolve, several emerging trends are shaping its global adoption. One major trend is the rise of digital technologies that enable circular business models, such as blockchain for supply chain transparency, artificial intelligence for material optimization, and 3D printing for sustainable manufacturing. Another key development is the increasing role of consumer behavior in driving circularity, with demand for sustainable products and services influencing corporate strategies. Governments are also implementing stricter regulations on waste and resource use, pushing industries to adopt circular practices. Additionally, financial institutions are beginning to recognize the economic benefits of circularity, leading to increased investment in circular startups and green bonds that support circular economy projects. These trends indicate that circular economy principles are becoming more deeply integrated into global economic systems, paving the way for a more sustainable future.

1.5 THE ROLE OF CIRCULAR ECONOMY IN ACHIEVING SDGS

1.5.1 Addressing Climate Change, Resource Scarcity, and Waste

The world is facing an unprecedented environmental crisis marked by climate change, resource scarcity, and excessive waste generation. These interconnected challenges threaten ecosystems, economies, and human well-being. Climate change, driven by greenhouse gas emissions from industrial activities, transportation, and deforestation, has led to rising global temperatures, extreme weather events, and disruptions to natural cycles. Simultaneously, the depletion of finite natural resources poses risks to economic stability, food security, and energy production. Waste generation, particularly from plastic pollution and industrial byproducts, exacerbates environmental degradation and places immense pressure on landfills and natural habitats.

The challenges of climate change, resource scarcity, and waste generation require immediate and coordinated action from governments, businesses, and individuals. Climate change mitigation efforts must focus on reducing greenhouse gas emissions, transitioning to renewable energy sources, and implementing adaptation strategies to protect vulnerable communities. Addressing resource scarcity involves adopting circular economy principles, promoting sustainable consumption, and developing alternative materials to reduce dependence on finite resources. Effective waste management solutions, including recycling, composting, and product redesign, are crucial in minimizing environmental impacts and promoting a more sustainable society. By embracing innovation, collaboration, and responsible decision-making, humanity can work towards a future where economic growth and environmental sustainability go hand in hand. The shift towards sustainable practices is not only necessary for the planet but also presents opportunities for new industries, job creation, and improved quality of life for future generations.

The Role of Climate Change in Environmental Degradation

Climate change has emerged as one of the most pressing environmental issues of the 21st century. The burning of fossil fuels for energy production, deforestation for agriculture, and industrial processes have significantly increased carbon dioxide and methane levels in the atmosphere. These greenhouse gases trap heat, leading to rising global temperatures and altered climate patterns. The consequences of climate change include more frequent and intense heatwaves, hurricanes, floods, and droughts, which threaten human settlements, infrastructure, and biodiversity. Melting glaciers and rising sea levels endanger coastal communities and small island nations, increasing the risk of displacement and loss of livelihoods.

Agriculture and food production are also heavily impacted by climate change. Shifts in temperature and precipitation patterns affect crop yields, leading to food shortages and increased prices. In some regions, prolonged droughts have resulted in desertification and soil degradation, making agricultural land unusable. Additionally, changing climate conditions have facilitated the spread of pests and diseases that affect both crops and livestock. To combat these challenges, efforts must focus on reducing greenhouse gas emissions through renewable energy adoption, reforestation programs, and sustainable agricultural practices. Governments and organizations must also invest in climate adaptation strategies, such as building resilient infrastructure and developing early warning systems for extreme weather events.

Resource Scarcity and the Urgent Need for Conservation

The depletion of natural resources is another critical issue that threatens long-term sustainability. The global population continues to grow, placing greater demands on essential resources such as water, minerals, forests, and fossil fuels. Overextraction and unsustainable consumption patterns have led to resource depletion, making it difficult to meet the needs of future generations. Water scarcity, for example, is a growing concern, with many regions experiencing severe droughts and declining freshwater availability. Industrial and agricultural activities often pollute water sources, further limiting access to clean and safe drinking water.

The overuse of finite minerals and metals, such as lithium, cobalt, and rare earth elements, presents challenges for industries that rely on these materials for manufacturing electronics, batteries, and renewable energy technologies. The demand for these resources is expected to rise as the transition to green technologies accelerates, necessitating more efficient extraction methods, recycling initiatives, and material alternatives. Sustainable forestry practices and afforestation projects can help address deforestation, ensuring the long-term availability of timber and preserving biodiversity.

To mitigate resource scarcity, businesses and policymakers must adopt circular economy principles, which focus on maximizing resource efficiency, promoting recycling, and designing products with longevity in mind. Governments can implement regulations that encourage sustainable resource management, such as imposing limits on resource extraction, incentivizing the use of recycled materials, and supporting research into alternative materials. Individuals can also contribute by reducing waste, adopting sustainable consumption habits, and supporting companies that prioritize environmental responsibility.

The Growing Challenge of Waste Management

Waste generation has reached alarming levels, with plastic pollution, electronic waste, and food waste becoming major environmental threats. The rapid increase in disposable consumer goods, single-use plastics, and fast fashion has contributed to overflowing landfills and environmental contamination. Plastics, in particular, have become a major concern due to their persistence in the environment. Every year, millions of tons of plastic waste end up in oceans, harming marine life and entering the food chain through microplastic contamination.

Electronic waste, or e-waste, is another growing issue as technological advancements lead to shorter product lifecycles. Many electronic devices contain hazardous substances such as lead, mercury, and cadmium, which pose health and environmental risks if not properly disposed of. The improper handling of e-waste often results in toxic materials leaching into soil and water, further exacerbating pollution problems. Sustainable e-waste management requires the establishment of efficient recycling systems, the implementation of take-back programs by manufacturers, and the promotion of repair and refurbishment initiatives.

Food waste also represents a significant environmental and social challenge. A large portion of food produced globally is wasted due to inefficiencies in supply chains, improper storage, and consumer behavior. Food waste not only contributes to greenhouse gas emissions from decomposition but also wastes valuable resources such as water, energy, and labor used in food production. Addressing food waste requires improving distribution systems, educating consumers on proper food storage, and implementing policies that encourage surplus food donation and composting.

Innovative Solutions for a Sustainable Future

Addressing climate change, resource scarcity, and waste requires innovative solutions that integrate technology, policy, and community engagement. Renewable energy technologies, such as solar, wind, and hydropower, play a crucial role in reducing dependence on fossil fuels and lowering carbon emissions. Advances in battery storage and smart grid systems enhance the efficiency and reliability of renewable energy sources, making them more viable alternatives to traditional energy production.

Circular economy models offer a promising approach to resource conservation and waste reduction. Businesses are increasingly adopting circular strategies, such as designing products for durability, implementing closed-loop manufacturing processes, and embracing product-as-a-service models. For example, companies in the fashion industry are exploring sustainable textiles, garment recycling programs, and rental clothing services to reduce textile waste and promote sustainable consumption.

Government policies and international cooperation are also essential in tackling these environmental challenges. Carbon pricing mechanisms, emissions trading schemes, and strict environmental regulations can incentivize industries to adopt cleaner production methods and invest in sustainable practices. Additionally, global agreements, such as the Paris Agreement, play a crucial role in setting emission reduction targets and promoting collaborative efforts to combat climate change.

Education and awareness campaigns are critical in fostering behavioral changes that support sustainability. Schools, businesses, and media organizations can promote eco-friendly habits, such as reducing single-use plastics, conserving energy, and supporting local and sustainable products. Grassroots movements and community-led initiatives also play an important role in driving environmental action and advocating for policy changes at local and national levels.

1.5.2 Aligning Circular Economy with the UN's Sustainable Development Goals

The circular economy presents a powerful framework for achieving the United Nations' Sustainable Development Goals by promoting responsible resource use, reducing environmental impact, and fostering economic and social resilience. Its alignment with goals related to climate action, resource efficiency, clean energy, and sustainable urban development highlights the transformative potential of circular strategies. Governments, businesses, and communities must collaborate to accelerate the adoption of circular economy practices, invest in innovation, and implement policies that encourage sustainability. As the world moves toward a more resource-conscious future, embracing circular principles will be essential in achieving a balanced and sustainable global economy while ensuring a healthier planet for future generations.

Circular Economy and Sustainable Development

Responsible Consumption and Production

One of the most direct connections between the circular economy and the SDGs is with Goal 12, which aims to ensure sustainable consumption and production patterns. The traditional linear economic model—based on the "take, make, dispose" approach—has led to significant resource depletion and environmental degradation. By shifting to a circular economy, industries can reduce waste, extend the lifecycle of products, and implement recycling and reuse strategies. Businesses can adopt sustainable supply chains, design products with longevity in mind, and minimize packaging waste, all of which contribute to achieving responsible consumption and production targets.

Climate Action

The circular economy also plays a crucial role in addressing climate change, which is the focus of Goal 13. Climate change is driven by greenhouse gas emissions resulting from industrial activities, energy production, and waste generation. Circular economy strategies, such as using renewable energy, improving energy efficiency, and reducing waste, can significantly lower carbon footprints. By transitioning to a circular system, industries can cut emissions associated with raw material extraction, transportation, and disposal. Policies that promote sustainable practices, such as carbon pricing and incentives for green innovation, further support the alignment of the circular economy with climate action goals.

Clean Water and Sanitation

Water scarcity and pollution are major global challenges that threaten ecosystems and human health. Goal 6 focuses on ensuring access to clean water and sanitation for all. The circular economy promotes water conservation through strategies such as water recycling, wastewater treatment, and rainwater harvesting. Industries can adopt closed-loop water systems that minimize water waste and pollution. Additionally, sustainable agricultural practices, such as precision irrigation and soil conservation, reduce water consumption while improving productivity. By integrating circular water management practices, communities can achieve long-term water security and reduce the impact of pollution on freshwater sources.

Affordable and Clean Energy

The transition to a circular economy is closely linked to Goal 7, which seeks to ensure access to affordable, reliable, sustainable, and modern energy for all. A circular economy promotes the use of renewable energy sources, such as solar, wind, and bioenergy, while reducing dependence on fossil fuels. Energy efficiency measures, such as smart grid technology and improved insulation, contribute to reducing energy waste. The adoption of decentralized energy systems, where waste heat and biomass are repurposed, supports both economic and environmental sustainability. By integrating circular energy solutions, communities can achieve cleaner energy access and reduce the overall environmental impact of energy production.

Decent Work and Economic Growth

A circular economy can stimulate economic growth while promoting decent work opportunities, which aligns with Goal 8. By shifting away from resource-intensive industries and fostering innovation in sustainable practices, new job opportunities emerge in sectors such as recycling, remanufacturing, and renewable energy. Small and medium-sized enterprises (SMEs) benefit from circular business models that encourage local sourcing, repair services, and shared ownership systems. The transition to a circular economy also fosters economic resilience by reducing dependency on finite resources, thereby protecting businesses from price volatility and supply chain disruptions. Additionally, policies that support sustainable entrepreneurship and workforce training in green industries contribute to long-term employment stability.

Industry, Innovation, and Infrastructure

Goal 9 emphasizes the need for resilient infrastructure, sustainable industrialization, and innovation. The circular economy drives innovation in materials science, waste management, and industrial processes, leading to more sustainable production methods. Technologies such as 3D printing, biodegradable materials, and blockchain for supply chain transparency are transforming industries. Sustainable infrastructure projects, such as green buildings and eco-friendly transportation systems, further support the transition to a circular economy. Governments and businesses that invest in research and development of circular solutions can enhance competitiveness and drive industrial transformation towards sustainability.

Sustainable Cities and Communities

Urbanization is accelerating globally, making Goal 11—focused on creating sustainable cities and communities—an essential priority. Circular economy strategies can help cities reduce waste, improve resource efficiency, and enhance urban resilience. Sustainable urban planning initiatives, such as eco-friendly public transportation, green spaces, and energy-efficient buildings, contribute to lower carbon emissions and improved quality of life. Waste management systems that prioritize recycling and composting help reduce landfill waste. Smart city technologies, such as sensor-based waste collection and energy-efficient lighting, support the circular economy by optimizing resource use and reducing environmental impact.

Life on Land

Deforestation, soil degradation, and biodiversity loss are significant threats to terrestrial ecosystems, making Goal 15 crucial for sustainability efforts. The circular economy encourages sustainable land use practices, including regenerative agriculture, afforestation, and responsible forestry management. By promoting biodegradable and sustainable materials, industries can reduce reliance on virgin resources that contribute to habitat destruction. Circular farming techniques, such as agroforestry and permaculture, enhance soil health and biodiversity while improving food security. Policies that support ecosystem restoration and conservation initiatives further align circular economy principles with the goal of protecting life on land.

Life below Water

Marine pollution, overfishing, and habitat destruction threaten ocean ecosystems, which is why Goal 14 focuses on conserving and sustainably using marine resources. The circular economy addresses these challenges by reducing plastic waste, promoting sustainable seafood practices, and implementing waste-to-energy solutions that prevent pollution. The development of biodegradable packaging and extended producer responsibility (EPR) programs for plastics contribute to reducing ocean contamination. Sustainable fishing policies and marine protected areas help restore marine biodiversity. By adopting circular strategies, industries and policymakers can minimize environmental damage to oceans and support the long-term health of marine ecosystems.

CHAPTER 2

Key Concepts and Principles of Circular Economy

2.1 THE 3RS: REDUCE, REUSE, AND RECYCLE

2.1.1 Reducing Resource Consumption and Waste Generation

The global economy has long relied on a linear model of production and consumption, which follows the pattern of extracting raw materials, manufacturing products, using them, and then discarding them as waste. This approach has led to excessive resource consumption, environmental degradation, and a growing waste crisis. In response to these challenges, there is an increasing shift towards sustainable practices that focus on reducing resource consumption and minimizing waste generation. By implementing strategies such as resource efficiency, circular economy principles, and sustainable design, businesses and individuals can contribute to a more sustainable future while preserving the planet's natural resources.

Reducing resource consumption and waste generation is essential for achieving environmental sustainability and mitigating the negative impacts of human activity on the planet. Through a combination of circular economy strategies, sustainable design, efficient resource management, and technological innovation, businesses and individuals can contribute to a more sustainable future. Government policies and consumer awareness also play a crucial role in driving change and promoting responsible consumption patterns. By adopting a holistic approach that integrates sustainability into all aspects of production and consumption, society can move towards a more resilient and resource-efficient economy that benefits both the environment and future generations.

The Need for Reducing Resource Consumption

The demand for natural resources has been rising steadily due to population growth, urbanization, and economic development. Many of these resources, including fossil fuels, minerals, and freshwater, are finite and are being depleted at an alarming rate. Overextraction of raw materials not only leads to resource scarcity but also contributes to environmental problems such as deforestation, loss of biodiversity, and climate change. To address these issues, efforts must be made to optimize resource use and promote responsible consumption patterns. Industries can adopt sustainable sourcing practices, develop energy-efficient manufacturing processes, and invest in renewable energy sources to reduce their reliance on non-renewable materials.

Circular Economy as a Solution

One of the most effective approaches to reducing resource consumption and waste generation is the adoption of a circular economy model. Unlike the traditional linear model, the circular economy focuses on keeping resources in use for as long as possible through recycling, refurbishment, and remanufacturing. By designing products for durability and repairability, companies can extend the lifespan of goods and reduce the need for virgin materials. Additionally, implementing closed-loop production systems allows industries to recover valuable materials from used products and reintegrate them into the manufacturing process. This not only conserves natural resources but also reduces waste and minimizes the environmental footprint of production activities.

Government Policies and Regulations

Government policies and regulations play a vital role in promoting sustainable resource consumption and waste reduction. Many countries have implemented policies that encourage businesses to adopt circular economy principles, such as extended producer responsibility (EPR) programs, which require manufacturers to take responsibility for the end-of-life management of their products. Waste reduction targets, recycling mandates, and bans on single-use plastics are also effective measures in addressing waste-related issues. Incentives for companies that invest in sustainable technologies, such as tax breaks and grants, further support the transition towards a more resource-efficient economy. By enforcing regulations and providing support for sustainable initiatives, governments can drive systemic change and encourage businesses and consumers to adopt more responsible practices.

The Role of Technology in Waste Reduction

Technological advancements are driving innovation in resource conservation and waste management. Smart waste collection systems, powered by artificial intelligence and data analytics, enable efficient waste sorting and recycling processes. Biotechnology solutions, such as enzyme-based recycling for plastics, offer new ways to break down waste materials into reusable components. Additionally, digital platforms that facilitate product sharing and rental services promote a shift towards a more circular economy by reducing the demand for new goods. These technological solutions are transforming waste management practices and providing scalable solutions to global resource challenges.

Business Models for Sustainability

New business models that prioritize sustainability are emerging as a response to the need for resource conservation and waste reduction. Subscription-based services, product-as-a-service models, and second-hand marketplaces are gaining popularity as consumers seek more sustainable alternatives to traditional ownership. Companies that embrace these models can reduce material waste while meeting customer demands for affordable and eco-friendly products. For example, clothing rental services allow consumers to access fashion without contributing to textile waste, while electronics refurbishment programs extend the lifespan of electronic devices. These innovative business approaches demonstrate how sustainability can be integrated into commercial success.

2.1.2 Reuse Strategies for Materials and Products

The concept of reuse has gained significant attention as a key strategy in reducing waste and promoting sustainability. Unlike recycling, which often involves breaking down materials to create new products, reuse focuses on extending the life of materials and products by repurposing them in their existing form. This approach not only conserves resources but also reduces energy consumption and environmental pollution associated with production and waste disposal. Reuse strategies for materials and products play a critical role in reducing waste, conserving resources, and promoting sustainability. From industrial symbiosis and reusable packaging to consumer habits and government policies, multiple stakeholders can contribute to extending the lifespan of products and minimizing environmental impact. While challenges remain, continued innovation, education, and policy support can accelerate the adoption of reuse practices on a global scale. By embracing a culture of reuse, societies can move closer to a circular economy where materials are valued, waste is minimized, and resources are used efficiently for the benefit of future generations.

The Importance of Reuse in Sustainability

Reuse plays a crucial role in the transition to a circular economy, where materials are kept in use for as long as possible. It helps reduce the demand for raw materials, which in turn lessens the environmental impact of extraction and processing. Reuse also decreases the volume of waste that ends up in landfills and incinerators, mitigating the release of greenhouse gases and harmful pollutants. Additionally, by prioritizing reuse over disposal, society can move away from a linear consumption model and adopt more responsible resource management practices that align with global sustainability goals.

Product Design for Reusability

One of the most effective ways to promote reuse is through sustainable product design. Manufacturers can design products with modular components that allow for easy repair, refurbishment, and repurposing. Durable materials and timeless designs can extend the lifespan of products, making them more suitable for multiple uses. Companies that prioritize reusability in their designs also contribute to reducing electronic waste, textile waste, and packaging waste. For example, modular smartphones enable users to replace individual components instead of discarding the entire device, and refillable packaging systems help reduce single-use plastic consumption.

Reusable Packaging Solutions

The packaging industry has traditionally relied on disposable materials, contributing significantly to global waste issues. However, the adoption of reusable packaging solutions is gaining traction among businesses and consumers. Companies are introducing returnable containers, refill stations, and deposit systems to reduce packaging waste. Glass bottles, metal tins, and compostable packaging materials offer durable and sustainable alternatives to single-use plastics. Some retailers have also implemented bulk purchasing systems that allow customers to bring their own containers, minimizing packaging waste at the source. By embracing reusable packaging, businesses can lower their environmental impact and promote responsible consumer behavior.

The Role of Businesses in Encouraging Reuse

Companies can drive significant change by integrating reuse strategies into their business models. Implementing product-as-a-service models, where consumers rent or lease products instead of purchasing them, encourages multiple uses of the same item. For example, furniture rental services allow individuals to use high-quality pieces without the need for constant replacement. Electronics manufacturers are also exploring trade-in programs that refurbish and resell used devices, ensuring that valuable materials remain in circulation.

Public Policies and Regulations Supporting Reuse

Governments play a crucial role in promoting reuse through policies and regulations. Many countries have introduced extended producer responsibility (EPR) programs that require manufacturers to take back and manage the end-of-life disposal of their products. Tax incentives and subsidies for businesses that implement reuse initiatives encourage sustainable practices. Some cities have also implemented zero-waste policies that emphasize reuse as a key component of waste management. By enacting regulations that support reuse, governments can create an enabling environment for sustainable resource management and circular economy practices.

Challenges to Reuse Implementation

Despite the benefits of reuse, several challenges hinder its widespread adoption. One major barrier is consumer behavior, as many individuals prefer the convenience of disposable products over reusable alternatives. The lack of infrastructure for collecting, sorting, and refurbishing used materials also limits reuse opportunities. Additionally, some industries face financial constraints in redesigning products for reusability or establishing take-back systems. Overcoming these challenges requires a combination of education, investment in reuse infrastructure, and collaboration between governments, businesses, and consumers to drive a cultural shift toward sustainable consumption.

The Future of Reuse Strategies

As awareness of environmental issues continues to grow, the future of reuse strategies looks promising. Technological advancements in materials science, digital tracking, and artificial intelligence are making it easier to identify and repurpose used products efficiently. Businesses are increasingly recognizing the economic potential of reuse models, leading to the expansion of second-hand markets and circular supply chains. Collaborative initiatives between industries, policymakers, and consumers will further drive innovation in reuse practices. By continuously improving reuse strategies and integrating them into mainstream consumption patterns, societies can work towards a more sustainable and resource-efficient future.

2.1.3 Recycling Technologies and Innovations

Recycling is the process of converting waste materials into new materials and objects. This concept often includes the recovery of energy from waste materials. The recyclability of a material depends on its ability to reacquire the properties it had in its original state. It is an alternative to "conventional" waste disposal that can save material and help lower greenhouse gas emissions. It can also prevent the waste of potentially useful materials and reduce the consumption of fresh raw materials, reducing energy use, air pollution (from incineration) and water pollution (from landfilling).

Recycling is a key component of modern waste reduction and is the third component of the "Reduce, Reuse, and Recycle" waste hierarchy. It promotes environmental sustainability by removing raw material input and redirecting waste output in the economic system. There are some ISO standards related to recycling, such as ISO 15270:2008 for plastics waste and ISO 14001:2015 for environmental management control of recycling practice.

Recyclable materials include many kinds of glass, paper, cardboard, metal, plastic, tires, textiles, batteries, and electronics. The composting and other reuse of biodegradable waste—such as food and garden waste—is also a form of recycling. Materials for recycling are either delivered to a household recycling center or picked up from curbside bins, then sorted, cleaned, and reprocessed into new materials for manufacturing new products.

In ideal implementations, recycling a material produces a fresh supply of the same material—for example, used office paper would be converted into new office paper, and used polystyrene foam into new polystyrene. Some types of materials, such as metal cans, can be remanufactured repeatedly without losing their purity. With other materials, this is often difficult or too expensive (compared with producing the same product from raw materials or other sources), so "recycling" of many products and materials involves their reuse in producing different materials (for example, paperboard). Another form of recycling is the salvage of constituent materials from complex products, due to either their intrinsic value (such as lead from car batteries and gold from printed circuit boards), or their hazardous nature (e.g. removal and reuse of mercury from thermometers and thermostats).

Health and Environmental Impact

Health Impact

- E-waste: According to the WHO (2023), "Every year millions of electrical and electronic devices are discarded ... a threat to the environment and to human health if they are not treated, disposed of, and recycled appropriately. Common items ... include computers ... e-waste are recycled using environmentally unsound techniques and are likely stored in homes and warehouses, dumped, exported or recycled under inferior conditions. When e-waste is treated using inferior activities, it can release as many as 1000 different chemical substances ... including harmful neurotoxicants such as lead." A paper in the journal Sustainable Materials & Technologies remarks upon the difficulty of managing e-waste, particularly from home automation products, which, due to their becoming obsolete at a high rate, are putting increasing strain on recycling systems, which have not adapted to meet the recycling needs posed by this type of product.
- Slag Recycling: Copper slag is obtained when copper and nickel ores are recovered from their source ores using a pyrometallurgical process, and these ores usually contain other elements which include iron, cobalt, silica, and alumina. An estimate of 2.2–3 tons of copper slag is generated per ton of copper produced, resulting in around 24.6 tons

of slag per year, which is regarded as waste. Environmental impact of slag include copper paralysis, which leads to death due to gastric hemorrhage, if ingested by humans. It may also cause acute dermatitis upon skin exposure. Toxicity may also be uptaken by crops through soil, consequently spreading animals and food sources and increasing the risk of cardiovascular diseases, cancer, cognitive impairment, chronic anemia, and damage to kidneys, bones, nervous system, brain and skin. Substituting gravel and grit in quarries has been more cost-effective, due to having its sources with better proximity to consumer markets. Trading between countries and establishment of blast furnaces is helping increase slag utilization, hence reducing wastage and pollution.

Environmental Impact

Economist Steven Landsburg, author of a paper entitled "Why I Am Not an Environmentalist", claimed that paper recycling actually reduces tree populations. He argues that because paper companies have incentives to replenish their forests, large demands for paper lead to large forests while reduced demand for paper leads to fewer "farmed" forests.

Fig: A Metal Scrap Worker is Pictured Burning Insulated Copper Wires for Copper Recovery at Agbogbloshie, Ghana

When foresting companies cut down trees, more are planted in their place; however, such farmed forests are inferior to natural forests in several ways. Farmed forests are not able to fix the soil as quickly as natural forests. This can cause widespread soil erosion and often requiring large amounts of fertilizer to maintain the soil, while containing little tree and wild-life biodiversity compared to virgin forests. Also, the new trees planted are not as big as the trees that were cut down, and the argument that there would be "more trees" is not compelling to forestry advocates when they are counting saplings.

In particular, wood from tropical rainforests is rarely harvested for paper because of their heterogeneity. According to the United Nations Framework Convention on Climate Change secretariat, the overwhelming direct cause of deforestation is subsistence farming (48% of deforestation) and commercial agriculture (32%), which is linked to food, not paper production.

Other non-conventional methods of material recycling, like Waste-to-Energy (WTE) systems, have garnered increased attention in the recent past due to the polarizing nature of their emissions. While viewed as a sustainable method of capturing energy from material waste feedstocks by many, others have cited numerous explanations for why the technology has not been scaled globally.

Legislation

Supply

For a recycling program to work, a large, stable supply of recyclable material is crucial. Three legislative options have been used to create such supplies: mandatory recycling collection, container deposit legislation, and refuse bans. Mandatory collection laws set recycling targets for cities, usually in the form that a certain percentage of a material must be diverted from the city's waste stream by a target date. The city is responsible for working to meet this target.

Container deposit legislation mandates refunds for the return of certain containers—typically glass, plastic and metal. When a product in such a container is purchased, a small surcharge is added that the consumer can reclaim when the container is returned to a collection point. These programs have succeeded in creating an average 80% recycling rate. Despite such good results, the shift in collection costs from local government to industry and consumers has created strong opposition in some areas—for example, where manufacturers bear the responsibility for recycling their products. In the European Union, the WEEE Directive requires producers of consumer electronics to reimburse the recyclers' costs.

An alternative way to increase the supply of recyclates is to ban the disposal of certain materials as waste, often including used oil, old batteries, tires, and garden waste. This can create a viable economy for the proper disposal of the products. Care must be taken that enough recycling services exist to meet the supply, or such bans can create increased illegal dumping.

Government-Mandated Demand

Four forms of legislation have also been used to increase and maintain the demand for recycled materials: minimum recycled content mandates, utilization rates, procurement policies, and recycled product labeling.

Both minimum recycled content mandates and utilization rates increase demand by forcing manufacturers to include recycling in their operations. Content mandates specify that a certain percentage of a new product must consist of recycled material. Utilization rates are a more flexible option: Industries can meet their recycling targets at any point of their operations, or even contract out recycling in exchange for tradable credits. Opponents to these methods cite their large increase in reporting requirements, and claim that they rob the industry of flexibility.

Governments have used their own purchasing power to increase recycling demand through "procurement policies". These policies are either "set-asides", which reserve a certain amount of spending for recycled products; or "price preference" programs that provide larger budgets when recycled items are purchased. Additional regulations can target specific cases: in the United States, for example, the Environmental Protection Agency mandates the purchase of oil, paper, tires and building insulation from recycled or re-refined sources whenever possible.

The final government regulation toward increased demand is recycled product labeling. When producers are required to label their packaging with the amount of recycled material it contains (including the packaging), consumers can make more educated choices. Consumers with sufficient buying power can choose more environmentally conscious options, prompting producers to increase the recycled material in their products and increase demand. Standardized recycling labeling can also have a positive effect on the supply of recyclates when it specifies how and where the product can be recycled.

Recyclates

"Recyclate" is a raw material sent to and processed in a waste recycling plant or materials-recovery facility so it can be used in the production of new materials and products. For example, plastic bottles can be made into plastic pellets and synthetic fabrics.

Quality of Recyclate

The quality of recyclates is one of the principal challenges for the success of a long-term vision of a green economy and achieving zero waste. It generally refers to how much of it is composed of target material, versus non-target material and other non-recyclable material. Steel and other metals have intrinsically higher recyclate quality; it is estimated that two-thirds of all new steel comes from recycled steel. Only target material is likely to be recycled, so higher amounts of non-target and non-recyclable materials can reduce the quantity of recycled products. A high proportion of non-target and non-recyclable material can make it more difficult to achieve "high-quality" recycling; and if recyclate is of poor quality, it is more likely to end up being down-cycled or, in more extreme cases, sent to other recovery options or landfilled. For example, to facilitate the remanufacturing of clear glass products, there are tight restrictions for colored glass entering the re-melt process. Another example is the downcycling of plastic, where products such as plastic food packaging are often downcycled into lower quality products, and do not get recycled into the same plastic food packaging.

Fig: Glass Recovered by Crushing only One Kind of Beer Bottle

The quality of recyclate not only supports high-quality recycling, but it can also deliver significant environmental benefits by reducing, reusing, and keeping products out of landfills. High-quality recycling can support economic growth by maximizing the value of waste material. Higher income levels from the sale of quality recyclates can return value significant to local governments, households and businesses. Pursuing high-quality recycling can also promote consumer and business confidence in the waste and resource management sector, and may encourage investment in it.

There are many actions along the recycling supply chain, each of which can affect recyclate quality. Waste producers who place non-target and non-recyclable wastes in recycling collections can affect the quality of final recyclate streams, and require extra efforts to discard those materials at later stages in the recycling process. Different collection systems can induce different levels of contamination. When multiple materials are collected together, extra effort is required to sort them into separate streams and can significantly reduce the quality of the final products.

Transportation and the compaction of materials can also make this more difficult. Despite improvements in technology and quality of recyclate, sorting facilities are still not 100% effective in separating materials. When materials are stored outside, where they can become wet, can also cause problems for re-processors. Further sorting steps may be required to satisfactorily reduce the amount of non-target and non-recyclable material.

Recycling Consumer Waste

Collection

Fig: A Three-Sided Bin at a Railway Station in Germany, intended to Separate Paper (Left) and Plastic Wrappings (Right) from other Waste (Back)

A number of systems have been implemented to collect recyclates from the general waste stream, occupying different places on the spectrum of trade-off between public convenience and government ease and expense. The three main categories of collection are drop-off centers, buy-back centers and curbside collection. About two-thirds of the cost of recycling is incurred in the collection phase.

Curbside Collection

Curbside collection encompasses many subtly different systems, which differ mostly on where in the process the recyclates are sorted and cleaned. The main categories are mixed waste collection, commingled recyclables, and source separation. A waste collection vehicle generally picks up the waste.

In mixed waste collection, recyclates are collected mixed with the rest of the waste, and the desired materials are sorted out and cleaned at a central sorting facility. This results in a large amount of recyclable waste (especially paper) being too soiled to reprocess, but has advantages as well: The city need not pay for the separate collection of recyclates, no public education is needed, and any changes to the recyclability of certain materials are implemented where sorting occurs.

Fig: A Recycling Truck Collecting the Contents of a Recycling Bin in Canberra, Australia

In a commingled or single-stream system, recyclables are mixed but kept separate from non-recyclable waste. This greatly reduces the need for post-collection cleaning, but requires public education on what materials are recyclable.

Source Separation

Source separation is the other extreme, where each material is cleaned and sorted prior to collection. It requires the least post-collection sorting and produces the purest recyclates. However, it incurs additional operating costs for collecting each material, and requires extensive public education to avoid recyclate contamination. In Oregon, USA, Oregon DEQ surveyed multi-family property managers; about half of them reported problems, including contamination of recyclables due to trespassers such as transients gaining access to collection areas. Source separation used to be the preferred method due to the high cost of sorting commingled (mixed waste) collection. However, advances in sorting technology have substantially lowered this overhead, and many areas that had developed source separation programs have switched to what is called co-mingled collection.

Fig: Emptying of Segregated Rubbish Containers in Tomaszow Mazowiecki, Poland

Buy-Back Centers

Fig: Reverse Vending machine in Tomaszów Mazowiecki, Poland

At buy-back centers, separated, cleaned recyclates are purchased, providing a clear incentive for use and creating a stable supply. The post-processed material can then be sold. If profitable, this conserves the emission of greenhouse gases; if unprofitable, it increases their emission. Buy-back centres generally need government subsidies to be viable. According to a 1993 report by the U.S. National Waste & Recycling Association, it costs an average $50 to process a ton of material that can be resold for $30.

Drop-Off Centers

Fig: A Drop-Off Center in the United Kingdom, where They are Generally Named Recycling Centres

Drop-off centers require the waste producer to carry recyclates to a central location—either an installed or mobile collection station or the reprocessing plant itself. They are the easiest type of collection to establish but suffer from low and unpredictable throughput.

Distributed Recycling

For some waste materials such as plastic, recent technical devices called recyclebots enable a form of distributed recycling called DRAM (distributed recycling additive manufacturing). Preliminary life-cycle analysis (LCA) indicates that such distributed recycling of HDPE to make filament for 3D printers in rural regions consumes less energy than using virgin resin, or using conventional recycling processes with their associated transportation.

Another form of distributed recycling mixes waste plastic with sand to make bricks in Africa. Several studies have looked at the properties of recycled waste plastic and sand bricks. The composite pavers can be sold at 100% profit while employing workers at 1.5× the minimum wage in the West African region, where distributed recycling has the potential to produce 19 million pavement tiles from 28,000 tons of plastic water sachets annually in Ghana, Nigeria, and Liberia. This has also been done with COVID19 masks.

Sorting

Once commingled recyclates are collected and delivered to a materials recovery facility, the materials must be sorted. This is done in a series of stages, many of which involve automated processes, enabling a truckload of material to be fully sorted in less than an hour. Some plants can now sort materials automatically; this is known as single-stream recycling. Automatic sorting may be aided by robotics and machine learning. In plants, a variety of materials is sorted including paper, different types of plastics, glass, metals, food scraps, and most types of batteries. A 30% increase in recycling rates has been seen in areas with these plants. In the US, there are over 300 materials recovery facilities.

Fig: Early Sorting of Recyclable Materials: Glass and Plastic Bottles in Poland

Initially, commingled recyclates are removed from the collection vehicle and placed on a conveyor belt spread out in a single layer. Large pieces of corrugated fiberboard and plastic bags are removed by hand at this stage, as they can cause later machinery to jam. Next, automated machinery such as disk screens and air classifiers separate the recyclates by weight, splitting lighter paper and plastic from heavier glass and metal. Cardboard is removed from mixed paper, and the most common types of plastic—PET (#1) and HDPE (#2)—are collected, so these materials can be diverted into the proper collection channels. This is usually done by hand; but in some sorting centers, spectroscopic scanners are used to differentiate between types of paper and plastic based on their absorbed wavelengths. Plastics tend to be incompatible with each other due to differences in chemical composition; their polymer molecules repel each other, similar to oil and water. Strong magnets are used to separate out ferrous metals such as iron, steel and tin cans. Non-ferrous metals are ejected by magnetic eddy currents: A rotating magnetic field induces an electric current around aluminum cans, creating an eddy current inside the cans that is repulsed by a large magnetic field, ejecting the cans from the stream.

Fig: A Recycling Point in New Byth, Scotland, with Separate Containers for Paper, Plastics, and Differently Colored Glass

Finally, glass is sorted according to its color: brown, amber, green, or clear. It may be sorted either by hand, or by a machine that uses colored filters to detect colors. Glass fragments smaller than 10 millimetres (0.39 in) cannot be sorted automatically, and are mixed together as "glass fines".

In 2003, San Francisco's Department of the Environment set a citywide goal of zero waste by 2020. San Francisco's refuse hauler, Recology, operates an effective recyclables sorting facility that has helped the city reach a record-breaking landfill diversion rate of 80% as of 2021. Other American cities, including Los Angeles, have achieved similar rates.

Recycling Industrial Waste

Although many government programs concentrate on recycling at home, 64% of waste in the United Kingdom is generated by industry. The focus of many recycling programs in industry is their cost-effectiveness. The ubiquitous nature of cardboard packaging makes cardboard a common waste product recycled by companies that deal heavily in packaged goods, such as retail stores, warehouses, and goods distributors. Other industries deal in niche and specialized products, depending on the waste materials they handle.

Fig: Mounds of Shredded Rubber Tires Ready for Processing

Glass, lumber, wood pulp and paper manufacturers all deal directly in commonly recycled materials; however, independent tire dealers may collect and recycle rubber tires for a profit. The waste produced from burning coal in a Coal-fired power station is often called fuel ash or fly ash in the United States. It is a very useful material and used in concrete construction. It exhibits Pozzolanic activity.

Levels of metals recycling are generally low. In 2010, the International Resource Panel, hosted by the United Nations Environment Programme (UNEP), published reports on metal stocks and their recycling rates. It reported that the increase in the use of metals during the 20th and into the 21st century has led to a substantial shift in metal stocks from below-ground to use in above-ground applications within society. For example, in the US, in-use copper grew from 73 to 238 kg per capita between 1932–1999. The report's authors observed that, as metals are inherently recyclable, metal stocks in society can serve as huge above-ground mines (the term "urban mining" has thus been coined). However, they found that the recycling rates of many metals are low. They warned that the recycling rates of some rare metals used in applications such as mobile phones, battery packs for hybrid cars and fuel cells, are so low that unless future end-of-life recycling rates are dramatically increased, these critical metals will become unavailable for use in modern technology.

The military recycles some metals. The U.S. Navy's Ship Disposal Program uses ship breaking to reclaim the steel of old vessels. Ships may also be sunk to create artificial reefs. Uranium is a dense metal that has qualities superior to lead and titanium for many military and industrial uses. Uranium left over from processing it into nuclear weapons and fuel for nuclear reactors is called depleted uranium, and is used by all branches of the U.S. military for the development of such things as armor-piercing shells and shielding.

The construction industry may recycle concrete and old road surface pavement, selling these materials for profit. Some rapidly growing industries, particularly the renewable energy and solar photovoltaic technology industries, are proactively creating recycling policies even before their waste streams have considerable volume, anticipating future demand.

Recycling of plastics is more difficult, as most programs are not able to reach the necessary level of quality. Recycling of PVC often results in downcycling of the material, which means only products of lower quality standard can be made with the recycled material.

E-waste is a growing problem, accounting for 20–50 million metric tons of global waste per year according to the EPA. It is also the fastest growing waste stream in the EU. Many recyclers do not recycle e-waste responsibly. After the cargo barge Khian Sea dumped 14,000 metric tons of toxic ash in Haiti, the Basel Convention was formed to stem the flow of hazardous substances into poorer countries. They created the e-Stewards certification to ensure that recyclers are held to the highest standards for environmental responsibility and to help consumers identify responsible recyclers. It operates alongside other prominent legislation, such as the Waste Electrical and Electronic Equipment Directive of the EU and the United States National Computer Recycling Act, to prevent poisonous chemicals from entering waterways and the atmosphere.

In the recycling process, television sets, monitors, cell phones, and computers are typically tested for reuse and repaired. If broken, they may be disassembled for parts still having high value if labor is cheap enough. Other e-waste is shredded to pieces roughly 10 centimetres (3.9 in) in size and manually checked to separate toxic batteries and capacitors, which contain poisonous metals. The remaining pieces are further shredded to 10 millimetres (0.39 in) particles and passed under a magnet to remove ferrous metals. An eddy current ejects non-ferrous metals, which are sorted by density either by a centrifuge or vibrating plates. Precious metals can be dissolved in acid, sorted, and smelted into ingots. The remaining glass and plastic fractions are separated by density and sold to re-processors. Television sets and monitors must be manually disassembled to remove lead from CRTs and the mercury backlight from LCDs.

Vehicles, solar panels and wind turbines can also be recycled. They often contain rare-earth elements (REE) and/or other critical raw materials. For electric car production, large amounts of REE's are typically required.

Whereas many critical raw elements and REE's can be recovered, environmental engineer Phillipe Bihouix Archived 6 September 2021 at the Wayback Machine reports that recycling of indium, gallium, germanium, selenium, and tantalum is still very difficult and their recycling rates are very low.

Plastic Recycling

Plastic recycling is the process of recovering scrap or waste plastic and reprocessing the material into useful products, sometimes completely different in form from their original state. For instance, this could mean melting down soft drink bottles and then casting them as plastic chairs and tables. For some types of plastic, the same piece of plastic can only be recycled about 2–3 times before its quality decreases to the point where it can no longer be used.

- Some plastics are remelted to form new plastic objects; for example, PET water bottles can be converted into polyester destined for clothing. A disadvantage of this type of recycling is that the molecular weight of the polymer can change further and the levels of unwanted substances in the plastic can increase with each remelt.
- A commercial-built recycling facility was sent to the International Space Station in late 2019. The facility takes in plastic waste and unneeded plastic parts and physically converts them into spools of feedstock for the space station additive manufacturing facility used for in-space 3D printing.
- For some polymers, it is possible to convert them back into monomers, for example, PET can be treated with an alcohol and a catalyst to form

a dialkyl terephthalate. The terephthalate diester can be used with ethylene glycol to form a new polyester polymer, thus making it possible to use the pure polymer again. In 2019, Eastman Chemical Company announced initiatives of methanolysis and syngas designed to handle a greater variety of used material.

Another process involves the conversion of assorted polymers into petroleum by a much less precise thermal depolymerization process. Such a process would be able to accept almost any polymer or mix of polymers, including thermoset materials such as vulcanized rubber tires and the biopolymers in feathers and other agricultural waste. Like natural petroleum, the chemicals produced can be used as fuels or as feedstock. A RESEM Technology plant of this type in Carthage, Missouri, US, uses turkey waste as input material. Gasification is a similar process but is not technically recycling since polymers are not likely to become the result. Plastic Pyrolysis can convert petroleum based waste streams such as plastics into quality fuels, carbons. Given below is the list of suitable plastic raw materials for pyrolysis:

- Mixed plastic (HDPE, LDPE, PE, PP, Nylon, Teflon, PS, ABS, FRP, PET etc.)
- Mixed waste plastic from waste paper mill
- Multi-layered plastic

Recycling Codes

Fig: Recycling Codes on Products

In order to meet recyclers' needs while providing manufacturers a consistent, uniform system, a coding system was developed. The recycling code for plastics was introduced in 1988 by the plastics industry through the Society of the Plastics Industry. Because municipal recycling programs traditionally have targeted packaging—primarily bottles and containers—the resin coding system offered a means of identifying the resin content of bottles and containers commonly found in the residential waste stream. In the United States, plastic products are printed with numbers 1–7 depending on the type of resin. Type 1 (polyethylene terephthalate) is commonly found in soft drink and water bottles. Type 2 (high-density polyethylene) is found in most hard plastics such as milk jugs, laundry detergent bottles, and some dishware. Type 3 (polyvinyl chloride) includes items such as shampoo bottles, shower curtains, hula hoops, credit cards, wire jacketing, medical equipment, siding, and piping. Type 4 (low-density polyethylene) is found in shopping bags, squeezable bottles, tote bags, clothing, furniture, and carpet. Type 5 is polypropylene and makes up syrup bottles, straws, Tupperware, and some automotive parts. Type 6 is polystyrene and makes up meat trays, egg cartons, clamshell containers, and compact disc cases. Type 7 includes all other plastics such as bulletproof materials, 3- and 5-gallon water bottles, cell phone and tablet frames, safety goggles and sunglasses. Having a recycling code or the chasing arrows logo on a material is not an automatic indicator that a material is recyclable but rather an explanation of what the material is. Types 1 and 2 are the most commonly recycled.

Cost–Benefit Analysis

In addition to environmental impact, there is debate over whether recycling is economically efficient. According to a Natural Resources Defense Council study, waste collection and landfill disposal creates less than one job per 1,000 tons of waste material managed; in contrast, the collection, processing, and manufacturing of recycled materials creates 6–13 or more jobs per 1,000 tons.

Table: Environmental Effects of Recycling

Material	Energy savings vs. new production	Air pollution savings vs. new production
Aluminium	95%	95%
Cardboard	24%	—
Glass	5–30%	20%
Paper	40%	73%
Plastics	70%	—
Steel	60%	—

According to the U.S. Recycling Economic Informational Study, there are over 50,000 recycling establishments that have created over a million jobs in the US. The National Waste & Recycling Association (NWRA) reported in May 2015 that recycling and waste made a $6.7 billion economic impact in Ohio, U.S., and employed 14,000 people. Economists would classify this extra labor used as a cost rather than a benefit since these workers could have been employed elsewhere; the cost effectiveness of creating these additional jobs remains unclear.

Sometimes cities have found recycling saves resources compared to other methods of disposal of waste. Two years after New York City declared that implementing recycling programs would be "a drain on the city", New York City leaders realized that an efficient recycling system could save the city over $20 million. Municipalities often see fiscal benefits from implementing recycling programs, largely due to the reduced landfill costs. A study conducted by the Technical University of Denmark according to the Economist found that in 83 percent of cases, recycling is the most efficient method to dispose of household waste. However, a 2004 assessment by the Danish Environmental Assessment Institute concluded that incineration was the most effective method for disposing of drink containers, even aluminium ones.

Fiscal efficiency is separate from economic efficiency. Economic analysis of recycling does not include what economists call externalities: unpriced costs and benefits that accrue to individuals outside of private transactions. Examples include less air pollution and greenhouse gases from incineration and less waste leaching from landfills. Without mechanisms such as taxes or subsidies, businesses and consumers following their private benefit would ignore externalities despite the costs imposed on society. If landfills and incinerator pollution is inadequately regulated, these methods of waste disposal appear cheaper than they really are, because part of their cost is the pollution imposed on people nearby. Thus, advocates have pushed for legislation to increase demand for recycled materials. The United States Environmental Protection Agency (EPA) has concluded in favor of recycling, saying that recycling efforts reduced the country's carbon emissions by a net 49 million metric tonnes in 2005. In the United Kingdom, the Waste and Resources Action Programme stated that Great Britain's recycling efforts reduce CO_2 emissions by 10–15 million tonnes a year. The question for economic efficiency is whether this reduction is worth the extra cost of recycling and thus makes the artificial demand creates by legislation worthwhile.

Certain requirements must be met for recycling to be economically feasible and environmentally effective. These include an adequate source of recyclates, a system to extract those recyclates from the waste stream, a nearby factory capable of reprocessing the recyclates, and a potential demand for the recycled products.

These last two requirements are often overlooked—without both an industrial market for production using the collected materials and a consumer market for the manufactured goods, recycling is incomplete and in fact only "collection".

Free-market economist Julian Simon remarked "There are three ways society can organize waste disposal: (a) commanding, (b) guiding by tax and subsidy, and (c) leaving it to the individual and the market". These principles appear to divide economic thinkers today.

Frank Ackerman favours a high level of government intervention to provide recycling services. He believes that recycling's benefit cannot be effectively quantified by traditional laissez-faire economics. Allen Hershkowitz supports intervention, saying that it is a public service equal to education and policing. He argues that manufacturers should shoulder more of the burden of waste disposal.

Paul Calcott and Margaret Walls advocate the second option. A deposit refund scheme and a small refuse charge would encourage recycling but not at the expense of illegal dumping. Thomas C. Kinnaman concludes that a landfill tax would force consumers, companies and councils to recycle more.

Most free-market thinkers detest subsidy and intervention, arguing that they waste resources. The general argument is that if cities charge the full cost of garbage collection, private companies can profitably recycle any materials for which the benefit of recycling exceeds the cost (e.g. aluminum) and do not recycle other materials for which the benefit is less than the cost (e.g. glass). Cities, on the other hand, often recycle even when they not only do not receive enough for the paper or plastic to pay for its collection, but must actually pay private recycling companies to take it off of their hands. Terry Anderson and Donald Leal think that all recycling programmes should be privately operated, and therefore would only operate if the money saved by recycling exceeds its costs. Daniel K. Benjamin argues that it wastes people's resources and lowers the wealth of a population. He notes that recycling can cost a city more than twice as much as landfills, that in the United States landfills are so heavily regulated that their pollution effects are negligible, and that the recycling process also generates pollution and uses energy, which may or may not be less than from virgin production.

Trade in Recyclates

Certain countries trade in unprocessed recyclates. Some have complained that the ultimate fate of recyclates sold to another country is unknown and they may end up in landfills instead of being reprocessed. According to one report, in America, 50–80 percent of computers destined for recycling are actually not recycled. There are reports of illegal-waste imports to China being dismantled and recycled solely for monetary gain, without consideration for workers' health or environmental damage. Although the Chinese government has banned these practices, it has not been able to eradicate them. In 2008, the prices of recyclable waste plummeted before rebounding in 2009. Cardboard averaged about £53/tonne from 2004 to 2008, dropped to £19/tonne, and then went up to £59/tonne in May 2009. PET plastic averaged about £156/tonne, dropped to £75/tonne and then moved up to £195/tonne in May 2009.

Certain regions have difficulty using or exporting as much of a material as they recycle. This problem is most prevalent with glass: both Britain and the U.S. import large quantities of wine bottled in green glass. Though much of this glass is sent to be recycled, outside the American Midwest there is not enough wine production to use all of the reprocessed material. The extra must be downcycled into building materials or re-inserted into the regular waste stream.

Similarly, the northwestern United States has difficulty finding markets for recycled newspaper, given the large number of pulp mills in the region as well as the proximity to Asian markets. In other areas of the U.S., however, demand for used newsprint has seen wide fluctuation. In some U.S. states, a program called RecycleBank pays people to recycle, receiving money from local municipalities for the reduction in landfill space that must be purchased. It uses a single stream process in which all material is automatically sorted.

Net Environmental Benefits

Critics dispute the net economic and environmental benefits of recycling over its costs, and suggest that proponents of recycling often make matters worse and suffer from confirmation bias. Specifically, critics argue that the costs and energy used in collection and transportation detract from (and outweigh) the costs and energy saved in the production process; also that the jobs produced by the recycling industry can be a poor trade for the jobs lost in logging, mining, and other industries associated with production; and that materials such as paper pulp can only be recycled a few times before material degradation prevents further recycling.

The amount of energy saved through recycling depends upon the material being recycled and the type of energy accounting that is used. Correct accounting for this saved energy can be accomplished with life-cycle analysis using real energy values, and in addition, exergy, which is a measure of how much useful energy can be used. In general, it takes far less energy to produce a unit mass of recycled materials than it does to make the same mass of virgin materials.

Some scholars use emergy (spelled with an m) analysis, for example, budgets for the amount of energy of one kind (exergy) that is required to make or transform things into another kind of product or service. Emergy calculations take into account economics that can alter pure physics-based results. Using emergy life-cycle analysis researchers have concluded that materials with large refining costs have the greatest potential for high recycle benefits. Moreover, the highest emergy efficiency accrues from systems geared toward material recycling, where materials are engineered to recycle back into their original form and purpose, followed by adaptive reuse systems where the materials are recycled into a different kind of product, and then by-product reuse systems where parts of the products are used to make an entirely different product.

Fig: Bales of Crushed Steel Ready for Transport to the Smelter

The Energy Information Administration (EIA) states on its website that "a paper mill uses 40 percent less energy to make paper from recycled paper than it does to make paper from fresh lumber." Some critics argue that it takes more energy to produce recycled products than it does to dispose of them in traditional landfill methods, since the curbside collection of recyclables often requires a second waste truck. However, recycling proponents point out that a second timber or logging truck is eliminated when paper is collected for recycling, so the net energy consumption is the same. An emergy life-cycle analysis on recycling revealed that fly ash, aluminum, recycled concrete aggregate, recycled plastic, and steel yield higher efficiency ratios, whereas the recycling of lumber generates the lowest recycle benefit ratio. Hence, the specific nature of the recycling process, the methods used to analyse the process, and the products involved affect the energy savings budgets.

It is difficult to determine the amount of energy consumed or produced in waste disposal processes in broader ecological terms, where causal relations dissipate into complex networks of material and energy flow.

- [C]ities do not follow all the strategies of ecosystem development. Biogeochemical paths become fairly straight relative to wild ecosystems, with reduced recycling, resulting in large flows of waste and low total energy efficiencies. By contrast, in wild ecosystems, one population's wastes are another population's resources, and succession results in efficient exploitation of available resources. However, even modernized cities may still be in the earliest stages of a succession that may take centuries or millennia to complete.

How much energy is used in recycling also depends on the type of material being recycled and the process used to do so. Aluminium is generally agreed to use far less energy when recycled rather than being produced from scratch. The EPA states that "recycling aluminum cans, for example, saves 95 percent of the energy required to make the same amount of aluminum from its virgin source, bauxite." In 2009, more than half of all aluminium cans produced came from recycled aluminium. Similarly, it has been estimated that new steel produced with recycled cans reduces greenhouse gas emissions by 75%.

- Every year, millions of tons of materials are being exploited from the earth's crust, and processed into consumer and capital goods. After decades to centuries, most of these materials are "lost". With the exception of some pieces of art or religious relics, they are no longer engaged in the consumption process. Where are they? Recycling is only an intermediate solution for such materials, although it does prolong the residence time in the anthroposphere. For thermodynamic reasons, however, recycling cannot prevent the final need for an ultimate sink.—*P. H. Brunner*

Economist Steven Landsburg has suggested that the sole benefit of reducing landfill space is trumped by the energy needed and resulting pollution from the recycling process. Others, however, have calculated through life-cycle assessment that producing recycled paper uses less energy and water than harvesting, pulping, processing, and transporting virgin trees. When less recycled paper is used, additional energy is needed to create and maintain farmed forests until these forests are as self-sustainable as virgin forests. Other studies have shown that recycling in itself is inefficient to perform the "decoupling" of economic development from the depletion of non-renewable raw materials that is necessary for sustainable development. The international transportation or recycle material flows through "... different trade networks of the three countries result in different flows, decay rates, and potential recycling returns". As global consumption of a natural resources grows, their depletion is inevitable. The best recycling can do is to delay; complete closure of material loops to achieve 100 percent recycling of nonrenewables is impossible as micro-trace materials dissipate into the environment causing severe damage to the planet's ecosystems. Historically, this was identified as the metabolic rift by Karl Marx, who identified the unequal exchange rate between energy and nutrients flowing from rural areas to feed urban cities that create effluent wastes degrading the planet's ecological capital, such as loss in soil nutrient production. Energy conservation also leads to what is known as Jevon's paradox, where improvements in energy efficiency lowers the cost of production and leads to a rebound effect where rates of consumption and economic growth increases.

Economic Costs

Journalist John Tierney notes that it is generally more expensive for municipalities to recycle waste from households than to send it to a landfill and that "recycling may be the most wasteful activity in modern America."

The amount of money actually saved through recycling depends on the efficiency of the recycling program used to do it. The Institute for Local Self Reliance argues that the cost of recycling depends on various factors, such as landfill fees and the amount of disposal that the community recycles. It states that communities begin to save money when they treat recycling as a replacement for their traditional waste system rather than an add-on to it and by "redesigning their collection schedules and/or trucks".

In some cases, the cost of recyclable materials also exceeds the cost of raw materials. Virgin plastic resin costs 40 percent less than recycled resin. Additionally, a United States Environmental Protection Agency (EPA) study that tracked the price of clear glass from 15 July to 2 August 1991, found that the average cost per ton ranged from $40 to $60 while a USGS report shows that the cost per ton of raw silica sand from years 1993 to 1997 fell between $17.33 and $18.10.

Comparing the market cost of recyclable material with the cost of new raw materials ignores economic externalities—the costs that are currently not counted by the market. Creating a new piece of plastic, for instance, may cause more pollution and be less sustainable than recycling a similar piece of plastic, but these factors are not counted in market cost. A life cycle assessment can be used to determine the levels of externalities and decide whether the recycling may be worthwhile despite unfavorable market costs. Alternatively, legal means (such as a carbon tax) can be used to bring externalities into the market, so that the market cost of the material becomes close to the true cost.

Working Conditions and Social Costs

Fig: Some People in Brazil Earn their Living by Collecting and Sorting Garbage and Selling them for Recycling

The recycling of waste electrical and electronic equipment can create a significant amount of pollution. This problem is specifically occurrent in India and China. Informal recycling in an underground economy of these countries has generated an environmental and health disaster. High levels of lead (Pb), polybrominated diphenylethers (PBDEs), polychlorinated dioxins and furans, as well as polybrominated dioxins and furans (PCDD/Fs and PBDD/Fs), concentrated in the air, bottom ash, dust, soil, water, and sediments in areas surrounding recycling sites. These materials can make work sites harmful to the workers themselves and the surrounding environment.

In some countries, recycling is performed by the entrepreneurial poor such as the karung guni, zabbaleen, the rag-and-bone man, waste picker, and junk man. With the creation of large recycling organizations that may be profitable, either by law or economies of scale, the poor are more likely to be driven out of the recycling and the remanufacturing job market. To compensate for this loss of income, a society may need to create additional forms of societal programs to help support the poor.

Like the parable of the broken window, there is a net loss to the poor and possibly the whole of a society to make recycling artificially profitable, e.g. through the law. However, in Brazil and Argentina, waste pickers/informal recyclers work alongside the authorities, in fully or semi-funded cooperatives, allowing informal recycling to be legitimized as a paid public sector job.

Because the social support of a country is likely to be less than the loss of income to the poor undertaking recycling, there is a greater chance for the poor to come in conflict with the large recycling organizations.

This means fewer people can decide if certain waste is more economically reusable in its current form rather than being reprocessed. Contrasted to the recycling poor, the efficiency of their recycling may actually be higher for some materials because individuals have greater control over what is considered "waste".

One labor-intensive underused waste is electronic and computer waste. Because this waste may still be functional and wanted mostly by those on lower incomes, who may sell or use it at a greater efficiency than large recyclers.

Some recycling advocates believe that laissez-faire individual-based recycling does not cover all of society's recycling needs. Thus, it does not negate the need for an organized recycling program. Local government can consider the activities of the recycling poor as contributing to the ruining of property.

Public Participation Rates

Changes that have been demonstrated to increase recycling rates include:

- Single-stream recycling
- Pay as you throw fees for trash

In a study done by social psychologist Shawn Burn, it was found that personal contact with individuals within a neighborhood is the most effective way to increase recycling within a community. In her study, she had 10 block leaders talk to their neighbors and persuade them to recycle. A comparison group was sent fliers promoting recycling. It was found that the neighbors that were personally contacted by their block leaders recycled much more than the group without personal contact.

As a result of this study, Shawn Burn believes that personal contact within a small group of people is an important factor in encouraging recycling. Another study done by Stuart Oskamp examines the effect of neighbors and friends on recycling. It was found in his studies that people who had friends and neighbors that recycled were much more likely to also recycle than those who did not have friends and neighbors that recycled.

Fig: Single-Stream Recycling Increases Public Participation Rates, but Requires Additional Sorting

Many schools have created recycling awareness clubs in order to give young students an insight on recycling. These schools believe that the clubs actually encourage students to not only recycle at school but at home as well.

Recycling of metals varies extremely by type. Titanium and lead have an extremely high recycling rates of over 90%. Copper and cobalt have high rates of recycling around 75%. Only about half of aluminum is recycled. Most of the remaining metals have recycling rates of below 35%, while 34 types of metals have recycling rates of under 1%.

"Between 1960 and 2000, the world production of plastic resins increased 25 times its original amount, while recovery of the material remained below 5 percent." Many studies have addressed recycling behaviour and strategies to encourage community involvement in recycling programs.

It has been argued that recycling behavior is not natural because it requires a focus and appreciation for long-term planning, whereas humans have evolved to be sensitive to short-term survival goals; and that to overcome this innate predisposition, the best solution would be to use social pressure to compel participation in recycling programs. However, recent studies have concluded that social pressure does not work in this context. One reason for this is that social pressure functions well in small group sizes of 50 to 150 individuals (common to nomadic hunter-gatherer peoples) but not in communities numbering in the millions, as we see today. Another reason is that individual recycling does not take place in the public view.

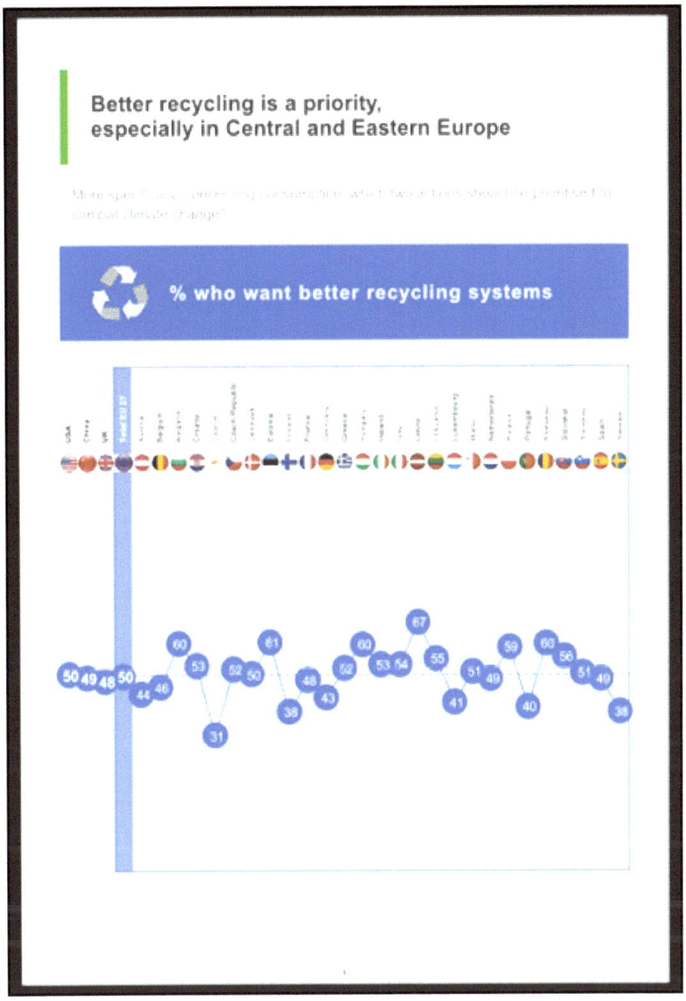

Fig: Better recycling is a priority in the European Union, especially in Central and Eastern Europe among respondents of the 2020-21 European Investment Bank Climate Survey

Embracing a Circular Economy through Advanced Sorting Technologies

By extending the lifespan of goods, parts, and materials, a circular economy seeks to minimize waste and maximize resource utilization. Advanced sorting techniques like optical and robotic sorting may separate and recover valuable materials from waste streams, lowering the requirement for virgin resources and accelerating the shift to a circular economy. Community engagement, such as education and awareness campaigns, may support the acceptance of recycling and reuse programs and encourage the usage of sustainable practices. One can lessen our influence on the environment, save natural resources, and generate economic possibilities by adopting a circular economy using cutting-edge sorting technology and community engagement. According to Melati et al., to successfully transition to a circular economy, legislative and regulatory frameworks must encourage sustainable practices while addressing possible obstacles and difficulties in putting these ideas into action.

2.2 CRADLE-TO-CRADLE AND CLOSED-LOOP SYSTEMS

2.2.1 Designing for Longevity and Reusability

In an era where resource conservation and waste reduction are becoming increasingly critical, designing for longevity and reusability has emerged as a key principle in sustainable development. This approach seeks to extend the lifespan of products, reduce the need for frequent replacements, and minimize environmental impact. By integrating durability, repairability, and adaptability into design, manufacturers can create products that remain functional and valuable for extended periods. Whether applied to consumer goods, industrial equipment, or infrastructure, designing for longevity and reusability aligns with the goals of the circular economy and promotes a more responsible use of resources.

Designing for longevity and reusability is a fundamental strategy in achieving a sustainable and circular economy. By prioritizing durable materials, modular designs, and multi-functional products, manufacturers can extend the lifespan of goods while reducing waste and resource consumption. Businesses, governments, and consumers all play a role in supporting this transition through sustainable practices, policies, and responsible consumption habits. While challenges remain, the growing awareness of environmental issues and advancements in sustainable technology are paving the way for a future where products are designed to last, be repaired, and be reused rather than discarded. By adopting longevity-focused design principles, society can create a more sustainable and efficient system that benefits both the environment and the economy.

The Importance of Designing for Longevity

Product longevity is essential in reducing the environmental and economic costs associated with frequent replacements. Short product lifecycles contribute to excessive resource consumption, pollution, and waste generation. When products are designed to last, they help conserve raw materials, decrease energy consumption during manufacturing, and reduce the burden on landfills. Moreover, durable products offer consumers better value for their money by eliminating the need for constant repurchasing. Businesses that prioritize longevity in their designs can also enhance customer loyalty and build a reputation for sustainability and quality.

Material Selection for Durability

The choice of materials plays a crucial role in determining the lifespan of a product. High-quality, durable materials can withstand wear and tear, reducing the need for frequent repairs or replacements. For example, stainless steel, tempered glass, and engineered wood are known for their longevity compared to lower-quality alternatives. In addition to durability, materials should also be chosen based on their environmental impact. Recyclable, biodegradable, or sustainably sourced materials help ensure that products remain in circulation for as long as possible without causing long-term harm to the planet. By prioritizing material selection in the design process, manufacturers can significantly enhance product longevity.

Modular and Repairable Design

Products designed with modularity and repairability in mind offer significant advantages in extending their lifespan. Modular designs allow for individual components to be replaced or upgraded without discarding the entire product. This approach is particularly relevant in electronics, where devices such as smartphones and laptops can be upgraded with new parts rather than being replaced entirely. Repairable designs, which ensure that parts can be easily accessed and replaced, further contribute to longevity. Companies that provide spare parts and repair guides empower consumers to maintain their products rather than dispose of them prematurely. As a result, modular and repairable designs contribute to waste reduction and resource efficiency.

Reusable and Multi-Functional Products

Designing products that can be reused in multiple ways enhances their value and reduces the need for single-use alternatives. Multi-functional products offer flexibility and adaptability, making them more appealing to consumers. For example, furniture with convertible features, such as sofa beds and expandable tables, serve multiple purposes and remain useful in different settings. Similarly, refillable containers and reusable packaging provide sustainable alternatives to disposable items. By integrating reusability into product design, businesses can create items that maintain their functionality across different use cases and lifecycles.

Extending the Lifespan of Consumer Goods

Many consumer products, including clothing, appliances, and vehicles, are often discarded before reaching the end of their functional life. Encouraging consumers to take better care of their possessions through proper maintenance, repair, and refurbishment can significantly extend product lifespans. Designing fashion items with durable fabrics and timeless styles prevents clothing from becoming obsolete. Similarly, designing appliances and vehicles with easily replaceable parts ensures that they can continue to function efficiently over time. By fostering a culture of durability and responsible ownership, society can shift away from the disposable mindset that contributes to excessive waste.

The Role of Businesses in Promoting Longevity

Businesses have a crucial role to play in designing for longevity and reusability. By prioritizing sustainability in their product development processes, companies can reduce waste and encourage responsible consumption. Many businesses are adopting circular business models, such as leasing or product-as-a-service models, where consumers rent products rather than owning them outright. This ensures that products are maintained, upgraded, and reused for extended periods rather than discarded after a single use. Furthermore, companies that offer warranties, maintenance services, and trade-in programs help extend the lifespan of their products and reduce overall environmental impact.

Government Regulations and Policies

Regulatory measures and policies can support the transition toward designing for longevity and reusability. Governments worldwide are introducing laws that require manufacturers to improve product durability, repairability, and recyclability. Right-to-repair legislation, for example, mandates that companies provide access to repair information and spare parts to consumers and independent repair shops. Additionally, policies that promote eco-design standards ensure that sustainability is integrated into product development from the outset. By implementing regulations that encourage long-lasting and reusable designs, policymakers can help drive systemic change across industries and reduce environmental harm.

Challenges in Implementing Longevity-Focused Design

Despite its many advantages, designing for longevity and reusability presents several challenges. One major obstacle is the economic model of planned obsolescence, where companies deliberately design products with a limited lifespan to encourage repeat purchases. Overcoming this requires a shift in business strategies and consumer demand for sustainable alternatives. Another challenge lies in balancing durability with affordability, as high-quality materials and design innovations can increase production costs. Additionally, technological advancements often lead to product replacements, particularly in the electronics industry, where newer models frequently render older devices obsolete. Addressing these challenges requires a combination of consumer awareness, corporate responsibility, and regulatory enforcement.

2.2.2 The Circular Supply Chain and Closed-Loop Production

As sustainability and resource efficiency gain prominence in global discussions, businesses and industries are shifting their focus toward circular supply chains and closed-loop production systems. Unlike traditional linear supply chains, which follow a take-make-dispose model, circular supply chains are designed to maximize resource utilization and minimize waste. Closed-loop production ensures that materials and products remain in use for as long as possible through processes like recycling, remanufacturing, and refurbishment. These systems play a vital role in promoting environmental sustainability, reducing reliance on finite resources, and fostering economic resilience.

The transition to circular supply chains and closed-loop production represents a significant step towards sustainable resource management and waste reduction. By rethinking traditional supply chain models, businesses can create value while minimizing environmental impact. Although challenges exist, technological advancements, government regulations, and changing consumer preferences are driving the shift towards circularity. Companies that embrace these principles will not only contribute to a more sustainable future but also enhance their competitiveness and resilience in a rapidly evolving global economy. As industries continue to innovate and adopt circular strategies, the integration of circular supply chains will become a cornerstone of responsible business practices worldwide.

Circular Supply Chains in Different Industries

The adoption of circular supply chains varies across industries, with some sectors making significant progress in implementing closed-loop systems. The electronics industry, for example, has embraced circularity through initiatives such as electronic waste recycling, modular smartphone designs, and trade-in programs that extend product lifespans. The fashion industry is also moving towards sustainable practices by promoting textile recycling, clothing rental services, and biodegradable fabrics. In the automotive sector, companies are integrating remanufactured components and designing vehicles with recyclable materials. The construction industry is exploring ways to repurpose building materials, reduce waste, and implement circular design principles. By adopting circular supply chain models, these industries can significantly reduce their environmental impact and create more resilient business operations.

Government Policies and Regulations Supporting Circularity

Governments play a crucial role in facilitating the shift towards circular supply chains through policies and regulations. Many countries have introduced extended producer responsibility (EPR) laws, which require manufacturers to take responsibility for the entire lifecycle of their products, including disposal and recycling. Regulatory frameworks promoting eco-design standards ensure that products are designed with longevity and recyclability in mind. Additionally, financial incentives such as tax benefits, grants, and subsidies encourage businesses to invest in circular economy initiatives. International agreements and collaborations also support circular supply chain development by promoting sustainable trade practices and resource efficiency. Strong government policies help create an environment where circular supply chains can thrive and drive long-term sustainability.

Consumer Awareness and Participation in Circular Supply Chains

Consumer behavior plays a significant role in the success of circular supply chains and closed-loop production. As awareness of sustainability issues grows, consumers are becoming more conscious of their purchasing decisions and actively seeking products with minimal environmental impact. Businesses can support this shift by providing transparent information on product sustainability, offering take-back programs, and encouraging responsible consumption. Education campaigns and eco-labeling initiatives also help inform consumers about the benefits of circular products. By fostering a culture of sustainability, consumers contribute to the demand for circular supply chains and drive businesses to adopt more responsible practices.

Future Trends in Circular Supply Chains and Closed-Loop Production

The future of circular supply chains and closed-loop production is expected to be shaped by advancements in technology, increased regulatory support, and evolving consumer expectations. The rise of artificial intelligence and machine learning will further optimize resource efficiency and predictive maintenance, reducing waste in manufacturing processes. Companies are likely to adopt more localized and decentralized production models to reduce transportation emissions and increase supply chain resilience. Additionally, innovations in biodegradable and renewable materials will continue to expand sustainable production options. As circularity becomes a mainstream business strategy, industries will move toward more holistic and interconnected supply chain systems that prioritize long-term environmental and economic benefits.

2.3 PRODUCT LIFE CYCLE ASSESSMENT (LCA)

2.3.1 Life Cycle Thinking in Circular Economy

The concept of sustainability has gained prominence in recent years as societies strive to minimize environmental degradation while ensuring economic prosperity. A crucial framework that supports this goal is the circular economy, which promotes the efficient use of resources through strategies such as recycling, reuse, and waste minimization. Within this model, life cycle thinking (LCT) plays a fundamental role by assessing the environmental impacts of products and services throughout their entire life span.

Life cycle thinking is a crucial pillar in the development of a successful circular economy. By considering the entire life cycle of products and services, LCT helps identify opportunities to minimize environmental impacts, optimize resource use, and promote sustainability. While challenges exist, advancements in technology, policy standardization, and consumer education can enhance LCT adoption. As global efforts to achieve sustainability intensify, integrating life cycle thinking into circular economy models will play a pivotal role in shaping a resource-efficient and environmentally responsible future.

Case Studies: Life Cycle Thinking in Action

Several companies and industries have successfully integrated life cycle thinking into circular economy strategies. One notable example is the electronics industry, where companies like Fairphone design modular smartphones with replaceable components, reducing electronic waste and extending product life spans. By adopting LCT, Fairphone ensures that materials are sourced responsibly and that end-of-life disposal is minimized.

The fashion industry has also embraced life cycle thinking to combat the environmental impact of fast fashion. Brands such as Patagonia and Stella McCartney prioritize sustainable materials, durable designs, and repair programs to extend garment life. Through LCT assessments, these companies identify ways to reduce water usage, carbon emissions, and textile waste, aligning with circular economy principles.

In the automobile sector, manufacturers like Tesla incorporate LCT by designing electric vehicles with recyclable batteries and energy-efficient production processes. By considering the entire life cycle, Tesla reduces reliance on fossil fuels and mitigates the negative environmental effects of traditional vehicle manufacturing.

2.3.2 Tools and Methodologies for LCA

Life Cycle Assessment (LCA) is a systematic approach used to evaluate the environmental impacts of a product, process, or service throughout its entire life cycle. It considers all stages, including raw material extraction, manufacturing, transportation, use, and disposal. By adopting LCA, businesses, policymakers, and researchers can make informed decisions to reduce environmental burdens and enhance sustainability. To conduct an effective LCA, various tools and methodologies have been developed, helping standardize data collection, impact assessment, and interpretation.

Life Cycle Assessment (LCA) is a critical tool for evaluating environmental impacts and supporting sustainable decision-making. The development of advanced LCA tools and methodologies has significantly improved the efficiency and accuracy of environmental assessments. Software tools such as SimaPro, GaBi, OpenLCA, and Umberto, along with databases like Ecoinvent and USLCI, provide essential resources for conducting LCA studies. Impact assessment methodologies such as ReCiPe, CML, TRACI, and ILCD help translate inventory data into meaningful sustainability indicators.

Despite existing challenges, ongoing advancements in digital technology and data integration hold the potential to enhance LCA practices further. By refining methodologies, improving data quality, and integrating circular economy principles, LCA will continue to play a pivotal role in achieving sustainability goals and promoting responsible resource management.

Life Cycle Assessment Methodology

The LCA methodology follows a structured process defined by international standards such as ISO 14040 and ISO 14044. It consists of four main phases: goal and scope definition, life cycle inventory (LCI), life cycle impact assessment (LCIA), and interpretation. These phases ensure a comprehensive assessment of environmental impacts associated with a product or service.

The goal and scope definition phase establishes the purpose of the LCA study, the functional unit (a quantified measure of the product's function), and the system boundaries. This phase determines which life cycle stages are included and what assumptions are made. The Life Cycle Inventory (LCI) phase involves collecting data on energy and material flows, emissions, and waste generated throughout the product's life cycle. This phase requires extensive databases and software tools to ensure accuracy.

Life Cycle Impact Assessment (LCIA) translates inventory data into potential environmental impacts using impact categories such as climate change, resource depletion, and toxicity. Various characterization models, including ReCiPe, CML, and TRACI, help quantify these impacts. The interpretation phase synthesizes the results, identifying hotspots and opportunities for improvement while ensuring consistency with the study's objectives.

Key Tools for Life Cycle Assessment

Several software tools have been developed to facilitate LCA studies, enabling researchers and businesses to conduct systematic analyses efficiently. These tools integrate extensive databases, modeling capabilities, and impact assessment methods to streamline the LCA process.

One of the most widely used LCA software tools is SimaPro. Developed by PRé Sustainability, SimaPro provides a comprehensive framework for conducting LCA studies, offering access to multiple databases such as Ecoinvent and USLCI.

It allows users to model complex life cycle systems, perform sensitivity analyses, and generate environmental impact reports. The software supports various LCIA methodologies, making it suitable for diverse industries and research applications.

Another prominent tool is GaBi, developed by Sphera. GaBi is known for its robust data management capabilities and its extensive database covering various industrial sectors. It enables users to conduct scenario analyses, optimize material and energy flows, and integrate sustainability metrics into decision-making processes. GaBi is widely used by corporations and policymakers for developing sustainability strategies.

OpenLCA is an open-source LCA tool that provides a flexible platform for conducting environmental assessments. It supports multiple databases and methodologies, making it an accessible alternative for researchers and organizations with limited resources. OpenLCA enables users to perform hotspot analyses, visualize results through graphical representations, and collaborate on LCA projects through a shared database. Another valuable tool is Umberto, which specializes in material flow analysis (MFA) and LCA. Umberto is particularly useful for industrial applications, allowing users to optimize resource efficiency and analyze environmental impacts in production processes. Its graphical modeling interface simplifies the representation of complex systems, making it a practical tool for businesses aiming to improve sustainability performance.

2.4 CIRCULAR BUSINESS MODELS

2.4.1 Product-as-a-Service (PaaS) and Leasing Models

Product-as-a-Service (PaaS)

Platform as a service (PaaS) or application platform as a service (aPaaS) or platform-based service is a cloud computing service model where users provision, instantiate, run and manage a modular bundle of a computing platform and applications, without the complexity of building and maintaining the infrastructure associated with developing and launching application(s), and to allow developers to create, develop, and package such software bundles.

Development and Uses

PaaS can be delivered in three ways:

- As a public cloud service from a provider, where the consumer controls software deployment with minimal configuration options, and the provider provides the networks, servers, storage, operating system (OS), middleware (e.g. Java runtime, .NET runtime, integration, etc.), database and other services to host the consumer's application.

- As a private service (software or appliance) behind a firewall.
- As software deployed on public infrastructure as a service.

The first public platform as a service was Zimki, launched by Fotango, a London-based company owned by Canon Europe. It was developed in 2005, had a beta launch in March 2006 and a public launch at EuroOSCON in 2006.

At the time of its closure, Zimki had several thousand developer accounts. It had demonstrated the technical viability of Platform as a Service, but also provided the first example of the perils of being dependent on a single provider. This was highlighted when the CEO (Simon Wardley, known for Wardley maps) announced at OSCON 2007 that Zimki would no longer be open-sourced and discussed the future of what was then called framework-as-a-service (later called platform-as-a-service) covering the importance of a market of providers based on an open-source reference model. The original intent of PaaS was to simplify the writing of code, with the infrastructure and operations handled by the PaaS provider. Originally, all PaaSes were in the public cloud. Because many companies did not want to have everything in the public cloud, private and hybrid PaaS options (managed by internal IT departments) were created.

PaaS provides an environment for developers and companies to create, host and deploy applications, saving developers from the complexities of infrastructure (setting up, configuring and managing elements such as servers and databases). PaaS can improve the speed of developing an app, and allow its user to focus on the application itself. With PaaS, the customer manages applications and data, while the provider (in public PaaS) or IT department (in private PaaS) manages runtime, middleware, operating system, virtualization, servers, storage and networking. Development tools provided by the vendor are customized according to the needs of the user. The user can choose to maintain the software, or have the vendor maintain it.

PaaS offerings may also include facilities for application design, application development, testing and deployment, as well as services such as team collaboration, web service integration, and marshalling, database integration, security, scalability, storage, persistence, state management, application versioning, application instrumentation, and developer community facilitation. Besides the service engineering aspects, PaaS offerings include mechanisms for service management, such as monitoring, workflow management, discovery and reservation.

Advantages and Disadvantages

The advantages of PaaS are primarily that it allows for higher-level programming with dramatically reduced complexity; the overall development of the application can be more effective, as it has built-in/self up-and-down ramping infrastructure resources; and maintenance and enhancement of the application is thus easier. Disadvantages of various PaaS providers as cited by their users include increased pricing at larger scales, lack of operational features, reduced control, and the difficulties of traffic routing systems.

Public, Private and Hybrid

There are several types of PaaS, including public, private and hybrid. PaaS was originally intended for applications on public cloud services, before expanding to include private and hybrid options. Public PaaS is derived from software as a service (SaaS), and is situated in cloud computing between SaaS and infrastructure as a service (IaaS). SaaS is software hosted in the cloud so that it does not reside or run on customer computers. IaaS provides virtual hardware from a provider with adjustable scalability. In IaaS, the server is managed by the user, whereas in PaaS by the provider. A private PaaS can typically be downloaded and installed either in a company's on-premises data center, or in a public cloud. Once the software is installed on one or more machines, the private PaaS arranges the application and database components into a single hosting platform. Hybrid PaaS is typically a deployment consisting of a mix of public and private deployments.

2.4.2 Take-Back Systems and Extended Producer Responsibility (EPR)

Take-Back Systems

A take-back system or simply takeback is one of the primary channels of waste collection, especially for e-waste, besides municipal sites. Take-back is the idea that manufacturers and sellers "take back" the products that are at the end of their lives. Take-back is aimed to reduce a business' environmental impacts on the earth and also increase efficiency and lower costs for their business models. "Take-back regulations have targeted a wide array of products including packaging, batteries, automobiles, and electronics", and economic value can be found from recycling or re-manufacturing such products. "The programs benefit municipalities by lowering their overall waste disposal costs and reducing the burden on landfill sites". Although for certain companies, the take-back system is mandatory under legislation, many do it voluntarily.

Take-back can be split up into:

- Store retailer take-back and
- Producer take-back.

It can be further split into two types:

- Recycling
- Re-manufacturing

Recycling

One major option of the take-back system includes store retailers or producers taking back the products that have been distributed to their consumers in order to recycle the materials of these products. The take-back system encourages businesses to redesign their products into ones that are easily recyclable, reducing the burden that virgin materials have on the environment for the present and the future. This also gives companies an alternative supply of raw minerals.

Re-Manufacturing

The other major option of the take-back system includes the store retailers or producers taking back their products in order to create new ones. This process uses the older products in order to restore it into products that are of the same quality as the new ones. By this process, companies save up to 85% of energy that would have been used to manufacture brand-new products.

Economic Effect

The take-back system has shown economic effects for many companies that have adapted it. An example is Xerox, a company that has saved over $200 million from their take-back program in a year alone. The system encourages companies to create products that are easy to dissemble and re-manufacture in order to cut costs and generate revenue through taking back older products. In this way, companies can use older products that would have otherwise been thrown away in order to renovate them, allowing for them to be sold again just as Sprint has, in order to save over a billion dollars. In Wisconsin, the development of a take-back system created many new jobs, started a few companies, and had brought revenue from e-waste processing.

Environmental Impact

The take-back system provides a more environmentally friendly system for those that inherit it. The system gives the responsibility of handling waste to the producer, meaning that they are to guarantee that their products are dealt with when they are at the end of their lives. By taking old products back, companies reduce their environmental footprint on the world as their products are influenced to become more easily recyclable. The system influences companies to redesign their products in ways that are more cost-effective when they recycle, reuse, or re-manufacture their products. Policies of the system can require companies into using a certain amount of recycled material in their products, which reduces the amount of recovered materials that end up in landfills or incineration.

Circular Economy

The take-back system can be a main component to the business model that is called the circular economy. The circular economy is a plan for a business or company that aims to use and reduce their waste in order to become sustainable on their own. The take-back system allows for this model to work as it allows companies to recycle old products in order to become more environmentally friendly, where materials are used from these old products in order to use as resources and encourage sustainability. Not only that, but for most companies, the take-back system shows to be a more cost-effective system as it effectively minimizes waste management costs.

Implementation of Take-Back Systems

- Collection: Due to a high cost in recycling but low amount of customer incentive, companies and countries refrain from adapting a take-back system. To fix this, e-waste could be taken aback by the producers for donations, for re-manufacturing, or for upgrades.
- Waste Regulation Legislation and Government Help: Without legislation, a prominent take-back system cannot be achieved because current e-waste regulation systems are "limited to private recycling of high-value waste with only limited consumer participation". Rules and regulations that would incentive and fix issues regarding the dumping of electronic waste into landfills and prevent the illegal exportation of electronic waste are important to achieve success in e-waste management. The government would need to support it by giving incentives and the correct infrastructure in order to create such a system.
- Initiatives: "Initiatives refer to programs or schemes required to promote effective collection, recycling and disposal of e-waste". Through these incentives, the government and producers of waste must promote e-waste management on their own by giving effort in collecting e-waste to recycle, renew, or reuse it.
- Awareness and Responsibility: Consumers of the products must become aware to how managing their waste affects the environment, and the lack of programs that help teach these aspects show to be big barriers to the effective management of waste. To manage the waste properly, consumers must begin to show responsibility in bringing in their e-waste, while companies such as the producers of these products must be responsible for taking it back and dealing with it.

Germany's Take-Back System

Germany had set in put a packaging ordinance on June 12, 1991. "It specifies mandatory quotas for recycling for glass, paper/paperboard/carton, tin plate, aluminum, plastic, and composites". The responsibility for handling waste was put onto the manufacturer and distributor. As a result of the ordinance, "in 1993, the beginning of the mandatory quotas, compared to 1992, there were 500,000 fewer tons of packaging" and "From 1993 to 1994, paper packaging recycling increased from 55% to 70.6%". The system showed to be a success, as it reduced waste and redesigned packaging to be more environmentally friendly simply from integrating a version of the take-back system.

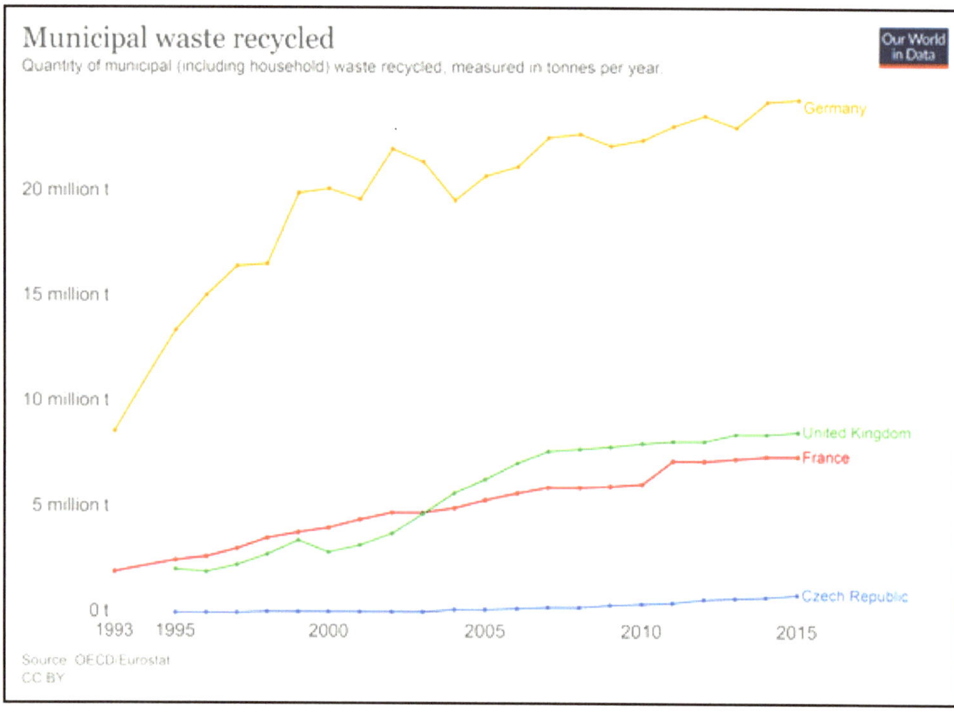

Fig: Germany at the Top of Most Municipal Waste Recycled

Issues

While the take-back system aims to create more eco-friendly businesses, there are reasons why it does not profoundly exist today. The main reason for this is the lack of incentives.

Being that there are products such as cars and computers that are unappealing to transport, the consumer finds it troubling and unappealing to bring these products back. Also, since many consumers see refurbished products as inferior and do not trust them, it is unappealing for companies to re-manufacture their own products for reselling purposes and thus cannot profit from it. Without the appropriate subsidies, in some cases it becomes more beneficial for a company to use virgin materials as opposed to recycling methods as it is cheaper, swaying some away from the take-back system.

Extended Producer Responsibility (EPR)

Extended producer responsibility (EPR) is a strategy to add all of the estimated environmental costs associated with a product throughout the product life cycle to the market price of that product, contemporarily mainly applied in the field of waste management. Such societal costs are typically externalities to market mechanisms, with a common example being the impact of cars.

Extended producer responsibility legislation is a driving force behind the adoption of remanufacturing initiatives because it "focuses on the end-of-use treatment of consumer products and has the primary aim to increase the amount and degree of product recovery and to minimize the environmental impact of waste materials". Passing responsibility to producers as polluters is not only a matter of environmental policy but also the most effective means of achieving higher environmental standards in product design.

Origin

The concept was first formally introduced in Sweden by Thomas Lindhqvist in a 1990 report to the Swedish Ministry of the Environment. In subsequent reports prepared for the Ministry, the following definition emerged: "[EPR] is an environmental protection strategy to reach an environmental objective of a decreased total environmental impact of a product, by making the manufacturer of the product responsible for the entire life-cycle of the product and especially for the take-back, recycling and final disposal."

Definition

Extended producer responsibility uses financial incentives to encourage manufacturers to design environmentally friendly products by holding producers responsible for the costs of managing their products at end of life. This policy approach differs from product stewardship, which shares responsibility across the chain of custody of a product, in that it attempts to relieve local governments of the costs of managing certain priority products by requiring manufacturers to internalize the cost of recycling within the product price. EPR is based on the principle that manufacturers (usually brand owners) have the greatest control over product design and marketing and have the greatest ability and responsibility to reduce toxicity and waste.

EPR may take the form of a reuse, buyback, or recycling program. The producer may also choose to delegate this responsibility to a third party, a so-called producer responsibility organization (PRO), which is paid by the producer for used-product management. In this way, EPR shifts the responsibility for waste management from government to private industry, obliging producers, importers and/or sellers to internalise waste management costs in their product prices and ensure the safe handling of their products. However, different stakeholders perceive the concept and the role of producers in various ways.

A good example of a producer responsibility organization is PRO Europe S.P.R.L. (Packaging Recovery Organisation Europe), founded in 1995, the umbrella organization for European packaging and packaging waste recovery and recycling schemes. Product stewardship organizations like PRO Europe are intended to relieve industrial companies and commercial enterprises of their individual obligation to take back used products through the operation of an organization which fulfills these obligations on a nationwide basis on behalf of their member companies. The aim is to ensure the recovery and recycling of packaging waste in the most economically efficient and ecologically sound manner. In many countries, this is done through the Green Dot trademark of which PRO Europe is the general licensor. In twenty-five nations, companies are now using the Green Dot as the financing symbol for the organization of recovery, sorting and recycling of sales packaging.

OECD Guidance Manuals

The OECD published a guidance manual about EPR in 2001 after several years of discussion by experts in this field, and updated it in 2016 to include developing countries' perspectives, based on experiences and policy changes.

Take-Back

In response to the growing problem of excessive waste, several countries adopted waste management policies in which manufacturers are responsible for taking back their products from end users at the end of the products' useful life, or partially financing a collection and recycling infrastructure. These policies were adopted due to the lack of collection infrastructure for certain products that contain hazardous materials, or due to the high costs to local governments of providing such collection services. The primary goals of these take-back laws therefore are to partner with the private sector to ensure that all waste is managed in a way that protects public health and the environment. The goals of take-back laws are to

- encourage companies to design products for reuse, recyclability, and materials reduction;
- correct market signals to the consumer by incorporating waste management costs into product price;
- promote innovation in recycling technology.

Take-back programs help promote these goals by creating incentives for companies to design products that minimize waste management costs, to design products that contain safer materials (so they do not need to be managed separately), or to design products that are easier to recycle and reuse (so recycling becomes more profitable). The earliest take-back activity began in Europe, where government-sponsored take-back initiatives arose from concerns about scarce landfill space and potentially hazardous substances in component parts. The European Union adopted a directive on Waste Electrical and Electronic Equipment (WEEE). The purpose of this directive is to prevent the production of waste electronics and also to encourage reuse and recycling of such waste. The directive requires the Member States to encourage design and production methods that take into account the future dismantling and recovery of their products. These take-back programs have been adopted in nearly every OECD country. In the United States, most of these policies have been implemented at the state level.

Plastic Bags

Recycling, banning, and taxation fails to adequately reduce the pollution caused by plastic bags. An alternative to these policies would be to increase extended producer responsibility. In the US, under the Clinton presidency, the President's Council on Sustainable Development suggested EPR in order to target different participants in the cycle of a product's life. This can, however, make the product more expensive since the cost must be taken into consideration before being put on the market, which is why it is not widely used in the United States currently. Instead, there is banning or taxation of plastic bags, which puts the responsibility on the consumers. In the United States, EPR is voluntary. What has been recommended is a comprehensive program which combines taxation, producer responsibility, and recycling to combat pollution.

Electronics

Many governments and companies have adopted extended producer responsibility to help address the growing problem of e-waste—used electrical and electronic equipment that contains materials that cannot be safely thrown away with regular household trash. In 2007, according to the Environmental Protection Agency, people threw away 2.5 million tons of cell phones, TVs, computers, and printers. Many governments have partnered with corporations in creating the necessary collection and recycling infrastructure.

The kinds of chemicals found in e-waste that are particularly dangerous to human health and the environment are lead, mercury, brominated flame-retardants, and cadmium. Lead is found in the screens of phones, TVs and computer monitors and can damage kidneys, nerves, blood, bones, reproductive organs, and muscles. Mercury is found in flat screen TVs, laptop screens, and fluorescent bulbs, and can cause damage to the kidneys and the nervous system. Brominated flame-retardants found in cables and plastic cases can cause cancer, disruption of liver function, and nerve damage. Cadmium is found in rechargeable batteries and can cause kidney damage and cancer. Poorer countries are dumping grounds for e-waste as many governments accept money for disposing of this waste on their lands. This causes increased health risks for people in these countries, especially ones who work or live close to these dumps.

In the United States, 25 states have implemented laws that require the recycling of electronic waste. Of those, 23 have incorporated some form of extended producer responsibility into their laws. According to analysis done by the Product Stewardship Institute, some states have not enacted EPR laws because of a lack of recycling infrastructure and funds for proper e-waste disposal. In contrast, according to a study of EPR legislation by the Electronics TakeBack Coalition (ETBC), states that have seen success in their e-waste recycling programs have done so because they have developed a convenient e-waste infrastructure or the state governments have instituted goals for manufacturers to meet.

Advocates for EPR also argue that including "high expectations for performance" into the laws, and ensuring that those are only minimum requirements, contribute to making the laws successful. The larger the scope of products that can be collected, the more e-waste will be disposed of properly.

Similar laws have been passed in other parts of the world as well. The European Union has taken steps to address some electronic waste management issues. They have restricted the use of harmful substances in member countries and have made it illegal to export waste. China banned the import of e-waste in 2000, and adopted EPR in 2012. This has proven to be difficult, however, because illegal smuggling of waste still occurs in the country. In order to dispose of e-waste in China today, a license is required and plants are held responsible for treating pollution. EPR laws in the U.S. still allow e-waste to be exported to China. The Institute of Electronics and Electrical Engineers (IEEE) has also proposed a deposit-refund system dealt with by producers.

Advantages:

- When producers face either the financial or physical burden of recycling their electronics after use, they may be incentivized to design more sustainable, less toxic, and more easily recyclable electronics. Using fewer materials and designing products to last longer can directly reduce producers' end-of-life costs. Thus, extended producer responsibility is often cited as one way to fight planned obsolescence, because it financially encourages manufacturers to design for recycling and make products last longer. In addition to fighting planned obsolescence, by allocating part of the financial responsibility for paying for and managing waste on the producer, the pressures placed on governments may be alleviated. Currently, many governments bear the weight of disposal and spend millions of dollars on collecting and removing electronic waste. However, these plans usually fail because governments do not have enough money to create and enforce them properly. Placing responsibility on producers to dispose of their products can give governments more freedom to create legislation which benefits sustainability with little cost to both parties, while also raising awareness about the issues EPR seeks to solve.

- One of the advantages of EPR is that it becomes more and more effective as the EPR policy puts pressure on countries that export their E-waste. The regulation of this E-waste forces infrastructure to deal with the waste or implement new ways of creating products from the producers. As more countries adopt these policies it restricts other countries from ignoring the issues. For example, when China stopped importing E-waste from the U.S., a build-up of waste was formed at ports. The lack of infrastructure around recycling E-waste in the US has been possible because of the ability to export and the negligence of producers. The pressure of this growing dump of E-waste forces countries to have their own infrastructure and will force more regulations from the government, state and federal, to be placed on producers.

Disadvantages:

- Some people have concerns about extended producer responsibility programs for complex electronics that can be difficult to safely recycle, such as lithium-ion polymer batteries. Others worry that such laws could increase the cost of electronics because producers would add recycling costs into the initial price tag. When companies are required to transport their products to a recycling facility, it can be expensive if the product contains hazardous materials and does not have a scrap value, such as with CRT televisions, which can contain up to five pounds of lead. Organizations and researchers against EPR claim that the mandate would slow innovation and impede technological progress.
- Other critics are concerned that manufacturers may use takeback programs to take secondhand electronics off the reuse market, by shredding rather than reusing or repairing goods that come in for recycling. Another argument against EPR is that EPR policies are not accelerating environmentally friendly designs because "manufacturers are already starting to moving toward reduced material-use per unit of output, reduced energy use in making and delivering each product, and improved environmental performance."

- The Reason Foundation argues that EPR is not clear in the way fees are established for the particular recycling processes. Fees are set in place to help incentivize recycling, but this may deter the use of manufacturing with better materials for the different electronic products. There are not set fees for certain materials, so confusion occurs when companies do not know what design features to include in their devices.

Fossil Fuels

A study suggests that applying the principle of extended producer responsibility to fossil fuels could deconflict energy security and climate policy at an affordable cost; in particular, authors suggested the responsibility could be used to establish the financing of CO_2 storage and nature-based solutions.

Implementation

EPR has been implemented in many forms, which may be classified into three major approaches:

- Mandatory.
- Negotiated.
- Voluntary.

It is perhaps because of the tendency of economic policy in market-driven economies not to interfere with consumers' preferences that the producer-centric representation is the dominant form of viewing the environmental impacts of industrial production: in statistics on energy, emissions, water, etc., impacts are almost always presented as attributes of industries ("on-site" or "direct" allocation) rather than as attributes of the supply chains of products for consumers. On a smaller scale, most existing schemes for corporate sustainability reporting include only impacts that arise out of operations controlled by the reporting company, and not supply-chain impacts According to this world view, "upstream and downstream [environmental] impacts are ... allocated to their immediate producers. The institutional setting and the different actors' spheres of influence are not reflected".

On the other hand, a number of studies have highlighted that final consumption and affluence, especially in the industrialised world, are the main drivers for the level and growth of environmental pressure. Even though these studies provide a clear incentive for complementing producer-focused environmental policy with some consideration for consumption-related aspects, demand-side measures to address environmental problems are rarely exploited.

The nexus created by the different views on impacts caused by industrial production is exemplified by several contributions to the discussion about producer or consumer responsibility for greenhouse gas emissions. Emissions data are reported to the IPCC as contributions of producing industries located in a particular country rather than as embodiments in products consumed by a particular population, irrespective of productive origin. However, especially for open economies, taking into account the greenhouse gases embodied in internationally traded commodities can have a considerable influence on national greenhouse gas balance sheets. Assuming consumer responsibility, exports have to be subtracted from, and imports added to national greenhouse gas inventories. In Denmark, for example, Munksgaard and Pedersen (2001) report that a significant amount of power and other energy-intensive commodities are traded across Danish borders, and that between 1966 and 1994 the Danish foreign trade balance in terms of CO_2 developed from a 7 Mt deficit to a 7 Mt surplus, compared to total emissions of approximately 60 Mt. In particular, electricity traded between Norway, Sweden and Denmark is subject to large annual fluctuations due to varying rainfall in Norway and Sweden. In wet years Denmark imports hydro-electricity whereas electricity from coal-fired power plants is exported in dry years. The official Danish emissions inventory includes a correction for electricity trade and thus applies the consumer responsibility principle.

Similarly, at the company level, "when adopting the concept of eco-efficiency and the scope of an environmental management system stated in for example ISO 14001, it is insufficient to merely report on the carbon dioxide emissions limited to the judicial borders of the company". 7 "Companies must recognise their wider responsibility and manage the entire life-cycle of their products ... Insisting on high environmental standards from suppliers and ensuring that raw materials are extracted or produced in an environmentally conscious way provides a start." A life-cycle perspective is also taken in EPR frameworks: "Producers of products should bear a significant degree of responsibility (physical and/or financial) not only for the environmental impacts of their products downstream from the treatment and disposal of their product, but also for their upstream activities inherent in the selection of materials and in the design of products." "The major impetus for EPR came from northern European countries in the late 1980s and early 1990s, as they were facing severe landfill shortages. [... As a result,] EPR is generally applied to post-consumer wastes which place increasing physical and financial demands on municipal waste management."

EPR has rarely been consistently quantified. Moreover, applying conventional life cycle assessment, and assigning environmental impacts to producers and consumers can lead to double-counting. Using input-output analysis, researchers have attempted for decades to account for both producers and consumers in an economy in a consistent way. Gallego and Lenzen demonstrate and discuss a method of consistently delineating producers' supply chains, into mutually exclusive and collectively exhaustive responsibilities to be shared by all agents in an economy. Their method is an approach to allocating responsibility across agents in a fully inter-connected circular system. Upstream and downstream environmental impacts are shared between all agents of a supply chain—producers and consumers.

2.4.3 Remanufacturing, Refurbishing, and Upcycling

Remanufacturing

Remanufacturing is "the rebuilding of a product to specifications of the original manufactured product using a combination of reused, repaired and new parts". It requires the repair or replacement of worn out or obsolete components and modules. Parts subject to degradation affecting the performance or the expected life of the whole are replaced. Remanufacturing is a form of a product recovery process that differs from other recovery processes in its completeness: a remanufactured machine should match the same customer expectation as new machines.

In 1995, the United States Environmental Protection Agency (EPA) implemented the Comprehensive Procurement Guideline (CPG) program to promote waste reduction and resource conservation through the use of materials recovered from solid waste, and to ensure that the materials collected in recycling programs will be used again in the manufacture of new products. The EPA is required to designate products that are or can be made with recovered materials, and to recommend practices for buying these products. Once a product is designated, state and federal procuring agencies are required to purchase it with the highest recovered material content level practicable.

In 2004, the EPA published its third CPG update (CPG IV) which designated seven additional products and revised three existing product designations. One of the new product categories to be added was Rebuilt Vehicular Parts. The EPA defines rebuilt vehicular parts as "vehicle parts that have been re-manufactured, reusing parts in their original form. Rebuilt parts undergo an extensive re-manufacturing and testing process and must meet the same industry specifications for performance as new parts."

In the UK, a market potential of up to 5.6 billion GBP has been identified in remanufacturing, with the benefits said to be improvement to business margins, revenues and security of supply. The United States remanufacturing industry grew by 15% between 2009 and 2011, and in 2020 it accounted for 2% of all manufacturing in the US and 1.9% in the European Union.

Definition

Many formal definitions of remanufacturing exist in the literature, but the first published report on remanufacturing, by R. Lund (1984), describes remanufacturing as "... an industrial process in which worn-out products are restored to like-new condition. Through a series of industrial processes in a factory environment, a discarded product is completely disassembled. Useable parts are cleaned, refurbished, and put into inventory. Then the product is reassembled from the old parts (and where necessary, new parts) to produce a unit fully equivalent and sometimes superior in performance and expected lifetime to the original new product".

Furthermore, the Automotive Parts Remanufacturers Association (APRA) realized that communication problems can arise when people from different countries with different language skills talk about remanufacturing. Certain terms can have different meanings as definitions between countries and individuals vary. In 2013, APRA was able to solve these communication problems by publishing a common translation list in many different languages in order to unite all those who deal with the automotive industry.

Rebuilding

Rebuilding is an old name for remanufacturing. It is still widely used by automotive industry. For example, the Automotive Parts Remanufacturers Association (APRA), have the new term in their name, but to be safe on their own website use the combined term 'rebuild/remanufacture'.

The term 'rebuilding' is also often used by railway companies; a steam locomotive may be rebuilt with a new boiler or a diesel locomotive may be rebuilt with a new engine. This saves money (by re-using the frame, and some other components, which still have years of useful life) and allows the incorporation of improved technology. For example, a new diesel engine may have lower fuel consumption, reduced exhaust emissions and better reliability. Recent examples include British Rail Class 57 and British Rail Class 43.

Types of Remanufacturing

There are three main types of remanufacturing activities, each with different operational challenges.

- Remanufacturing without identity loss With this method, a current machine is built on yesterday's base, receiving all enhancements, expected life and warranty of a new machine. The physical structure (the chassis or frame) is inspected for soundness. The whole product is refurbished and critical modules are overhauled, upgraded or replaced. Any defects in the original design are eliminated. This is the case for customized remanufacturing of machine tools, airplanes, computer mainframes, large medical equipment and other capital goods. Because of its uniqueness, this product recovery is characterized as a project.

- Remanufacturing with loss of original product identity With this method, used goods are disassembled into pre-determined components and repaired to stock, ready to be reassembled into a remanufactured product. This is the case when remanufacturing automobile components, photocopiers, toner cartridges, furniture, ready-to-use cameras and personal computers. Once the product is disassembled and the parts are recovered, the process concludes with an operation similar to original manufacturing. Disassembled parts are inventoried, just like purchased parts and made available for final assembly. Remanufacturing with loss of original product identity encompasses some unique challenges in inventory management and disassembly sequence development. Some of the open questions relate to the commonality of parts in products of different generations, the uncertainty in the supply of used products, and their relationship with production planning. The National Center for Remanufacturing and Resource Recovery (C3R) at Rochester Institute of Technology is researching remanufacturing processes including testing standards for remanufactured products.
- Repetitive remanufacturing without identity loss In this method, there is the additional challenge of scheduling the sequence of dependent processes and identifying the location of inventory buffers. There is a fine line between repetitive remanufacturing without loss of identity and product overhaul. The final output has an as-new appearance and is covered by a warranty comparable to that of a new product.

Remanufacturing by Recoating of Worn Engine Parts

In addition to these is a less significant type of remanufacturing, remanufacturing by recoating of worn engine parts. This type of remanufacturing serves many engine parts and other large and expensive components that become worn after a period of use. An example is the engine block, in particular the cylinder engine bores, which must withstand combustion. Instead of disposing of engine blocks, remanufacturing enables re-use by coating them with plasma transferred wire arc spraying (PTWA). Remanufacturing by recoating of parts is also popular in aviation and with geothermal pipe.

Refurbishing

Refurbishing is a critical practice that involves restoring, repairing, or upgrading products, machinery, and infrastructure to extend their lifespan and improve performance. It is widely used in various industries, including electronics, automobiles, furniture, and construction. As sustainability and resource efficiency become more pressing global concerns, refurbishing has gained prominence as a key strategy to reduce waste, conserve raw materials, and lower environmental impacts. This process not only benefits businesses and consumers by offering cost-effective alternatives to new purchases but also contributes to a circular economy by keeping products in use for longer periods. Refurbishing is a vital practice that contributes to sustainability, economic efficiency, and the circular economy. By extending the life of products, reducing waste, and offering cost-effective alternatives to new purchases, refurbishing benefits both businesses and consumers. Its applications span industries such as electronics, automotive, construction, and healthcare, demonstrating its widespread importance.

While challenges such as quality perception, regulatory compliance, and technological obsolescence remain, innovations in repair technologies and supportive government policies are driving growth in the refurbishing industry. As society continues to prioritize sustainability, refurbishing will play an increasingly significant role in shaping a more resource-efficient future. Encouraging further adoption of refurbishing practices will be crucial in reducing environmental impact, creating jobs, and fostering a more circular and sustainable economy.

The Process of Refurbishing

Refurbishing typically follows a structured process that includes inspection, disassembly, cleaning, repairing, replacing components, and reassembling. The first step involves assessing the condition of the product to determine the extent of refurbishment needed. In the case of electronic devices, this may include testing components, identifying faults, and evaluating software functionality. For furniture or machinery, it may involve checking for structural damage and wear.

Once the assessment is complete, the item is disassembled to allow for thorough cleaning and repairs. Cleaning removes accumulated dirt, rust, or contaminants that may affect performance. Damaged or outdated components are repaired or replaced with new or refurbished parts. In some cases, upgrades are incorporated to enhance functionality, such as adding new software to refurbished laptops or applying modern finishes to furniture.

Reassembly follows, ensuring that the product meets quality and safety standards before it is tested for functionality. Rigorous testing ensures that the refurbished item performs as expected. Once approved, the product is often repackaged and resold or reintroduced into circulation.

Applications of Refurbishing

Refurbishing is applied across multiple industries, each with its unique processes and challenges. The electronics industry is one of the largest adopters of refurbishing, particularly for smartphones, laptops, and home appliances. Companies such as Apple and Dell offer certified refurbished products, which undergo extensive testing and quality assurance to ensure they perform like new devices. These products provide consumers with affordable alternatives while reducing electronic waste, a significant environmental concern.

The automotive industry also heavily relies on refurbishing, especially for used vehicles, engines, and spare parts. Auto refurbishing involves reconditioning old vehicles, repairing critical systems, and sometimes upgrading components such as engines, transmissions, and interiors. This practice extends the life of vehicles, making transportation more affordable and reducing the demand for new car production, which has a substantial environmental footprint.

In the construction and furniture industries, refurbishing is used to restore old buildings, fixtures, and furnishings. Refurbished office furniture, for example, is an increasingly popular option for businesses seeking sustainable and cost-effective workplace solutions. In construction, refurbishing materials such as doors, windows, and steel structures helps conserve resources and reduce construction waste. Medical equipment refurbishing is another vital application, providing healthcare facilities with reliable, lower-cost alternatives to new equipment. High-value devices such as MRI machines, ultrasound systems, and patient monitors are often refurbished and resold, ensuring accessibility to advanced medical technology in regions with budget constraints.

Benefits of Refurbishing

One of the most significant benefits of refurbishing is its positive environmental impact. By extending the life of products, refurbishing reduces the demand for raw materials and minimizes waste. The electronics industry, for example, contributes significantly to global e-waste, but refurbishing helps curb this problem by reusing and repurposing existing devices.

From an economic perspective, refurbishing presents cost savings for both businesses and consumers. Refurbished products are typically sold at lower prices than new items while maintaining similar performance levels. For businesses, refurbishing assets such as machinery and office equipment helps optimize investment, allowing organizations to maximize value from existing resources.

Job creation is another benefit, as refurbishing requires skilled labor, including technicians, engineers, and quality control experts. The growth of refurbishing industries has led to employment opportunities in sectors ranging from electronics repair to automotive restoration and furniture refinishing.

Moreover, refurbishing plays a crucial role in promoting the circular economy by encouraging product reuse rather than disposal. This shift reduces landfill waste, lowers energy consumption associated with manufacturing new products, and supports sustainable consumption patterns.

Upcycling

Upcycling, also known as creative reuse, is the process of transforming by-products, waste materials, useless, or unwanted products into new materials or products perceived to be of greater quality, such as artistic value or environmental value. Upcycling is the opposite of downcycling, which is the other part of the recycling process. Downcycling involves converting materials and products into new materials, sometimes of lesser quality. Most recycling involves converting or extracting useful materials from a product and creating a different product or material. The terms upcycling and downcycling were first used in print in an article in SalvoNEWS by Thornton Kay quoting Reiner Pilz and published in 1994.

- We talked about the impending EU Demolition Waste Streams directive. "Recycling," he said, "I call it downcycling. They smash bricks, they smash everything. What we need is upcycling, where old products are given more value, not less." He despairs of the German situation and recalls the supply of a large quantity of reclaimed woodblock from an English supplier for a contract in Nuremberg, while just down the road a load of similar block was scrapped. In the road outside his premises was the result of the Germans' demolition "waste" recycling. It was a pinky looking aggregate with pieces of handmade brick, old tiles, and discernible parts of useful old items mixed with crushed concrete. Is this the future for Europe?

Upsizing was the title of the German edition of a book about upcycling, first published in English in 1998 by Gunter Pauli and given the revised title of Upcycling in 1999. The German edition was adapted to the German language and culture by Johannes F. Hartkemeyer, then Director of the Volkshochschule in Osnabrück. The concept was later incorporated by William McDonough and Michael Braungart in their 2002 book Cradle to Cradle: Remaking the Way We Make Things. They state that the goal of upcycling is to prevent wasting potentially useful materials by making use of existing ones. This reduces the consumption of new raw materials when creating new products. Reducing the use of new raw materials can result in a reduction of energy usage, air pollution, water pollution and even greenhouse gas emissions.

This is a significant step towards regenerative design culture where the end products are cleaner, healthier, and usually have a better value than the material inputs. For example, during the recycling process of plastics other than those used to create bottles, many different types of plastics are mixed, resulting in a hybrid. This hybrid is used in the manufacturing of plastic lumber applications. However, unlike the engineered polymer ABS which hold properties of several plastics well, recycled plastics suffer phase-separation that causes structural weakness in the final product. In 2009, Belinda Smith from Reuters wrote that upcycling had increased in the rich countries but observed that upcycling was a necessity in poorer ones:

- Supporters of the environmentally friendly practice of upcycling say people in developing countries have effectively been upcycling for years, using old packaging and clothing in new ways, although more out of need than for the environment. But upcycling is now taking off in other countries, reflecting an increased interest in eco-friendly products, particularly ones that are priced at an affordable level and proving profitable for the manufacturers. "If upcycling is going to become mainstream, then the corporate world needs to see that it can be profitable," said Albe Zakes, spokesman of U.S. company TerraCycle which specializes in finding new uses for discarded packaging. A growing number of companies are focusing on upcycling although the trend is still in its infancy with industry-wide figures yet to be produced.

Upcycling has shown significant growth across the United States and the World. For example, the number of products on Etsy, Pinterest or Upcycle Studio tagged with the word "upcycled" increased from about 7,900 in January 2010 to nearly 30,000 a year later. As of April 2013, that number stood at 263,685.

Material downcycling occurs when it is either not possible or uneconomic to restore materials to their original quality, for example, when wrought aluminium alloys are melted to produce lower-grade casting alloys. Material upcycling, in the thermodynamic sense, is only possible if even more energy is added to upgrade the material quality. Two guiding questions to ask when assessing recovering for waste materials or products are: How much energy is required to restore the recovered material back to the desired material or product?, and, How does this quantity compare with obtaining the desired material or product from virgin or primary sources? In some cases, little energy is required to reuse a discarded product, for example, secondhand clothing. In other cases, the energy required to recover the materials is more than the energy required to process virgin material.

Recycling and Upcycling

While recycling usually means the materials are remade into their original form, e.g., recycling plastic bottles into plastic polymers, which then produce plastic bottles through the manufacturing process, upcycling adds more value to the materials, as the name suggested. According to Watson & Wolfe "Upcycling, also known as creative reuse, is the process of transforming by-products, waste materials, useless, or unwanted products into new materials or products perceived to be of greater quality, such as artistic value or environmental value."

Similarly, recycle art may refer to art pieces using used materials in their original form while upcycle art may involve a transformation process such as breaking down, reforming, reassembling, and the like.

A common concept in Recycling is the 3Rs, which represent Reduce, Reuse, and Recycle. According to The Upcycle Artist's Handbook: A Comprehensive Guide to Creating Art from Waste published by Upcycle Art And Craft Society (UAACS). They coined a 3Rs principle for upcycling: Rethink, Reform, and Reborn.

"Rethink" involves reevaluating something and looking at an item from a new perspective. It means seeing the potential for repurposing, giving it a new function, or exploring other creative possibilities for that material. "Reform" involves physically altering the item, either by dismantling it, combining it with other materials, or using different techniques to change its form. This transformation of existing materials creates a new structure that better suits the artist's creative vision. "Reborn" is the final outcome when the upcycled item is given new life or purpose. It's like a resurrection of cast-offs that are given a second life"

Potential Technologies

The worldwide plastic production was 280 million tons in 2011 and production levels are growing every year. Its haphazard disposal causes severe environmental damage, such as the creation of the Great Pacific Garbage Patch. In 2018, global annual plastic consumption grew to over 320 million tons. In order to solve this problem, the employment of modern technologies and processes to reuse the waste plastic as a cheap substrate is under research. The goal is to bring this material from the waste stream back into the mainstream by developing processes, which will create an economic demand for them.

One approach in the field involves the conversion of waste plastics (like LDPE, PET, and HDPE) into paramagnetic, conducting microspheres or into carbon nano-materials by applying high temperatures and chemical vapor deposition. On a molecular level, the treatment of polymers like polypropylene or thermoplastics with electron beams (doses around 150 kGy) can increase material properties like bending strength and elasticity and provides an eco-friendly and sustainable way to upcycle them. Active research is being carried out for the biotransformation upcycling of plastic waste (e.g., polyethylene terephthalate and polyurethane) into PHA bioplastic using bacteria. PET could be converted into the biodegradable PHA by using a combination of temperature and microbial treatment. First it gets pyrolized at 450 °C and the resulting terephthalic acid is used as a substrate for microorganisms, which convert it finally into PHA. Similar to the aforementioned approach is the combination of nano-materials like carbon nanotubes with powdered orange peel as a composite material. This might be used to remove synthetic dyes from wastewater. Biotechnology companies have recently shifted focus towards the conversion of agricultural waste, or biomass, to different chemicals or commodities. One company in particular, BioTork, has signed an agreement with the State of Hawaii and the USDA to convert the unmarketable papayas in Hawaii into fish feed. As part of this Zero Waste Initiative put forth by the State of Hawaii, BioTork will upcycle the otherwise wasted biomass into fish feed.

2.5 SYSTEMS THINKING AND DESIGN FOR CIRCULARITY

2.5.1 Interconnectedness of Materials, Energy, and Products

The modern industrial world is built on a complex web of interactions between materials, energy, and products. These three components form the foundation of economic activities and technological advancements, influencing everything from manufacturing processes to environmental sustainability. Understanding their interconnectedness is essential for optimizing resource use, reducing environmental impact, and advancing toward a more sustainable and circular economy. Materials serve as the building blocks of products, energy powers their transformation, and the final products shape consumer demand and market dynamics. The relationship between these elements highlights the importance of efficient resource management, innovation, and policy development to ensure long-term economic and environmental stability.

The interconnectedness of materials, energy, and products is a fundamental aspect of modern industrial and economic systems. Understanding these relationships is essential for optimizing resource use, reducing environmental impact, and transitioning toward a sustainable future. Materials provide the foundation for production, energy drives their transformation, and products serve as the tangible outcomes that shape consumption patterns.

Adopting circular economy principles, integrating renewable energy, and investing in sustainable material innovations are critical steps toward strengthening these interconnections. While challenges such as high energy demands, economic constraints, and technological limitations exist, ongoing advancements and policy support can drive progress. By fostering a holistic approach to resource management, industries and societies can create a more efficient, resilient, and environmentally responsible future.

Materials as the Foundation of Industrial Processes

Materials are at the core of industrial production, providing the essential inputs needed to manufacture goods and infrastructure. They include raw materials such as metals, polymers, ceramics, and composites, each with unique properties suited to specific applications. The extraction, processing, and refinement of these materials require significant energy inputs and have direct environmental consequences.

For instance, the production of steel, a fundamental material in construction and manufacturing, involves intensive mining of iron ore and high-temperature processing that consumes substantial amounts of energy. Similarly, the production of plastics depends on petroleum-derived feedstocks, which not only require extraction and refining but also involve energy-intensive polymerization processes. The demand for advanced materials, such as rare earth elements used in electronics and renewable energy technologies, further complicates the material-energy relationship due to the geopolitical and environmental challenges associated with their extraction and processing. Optimizing material use and promoting sustainable sourcing strategies can significantly reduce energy consumption and waste generation. Recycling and reusing materials also play a crucial role in minimizing environmental impact. By integrating circular economy principles, industries can extend the lifecycle of materials and decrease dependence on virgin resources.

2.5.2 Circular Economy Design Guidelines

Circular economy design guidelines provide a framework for creating products, services, and systems that prioritize resource efficiency, waste reduction, and long-term sustainability. Unlike the traditional linear economy, which follows a take-make-dispose model, a circular economy focuses on designing products that can be reused, repaired, remanufactured, and recycled. Implementing circular design principles helps industries minimize environmental impact, optimize material use, and contribute to economic resilience.

Circular economy design guidelines offer a roadmap for creating products and systems that align with sustainability goals while maintaining functionality and economic viability. By designing for longevity, selecting sustainable materials, ensuring repairability, and optimizing energy efficiency, businesses can reduce environmental impact and contribute to a more resource-efficient economy. Integrating circular business models and engaging consumers in sustainable practices further strengthens the transition toward a circular economy. Overcoming challenges through innovation and collaboration will be key to making circular design the standard for future product development and consumption.

Designing for Longevity

One of the fundamental principles of circular economy design is ensuring product longevity. Designing durable products reduces the frequency of replacement and extends their lifecycle, thereby minimizing resource consumption. High-quality materials, robust engineering, and modular designs enhance durability and make maintenance easier. For example, modular smartphones allow users to replace individual components rather than discarding the entire device, reducing electronic waste. Similarly, durable textiles and furniture designed for extended use contribute to a circular approach by delaying product obsolescence and decreasing the demand for raw materials.

Material Selection and Resource Efficiency

Choosing the right materials plays a crucial role in circular design. Sustainable materials should be renewable, non-toxic, and recyclable to ensure they can be reintegrated into the production cycle at the end of their life. Designers must consider the entire lifecycle of materials, from extraction and processing to disposal and reuse. Utilizing bio-based, biodegradable, or recycled materials reduces dependency on finite resources and mitigates environmental harm. Lightweight materials can also improve energy efficiency in transportation and logistics, further reducing the environmental footprint of products.

Design for Disassembly and Repairability

Products designed for easy disassembly and repair help extend their useful life and facilitate component reuse. Incorporating standardized fasteners, modular parts, and accessible design features allows consumers and technicians to replace or upgrade components rather than discarding the entire product. This approach is particularly relevant in the electronics, automotive, and furniture industries, where repairability can significantly enhance product lifespan. Companies like Fairphone have embraced repairable design, offering replaceable batteries and modular components to ensure longevity and reduce waste.

Closing the Loop with Recycling and Reuse

Effective circular design considers the end-of-life phase and ensures that materials can be reclaimed and reintroduced into the production cycle. Designing for recyclability involves selecting mono-material components, avoiding hazardous substances, and integrating clear labeling to facilitate sorting and recycling. Product take-back programs and closed-loop manufacturing systems help recover valuable materials and prevent waste from entering landfills. For example, Nike's Move to Zero initiative incorporates recycled materials into footwear production, reducing the need for virgin resources while promoting circular practices.

Energy Efficiency and Low-Impact Manufacturing

Circular economy design goes beyond material selection and product longevity; it also considers the energy efficiency of production processes. Manufacturing techniques that minimize energy consumption and reduce carbon emissions contribute to sustainable product design. Implementing renewable energy sources, optimizing supply chain logistics, and using energy-efficient manufacturing technologies all help lower environmental impact. Life cycle assessments (LCAs) can identify areas where energy use can be reduced, guiding designers toward more sustainable production methods.

Business Models Supporting Circular Design

Adopting circular economy design principles requires a shift in business models. Companies must transition from selling products to offering services that emphasize longevity and reuse. Leasing, product-as-a-service, and subscription models encourage manufacturers to create durable and maintainable products while generating long-term value. For instance, Philips offers lighting-as-a-service, where businesses lease lighting systems rather than purchasing fixtures, ensuring efficient use and maintenance. Such models drive sustainable consumption patterns and reduce waste generation.

Consumer Engagement and Education

For circular economy design to be successful, consumer participation is essential. Educating consumers about the benefits of repairability, recycling, and sustainable consumption encourages responsible product use. Clear communication through eco-labeling, sustainability certifications, and repair guides empowers consumers to make informed choices. Companies that involve consumers in sustainability initiatives, such as take-back programs or repair workshops, foster a culture of circularity and encourage behavioral shifts toward responsible consumption.

Challenges and Opportunities in Circular Design

Despite its benefits, circular economy design faces several challenges. Many industries still rely on traditional linear production models, making the transition to circular practices complex and resource-intensive. Regulatory barriers, economic feasibility, and consumer resistance to refurbished or recycled products also pose hurdles. However, advancements in material science, digital technology, and policy incentives present opportunities to overcome these challenges. Innovations such as blockchain for supply chain transparency, AI-driven material optimization, and government-backed circular economy initiatives drive the adoption of sustainable design practices.

CHAPTER

Circular Economy in Key Sectors 3

3.1 CIRCULAR ECONOMY IN MANUFACTURING AND INDUSTRIAL SECTORS

3.1.1 Resource Efficiency in Manufacturing Processes

Resource efficiency in manufacturing processes is a crucial aspect of sustainable industrial development. It involves optimizing the use of materials, energy, water, and other resources to minimize waste and environmental impact while maintaining productivity and profitability. As global demand for products continues to rise, manufacturers face increasing pressure to adopt resource-efficient practices that reduce costs, improve operational efficiency, and enhance environmental sustainability. Implementing resource efficiency strategies in manufacturing not only contributes to economic resilience but also supports broader sustainability goals such as reducing carbon emissions and conserving natural resources.

Resource efficiency in manufacturing processes is essential for achieving sustainability, reducing environmental impact, and improving economic performance. By optimizing material use, enhancing energy efficiency, conserving water, and implementing lean manufacturing practices, industries can minimize waste and maximize productivity. Sustainable supply chain management, digitalization, and eco-design further contribute to resource-efficient manufacturing. Although challenges exist, regulatory support, technological advancements, and market incentives provide opportunities for industries to transition toward more sustainable production models. Embracing resource efficiency not only benefits businesses but also contributes to a more resilient and sustainable global economy.

Optimizing Material Use and Waste Reduction

Efficient material use is fundamental to resource efficiency in manufacturing. Industries must focus on minimizing raw material consumption and reducing production waste through innovative design and advanced manufacturing techniques. By implementing precision engineering, lean manufacturing, and computer-aided design (CAD), manufacturers can optimize material usage and eliminate excess waste. The adoption of advanced cutting and shaping technologies, such as laser cutting and 3D printing, allows for precise material usage, reducing offcuts and scrap. Additionally, reusing by-products and recycling manufacturing waste into new production cycles help close the resource loop and reduce dependency on virgin materials.

Energy Efficiency in Production Processes

Energy consumption is a significant factor in manufacturing, and improving energy efficiency can lead to substantial cost savings and environmental benefits. Manufacturers can optimize energy use by investing in energy-efficient machinery, implementing smart automation, and utilizing renewable energy sources. Integrating energy management systems (EMS) enables real-time monitoring and optimization of energy consumption, ensuring that production processes operate at peak efficiency. The adoption of waste heat recovery systems further enhances energy efficiency by capturing and repurposing heat generated during manufacturing. Implementing energy-efficient lighting, HVAC systems, and motor-driven equipment also contributes to reducing overall energy consumption and carbon emissions.

Water Conservation and Sustainable Water Management

Water is an essential resource in manufacturing, used for cooling, cleaning, and processing. Implementing water-efficient practices helps reduce consumption and minimize wastewater generation. Closed-loop water recycling systems allow industries to treat and reuse water multiple times, decreasing reliance on freshwater sources. Advanced filtration and wastewater treatment technologies help remove contaminants and improve water quality for reuse. Additionally, adopting dry manufacturing techniques and optimizing cooling processes reduces water consumption while maintaining operational efficiency. Sustainable water management strategies contribute to environmental protection and ensure long-term resource availability for industrial operations.

Process Optimization and Lean Manufacturing

Lean manufacturing principles focus on eliminating waste, improving efficiency, and enhancing productivity. By streamlining production processes and reducing inefficiencies, manufacturers can optimize resource use and lower operational costs. Process automation, robotics, and real-time data analytics play a crucial role in improving efficiency by minimizing errors, reducing downtime, and enhancing production accuracy. Implementing just-in-time (JIT) manufacturing reduces excess inventory and material waste by ensuring that resources are used only when needed. Continuous process improvement through Six Sigma and Kaizen methodologies further enhances resource efficiency by identifying and addressing inefficiencies in production workflows.

Sustainable Supply Chain Management

A resource-efficient manufacturing process extends beyond the factory floor to encompass the entire supply chain. Sustainable supply chain management involves sourcing raw materials responsibly, reducing transportation emissions, and optimizing logistics. Partnering with suppliers who follow sustainable practices ensures that materials are sourced ethically and with minimal environmental impact. Implementing digital supply chain management systems improves transparency, enabling manufacturers to track resource use and optimize procurement decisions. By adopting circular supply chain models, industries can facilitate the reuse and recycling of materials, further reducing resource consumption and waste generation.

Waste-to-Value Approaches and Industrial Symbiosis

Waste-to-value approaches transform production waste into valuable resources, creating opportunities for additional revenue streams and resource conservation. Industrial symbiosis, where waste or by-products from one manufacturing process serve as raw materials for another, enhances resource efficiency and promotes collaboration between industries. For example, waste heat from power plants can be used for district heating, and agricultural residues can be repurposed into bio-based materials. By viewing waste as a resource rather than a disposal problem, manufacturers can develop innovative solutions that reduce environmental impact and improve economic viability.

Digitalization and Smart Manufacturing

The integration of digital technologies in manufacturing, known as smart manufacturing or Industry 4.0, enhances resource efficiency by optimizing production processes and reducing waste. Internet of Things (IoT) sensors, artificial intelligence (AI), and big data analytics enable real-time monitoring and predictive maintenance, ensuring that machinery operates at optimal performance levels. Digital twins, which create virtual replicas of manufacturing processes, allow manufacturers to simulate and optimize production before implementation, minimizing resource use and reducing trial-and-error waste. The use of blockchain technology improves supply chain transparency, ensuring responsible sourcing and reducing inefficiencies in procurement and distribution.

Eco-Design and Sustainable Product Development

Designing products with sustainability in mind contributes to overall resource efficiency. Eco-design principles focus on minimizing material use, improving product durability, and enhancing end-of-life recyclability. By considering the entire product lifecycle, manufacturers can create items that require fewer resources, generate less waste, and have lower environmental impact. Lightweight materials, biodegradable components, and modular designs enhance product sustainability. Extended producer responsibility (EPR) policies encourage manufacturers to take accountability for their products' end-of-life management, ensuring that materials are recovered and reintegrated into new production cycles.

Regulatory Compliance and Policy Incentives

Governments and regulatory bodies play a crucial role in promoting resource efficiency in manufacturing. Environmental regulations, emissions targets, and resource management policies drive industries to adopt sustainable practices. Incentives such as tax credits, grants, and subsidies support businesses in investing in energy-efficient technologies and sustainable production methods. International frameworks, such as the European Green Deal and the United Nations Sustainable Development Goals (SDGs), provide guidelines for industries to align their operations with global sustainability objectives. Compliance with these regulations not only enhances corporate reputation but also ensures long-term business viability in an increasingly eco-conscious market.

Challenges and Opportunities in Resource Efficiency

While resource efficiency in manufacturing offers significant benefits, several challenges must be addressed. The transition to sustainable practices requires substantial investment in new technologies, process optimization, and workforce training. Small and medium-sized enterprises (SMEs) may face financial and technical barriers in adopting resource-efficient solutions. Additionally, balancing resource efficiency with cost-effectiveness and production demands presents an ongoing challenge. However, the growing focus on sustainability, advancements in technology, and increasing consumer demand for eco-friendly products create opportunities for innovation and competitiveness. Businesses that prioritize resource efficiency can gain a competitive advantage, reduce operational risks, and enhance long-term profitability.

3.1.2 Industrial Symbiosis and Collaborative Models

Industrial Symbiosis

Industrial symbiosis a subset of industrial ecology. It describes how a network of diverse organizations can foster eco-innovation and long-term culture change, create and share mutually profitable transactions—and improve business and technical processes.

Although geographic proximity is often associated with industrial symbiosis, it is neither necessary nor sufficient—nor is a singular focus on physical resource exchange. Strategic planning is required to optimize the synergies of co-location. In practice, using industrial symbiosis as an approach to commercial operations—

using, recovering and redirecting resources for reuse—results in resources remaining in productive use in the economy for longer. This in turn creates business opportunities, reduces demands on the earth's resources, and provides a stepping-stone towards creating a circular economy.

Industrial symbiosis is a subset of industrial ecology, with a particular focus on material and energy exchange. Industrial ecology is a relatively new field that is based on a natural paradigm, claiming that an industrial ecosystem may behave in a similar way to the natural ecosystem wherein everything gets recycled, albeit the simplicity and applicability of this paradigm has been questioned.

Eco-industrial development is one of the ways in which industrial ecology contributes to the integration of economic growth and environmental protection. Some of the examples of eco-industrial development are:

- Circular economy (single material and/or energy exchange).
- Greenfield eco-industrial development (geographically confined space).
- Brownfield eco-industrial development (geographically confined space).
- Eco-industrial network (no strict requirement of geographical proximity).
- Virtual eco-industrial network (networks spread in large areas e.g. regional network).
- Networked Eco-industrial System (macro level developments with links across regions).

Industrial symbiosis engages traditionally separate industries in a collective approach to competitive advantage involving physical exchange of materials, energy, water, and/or by-products. The keys to industrial symbiosis are collaboration and the synergistic possibilities offered by geographic proximity". Notably, this definition and the stated key aspects of industrial symbiosis, i.e., the role of collaboration and geographic proximity, in its variety of forms, has been explored and empirically tested in the UK through the research and published activities of the National Industrial Symbiosis Programme.

Industrial symbiosis systems collectively optimize material and energy use at efficiencies beyond those achievable by any individual process alone. IS systems such as the web of materials and energy exchanges among companies in Kalundborg, Denmark have spontaneously evolved from a series of micro innovations over a long time scale; however, the engineered design and implementation of such systems from a macro planner's perspective, on a relatively short time scale, proves challenging.

Often, access to information on available by-products is difficult to obtain. These by-products are considered waste and typically not traded or listed on any type of exchange. Only a small group of specialized waste marketplaces addresses this particular kind of waste trading.

Collaborative Models

In psycholinguistics, the collaborative model (or conversational model) is a theory for explaining how speaking and understanding work in conversation, specifically how people in conversation coordinate to determine definite references.

The model was initially proposed in 1986 by psycholinguists Herb Clark and Deanna Wilkes-Gibbs. It asserts that conversation partners must act collaboratively to reach a mutual understanding – i.e. the speaker must tailor their utterances to better suit the listener, and the listener must indicate to the speaker that they have understood. In this ongoing process, both conversation partners must work together in order to establish what a given noun phrase is referring to. The referential process can be initiated by the speaker using one of at least six types of noun phrases: the elementary noun phrase, the episodic noun phrase, the installment noun phrase, the provisional noun phrase, the dummy noun phrase, and/or the proxy noun phrase. Once this presentation is made, the listener must accept it either through presupposing acceptance (i.e. letting the speaker continue uninterrupted) or asserting acceptance (i.e. through a continuer such as "yes", okay", or a head nod). The speaker must then acknowledge this signal of acceptance. In this process, presentation and acceptance goes back and forth, and some utterances can simultaneously be both presentations and acceptances. This model also posits that conversationalists strive for minimum collaborative effort by making references based more on permanent properties than temporary properties and by refining perspective on referents through simplification and narrowing .

Clark and Wilkes-Gibbs

Clark and Wilkes-Gibbs criticized the literary model in their 1986 paper; they asserted that the model failed to account for the dynamic nature of verbal conversations.

- "First, in conversation unlike writing, speakers have limited time for planning and revision. They need to overcome this limitation, and in doing so they may exploit techniques possible only in conversational settings. Second, speech is evanescent. The listener has to attend to, hear, and try to understand an utterance at virtually the same time it is being issued. That requires a type of process synchronization not found in reading. And third, listeners in conversations aren't mute or invisible

> during an utterance. Speakers may alter what they say midcourse based on what addressees say and do."

In the same paper, they proposed the Collaborative Model as an alternative. They believed this model was more able to explain the aforementioned features of conversation. They had conducted an experiment to support this theory and also to further determine how the acceptance process worked. The experiment consisted of two participants seated at tables separated by an opaque screen. On the tables in front of each participant were a series of Tangram figures arranged in different orders. One participant, called the director, was tasked with getting the other participant, called the matcher, to accurately match his configuration of figures through conversation alone. This process was to be repeated 5 additional times by the same individuals, playing the same roles.

The collaborative model they proposed allowed them to make several predictions about what would happen. They predicted that it would require many more words to establish reference the first time, as the participants would need to use non-standard noun phrases which would make it difficult to determine which figures were being talked about. However, they hypothesized that later references to the same figures would take fewer words and a shorter amount of time, because by this point definite reference would have been mutually established, and also because the subjects would be able to rely on established standard noun phrases.

The results of the study confirmed many of their beliefs, and outlined some of the processes of collaborative reference, including establishing the types of noun phrases used in presentation, and their frequency.

Steps in Collaborating Reference

The following actions were observed in participants working towards mutual acceptance of a reference;

- Initiating or proposing a reference.
- Passing judgement on the reference.
- Refashioning a noun phrase.
- Accepting the reference.

Grounding

Grounding is the final stage in the collaborative process. The concept was proposed by Herbert H. Clark and Susan E. Brennan in 1991. It comprises the collection of "mutual knowledge, mutual beliefs, and mutual assumptions" that is essential for communication between two people. Successful grounding in communication requires parties "to coordinate both the content and process".

The parties engaging in grounding exchange information over what they do or do not understand over the course of a communication and they will continue to clarify concepts until they have agreed on grounding criterion. There are generally two phases in grounding:

- Presenting utterance(s)—speaker presents utterance to addressee.
- Accepting utterance(s)—addressee accepts utterance by providing evidence of understanding.

3.2 CIRCULAR ECONOMY IN THE BUILT ENVIRONMENT

3.2.1 Circular Construction and Demolition Practices

Circular construction and demolition practices are integral to creating a sustainable built environment. These practices focus on minimizing waste, optimizing resource use, and promoting material reuse and recycling in the construction industry. Unlike the traditional linear approach, which follows a take-make-dispose model, circular construction aims to close the loop by designing buildings for adaptability, reusability, and sustainability.

Circular construction and demolition practices offer a sustainable solution to the environmental and economic challenges posed by traditional construction methods. By designing for deconstruction, optimizing material use, minimizing waste, and integrating energy-efficient solutions, the industry can significantly reduce its ecological footprint. Policy support, technological innovation, and circular business models further drive the transition toward a more sustainable built environment. While challenges remain, the opportunities presented by circular construction contribute to a more resilient, resource-efficient, and environmentally responsible future for the construction industry.

Designing for Deconstruction and Reuse

A key principle of circular construction is designing buildings with future deconstruction and material reuse in mind. This approach ensures that materials can be easily disassembled and repurposed at the end of a building's life cycle. Modular construction, standardized components, and non-permanent fastening methods facilitate easy disassembly. Using materials that can be separated without damage, such as prefabricated concrete panels and steel structures with bolted connections, allows for efficient reuse. Designing for adaptability also ensures that buildings can be modified to meet changing needs, extending their lifespan and reducing demolition waste.

Material Selection and Resource Efficiency

Sustainable material selection plays a crucial role in circular construction. Using recycled, renewable, and low-impact materials reduces the demand for virgin resources and minimizes environmental degradation. Recycled concrete, reclaimed wood, and repurposed steel are examples of materials that contribute to a circular approach. Additionally, bio-based materials such as bamboo, hempcrete, and mycelium-based insulation provide sustainable alternatives with lower carbon footprints. Implementing resource-efficient strategies, such as optimizing material use and reducing offcuts through precise planning, further enhances sustainability in construction.

Waste Reduction in Construction Processes

Minimizing construction waste is essential for circularity. By adopting lean construction principles, project managers can optimize workflows, reduce excess materials, and improve efficiency. Digital technologies, such as Building Information Modeling (BIM), help streamline construction processes by enabling precise material estimation and reducing errors. Prefabrication and off-site manufacturing also contribute to waste reduction by improving material efficiency and reducing on-site construction waste. By implementing circular procurement policies that prioritize recycled and reusable materials, construction firms can actively support waste minimization efforts.

Demolition Waste Management and Recycling

Demolition generates a significant amount of waste, but circular practices aim to recover and recycle materials instead of sending them to landfills. Deconstruction, a selective dismantling process, allows for the recovery of valuable materials such as bricks, glass, metals, and wood. Advanced sorting technologies, including robotic demolition and AI-powered material recognition, improve the efficiency of material recovery. Crushed concrete can be repurposed as aggregate for new construction projects, while reclaimed bricks and wood can be used for renovation and restoration. Establishing demolition waste sorting facilities and promoting on-site material segregation enhance recycling rates and reduce disposal costs.

Circular Business Models in Construction

The transition to circular construction requires innovative business models that prioritize long-term resource efficiency. Leasing materials instead of outright purchasing them ensures that valuable resources remain in circulation. For example, companies can lease structural components, lighting systems, and flooring materials with take-back programs for reuse or refurbishment. Product-as-a-service models encourage manufacturers to maintain responsibility for the lifecycle of building materials, ensuring that they are collected and repurposed at the end of use. Implementing deposit-refund schemes for construction materials further incentivizes material recovery and reduces waste.

Energy Efficiency and Carbon Reduction

Circular construction not only focuses on material efficiency but also integrates energy-efficient practices to reduce carbon emissions. Passive design strategies, such as maximizing natural lighting, optimizing ventilation, and using high-performance insulation, reduce the energy demands of buildings. Renewable energy integration, including solar panels and geothermal heating systems, further enhances sustainability. The embodied carbon of construction materials is also a critical consideration; using low-carbon materials and carbon sequestration techniques, such as carbon-storing concrete, helps mitigate the overall environmental impact of buildings. Retrofitting existing structures for improved energy performance extends their lifespan and reduces the need for new construction.

3.2.2 Reuse and Recycling of Building Materials

The reuse and recycling of building materials play a crucial role in promoting sustainability in the construction industry. Traditional construction and demolition (C&D) practices generate significant waste, placing strain on landfills and natural resources. A circular approach that prioritizes material recovery, reuse, and recycling helps mitigate environmental impacts, reduce costs, and enhance resource efficiency.

The reuse and recycling of building materials are essential components of a sustainable construction industry. By prioritizing material recovery, embracing innovative technologies, and implementing supportive policies, the industry can significantly reduce waste, lower costs, and minimize environmental impact. Overcoming challenges through standardized quality control measures, improved logistics, and financial incentives will further accelerate the transition toward a circular construction model. Designing buildings for deconstruction, integrating modular construction techniques, and promoting cross-sector collaboration are critical steps in achieving long-term sustainability. As the demand for greener construction practices grows, embracing reuse and recycling strategies will play a pivotal role in shaping a more resilient and resource-efficient built environment.

The Importance of Material Reuse in Construction

Reusing building materials involves salvaging and repurposing elements from existing structures instead of discarding them. This approach reduces the demand for virgin resources, lowers carbon emissions associated with material production, and minimizes landfill waste. Commonly reused materials include wood, bricks, concrete, steel, and glass. Salvaging and reusing materials not only preserve their embedded energy but also contribute to cost savings for construction projects. By designing buildings for disassembly, incorporating modular components, and implementing deconstruction techniques, the industry can maximize material reuse potential and extend the lifecycle of construction resources.

Deconstruction vs. Demolition: Maximizing Material Recovery

Deconstruction is a strategic dismantling process that allows for the careful removal and preservation of building materials for reuse. Unlike traditional demolition, which involves the rapid destruction of structures, deconstruction prioritizes material recovery, reducing waste and landfill contributions. Selective deconstruction techniques enable the extraction of valuable components such as wooden beams, metal fixtures, and masonry units. When executed properly, deconstruction can recover up to 90% of a building's materials for reuse or recycling. The integration of deconstruction practices into construction projects helps promote a circular economy and encourages sustainable material management.

Recycling of Building Materials: Transforming Waste into Resources

Recycling involves processing construction waste into new materials that can be reintegrated into the building industry. Various recycling methods exist for different materials, ensuring that construction waste does not end up in landfills. Concrete, for example, can be crushed and reused as aggregate for new concrete production or road construction. Steel and aluminum are highly recyclable and can be melted down and reshaped into new structural components. Glass from windows and facades can be processed and reused in new glass products. Asphalt from roads and roofing materials can be reclaimed and incorporated into new paving applications. By implementing effective recycling systems, the construction industry can significantly reduce its environmental footprint and conserve natural resources.

Challenges in Reusing and Recycling Building Materials

Despite its numerous benefits, the reuse and recycling of building materials present several challenges. One of the primary obstacles is the lack of standardized processes for material recovery and quality assurance. Reused materials must meet structural and safety standards, which can be difficult to ensure without proper certification systems. Additionally, the logistics of material collection, sorting, and transportation can be complex and costly. Limited awareness and resistance to change within the industry further hinder the widespread adoption of material reuse and recycling practices. Addressing these challenges requires the development of clear regulations, financial incentives, and innovative technologies that facilitate efficient material recovery and reintegration into new construction projects.

Technological Innovations Supporting Material Reuse and Recycling

Advancements in technology are playing a key role in improving material reuse and recycling efforts. Digital platforms and material tracking systems enable better inventory management of reclaimed building components, allowing stakeholders to source and procure reused materials efficiently. Building Information Modeling (BIM) helps assess material lifecycles, identify reusable components, and optimize material recovery strategies. Robotics and automated sorting systems enhance the efficiency of material processing by accurately separating reusable and recyclable materials from construction waste. Emerging technologies such as 3D printing using recycled materials are opening new possibilities for sustainable construction. By leveraging these innovations, the industry can streamline material recovery processes and increase the feasibility of reuse and recycling initiatives.

Economic and Environmental Benefits of Reusing and Recycling Building Materials

The economic advantages of material reuse and recycling are significant, offering cost savings for construction projects while creating new business opportunities. Salvaging and repurposing materials reduce the need for expensive raw materials, lowering overall project expenses. The establishment of secondary material markets creates revenue streams for businesses specializing in reclaimed building materials. From an environmental perspective, reusing and recycling building materials help reduce greenhouse gas emissions associated with material extraction, processing, and transportation. Diverting construction waste from landfills conserves space and minimizes pollution, contributing to a healthier environment. The overall reduction in resource depletion supports long-term sustainability goals and promotes a more circular construction industry.

3.2.3 Modular Construction and Design for Disassembly

Fig: Algeco School Built Using Pre-Fabricated Modular Construction

Modular construction is a construction technique which involves the prefabrication of 2D panels or 3D volumetric structures in off-site factories and transportation to construction sites for assembly. This process has the potential to be superior to traditional building in terms of both time and costs, with claimed time savings of between 20 and 50 percent faster than traditional building techniques.

It is estimated that by 2030, modular construction could deliver US$22 billion in annual cost savings for the US and European construction industry, helping fill the US$1.6 trillion productivity gap. The current need for standardized, repeatable 3D volumetric housing pre-fabricated units and designs for student accommodations, affordable housing and hotels is driving demand for modular construction.

Advantages

In a 2018 Practice Note, the NEC states that the benefits obtained from offsite construction mainly relate to the creation of components in a factory setting, protected from the weather and using manufacturing techniques such as assembly lines with dedicated and specialist equipment. Through the use of appropriate technology, modular construction can:

- increase the speed of construction by increasing the speed of manufacture of the component parts;
- reduce waste;
- increase economies of scale;
- improve quality leading to reduction in the whole life costs of assets;
- reduce environmental impact such as dust and noise; and
- reduce accidents and ill health by reducing the amount of construction work taking place at site.

Disadvantages

In contrast to the benefits mentioned earlier, modular construction presents two significant obstacles:

- Logistical Challenges: The transportation of completed modules to the construction site demands meticulous organization and synchronization, often incurring substantial costs.
- Constraints on Size: The manufacturing and transportation procedures may place limitations on the dimensions of individual modular components. This can impact the room sizes in the building, potentially influencing the overall architectural design.

Time

Modular construction has consistently been at least 20 percent faster than traditional on-site builds. Currently, the design process of modular construction projects tends to take longer than that of traditional building. This is because modular construction is a fairly new technology and not many architects and engineers have experience working with it. In fewer words, the industry has not yet learned how to work this way. It is expected of design firms to develop module libraries which would assist in the automation of this process. These modules libraries would hold various pre-designed 2D panels and 3D structures which would be digitally assembled to create standardized structures.

The foundations of a structure are a crucial part of its rigidity. The magnitude and complexity of such will vary depending on the size, and overall weight of the structure. Therefore, the weight difference of a traditionally built house and a prefabricated structure will mean that foundations needed will be smaller and faster to build. Off-site manufacturing is the pinnacle of modular construction. The ability to coordinate and repeat activities in a factory along with the increased help of automation result in largely faster manufacturing times than those of on-site building. A large time saver is the ability to parallelly work on the foundation of a structure and the manufacturing of the structure itself. This would be impossible with traditional construction. The on-site construction is radically simplified. The assembly of pre-fabricated components is as simple as assembling the 3D modules, and connecting the services to main site connections. A team of five workers can assemble up to six 3D modules, or the equivalent of 270 square meters of finished floor area, in a single work day.

Production Algorithms

Since the technology required to manufacture the components of modular construction, the prefabricated parts of modular buildings are carried out by modular factories. To optimize time, modular factories consider the specifications and resources of the project and adapt a scheduling algorithm to fulfill the needs of this unique project. However, current scheduling methods assume the quantity of resources will never reach zero, therefore representing an unrealistic work cycle.

A modular factory handling a single project at any given point is rare, and would produce low returns. Hyun and Lee's research propose a Genetic Algorithm (GA) scheduling model which takes into consideration various project's characteristics and shares resources. The production sequence of this algorithm would be largely affected by which modules need to be transported to which site and the dates they should arrive. After considering the variables of production, transportation and on-site assembly the objective function is:

$$min\Sigma(S),\ldots S = S_i + P_i - E_i$$

Where S_i is the number of stocked units per day, P_i is the number of units per day and E_i is number of units installed per day. Production algorithms are continuously being developed to further accelerate the production of modular construction buildings, enlarging the time saving gap with traditional construction methods.

Cost

Modular construction can yield up to 20 percent of the total project cost in savings. However, there is also a risk of it increasing the cost by 10 percent. This occurs when the savings in the labor area of construction are outweighed by the increase in costs of the logistics area and materials. The pre-fabrication of components used in modular construction have a higher logistics cost than traditional building. Since the panels or 3D structures have to be manufactured in a factory and transported to the construction site, new variables which alter the flow of construction are presented.

Transportation

Transportation of fabricated components is naturally more expensive than that of raw materials. For one, even a number of 2D panels stacked together are much harder to transport than the raw cement, wood or material used to build them. Panels run a high risk of suffering minor or major damage when being transported through land. If a panel were to be damaged, it would likely have to be replaced entirely. The factory would need to temporarily stop production of other panels to replace this one, increasing the overall manufacturing hours and therefore cost. On top of the manufacturing hours, the transportation hours would also be increased, increasing yet another cost. Regardless, the transportation of 2D panels is still a good alternative to on-site construction.

Transportation reaches its peak cost when shipping 3D volumetric structures. While 1 m^2 of 2D floor space takes approximately US$8 to transport 250 km, its equivalent in 3D floor space takes US$45. Adding to this the replacement cost if the structure gets damaged during transport creates a large cost increase.

Construction

Assembling components in a factory off-site means that workers can use the repeatability of the structures as well as the use of automation to facilitate the manufacturing process. By standardizing the overall design of structures, work which would usually require expensive workers with specific skills (e.g. mechanical, electrical and plumbing) can be completed by low-cost manufacturers, decreasing the total salaries cost. As very little manufacturing occurs on-site, up to 80% of traditional labor activity can be moved off-site to the module factory. This leads to a lower number of sub-contractors needed, further decreasing overall total salaries cost. Overall, the larger the labor-intensive portion of a project, the larger the savings will be if modular construction is used. Project such as student accommodations, hotels and affordable housing are great candidates for modular construction. The repeatability of their structures leads to faster manufacturing times and therefore less overall cost. Meanwhile, if the project is (for example) a modern beach house with highly irregular wall spaces and ceilings, traditional construction methods may be preferable. As the industry continues to adapt and grow, these repeatable designs could one day be modified and adapted to fit all kinds of structures at decreased costs.

3.3 CIRCULAR ECONOMY IN AGRICULTURE AND FOOD SYSTEMS

3.3.1 Regenerative Agriculture and Soil Health

Regenerative Agriculture

Regenerative agriculture is a conservation and rehabilitation approach to food and farming systems. It focuses on topsoil regeneration, increasing biodiversity, improving the water cycle, enhancing ecosystem services, supporting biosequestration, increasing resilience to climate change, and strengthening the health and vitality of farm soil.

Fig: Hoverfly at Work

Regenerative agriculture is not a specific practice. It combines a variety of sustainable agriculture techniques. Practices include maximal recycling of farm waste and adding composted material from non-farm sources. Regenerative agriculture on small farms and gardens is based on permaculture, agroecology, agroforestry, restoration ecology, keyline design, and holistic management. Large farms are also increasingly adopting regenerative techniques, using "no-till" and/or "reduced till" practices. As soil health improves, input requirements may decrease, and crop yields may increase as soils are more resilient to extreme weather and harbor fewer pests and pathogens. Regenerative agriculture mitigates climate change through carbon dioxide removal from the atmosphere and sequestration. Along with reduction of carbon emissions, carbon sequestration is gaining popularity in agriculture, and individuals as well as groups are taking action to fight climate change.

History

Regenerative agriculture is based on various agricultural and ecological practices, with a particular emphasis on minimal soil disturbance and the practice of composting. Similar ideas focus on "sea minerals." His work led to innovations in no-till practices, such as slash and mulch in tropical regions. Sheet mulching is a regenerative agriculture practice that smothers weeds and adds nutrients to the soil below.

In the early 1980s, the Rodale Institute began using the term 'regenerative agriculture'. Rodale Publishing formed the Regenerative Agriculture Association, which began publishing regenerative agriculture books in 1987 and 1988.

- By marching forward under the banner of sustainability we are, in effect, continuing to hamper ourselves by not accepting a challenging enough goal. I am not against the word sustainable, rather I favor regenerative agriculture.—*Robert Rodale*

However, the institute stopped using the term in the late 1980s, and it only appeared sporadically (in 2005 and 2008), until they released a white paper in 2014, titled "Regenerative Organic Agriculture and Climate Change". The paper's summary states, "we could sequester more than 100% of current annual CO_2 emissions with a switch to common and inexpensive organic management practices, which we term 'regenerative organic agriculture.'" The paper described agricultural practices, like crop rotation, compost application, and reduced tillage, that are similar to organic agriculture methods.

In 2002, Storm Cunningham documented the beginning of what he called "restorative agriculture" in his first book, The Restoration Economy. Cunningham defined restorative agriculture as a technique that rebuilds the quantity and quality of topsoil, while also restoring local biodiversity (especially native pollinators) and watershed function. Restorative agriculture was one of the eight sectors of restorative development industries/disciplines in The Restoration Economy.

Fig: Newly Planted Soybean Plants are Emerging from the Residue Left Behind from a Prior Wheat Harvest. This Demonstrates Crop Rotation and No-Till Planting

Developments (Since 2010)

Regenerative agriculture has showed up in academic research since the early to mid 2010s in the fields of environmental science, plant science, and ecology. As the term expands in use, many books have been published on the topic and several organizations started to promote regenerative agriculture techniques. Allan Savory gave a TED talk on fighting and reversing climate change in 2013. He also launched The Savory Institute, which educates ranchers on methods of holistic land management. Abe Collins created LandStream to monitor ecosystem performance in regenerative agriculture farms. Eric Toensmeier had a book published on the subject in 2016. However, researchers at Wageningen University in the Netherlands found there to be no consistent definition of what people referencing "regenerative agriculture" meant. They also found that most of the work around this topic were instead the authors' attempt at shaping what regenerative agriculture meant.

In 2011, the (not for profit) Mulloon Institute was founded in New South Wales, Australia, to develop and promote regenerative practices to reclaim land as water-retentive areas by slowing the loss of water from land. The members of the Institute created a 22-weir in-stream project with neighbours over 2 kilometers of Mulloon Creek. A study indicates that the outcomes were positive but relatively unpredictable, and that suitability of ground conditions on site was a key for success. Bottom-up change in the context of Australian regenerative agriculture is a complex set of narratives and barriers to change affecting farmers. A West Australian government funded survey of land hydration was conducted by the Mulloon Institute in June 2022, which concluded that water retention projects supported the regeneration of native plant species.

Founded in 2013, 501(c)3 non-profit Kiss the Ground was one of the first to publicize the term to a broader audience. Today the group runs a series of media, farmland, education, and policy programs to raise awareness around soil health and support farmers who aim to transition from conventional to regenerative land management practices. The film Kiss the Ground, executive produced by Julian Lennon and Gisele Bündchen and narrated by Woody Harrelson, was released in 2020. A follow-up documentary, Common Ground, premiered in 2023 and was the recipient of the 2023 Human/Nature Award at the Tribeca Film Festival.

Not all regenerative systems emphasize ruminants. In 2017, Reginaldo Haslett Marroquin published "In the Shadow of Green Man" with Per Andreeason, which detailed Haslett Marroquin's early life as a campesino in Guatemala and how these experiences led him to develop regenerative poultry agroforestry systems that are now being practiced and expanding in the United States and elsewhere.

Several large corporations have also announced regenerative agriculture initiatives in the last few years. In 2019, General Mills announced an effort to promote regenerative agriculture practices in their supply chain. The farming practices have received criticism from academic and government experiments on sustainability in farming. In particular, Gunsmoke Farm partnered with General Mills to transition to regenerative agriculture practices and become a teaching hub for others. Experts from the area have expressed concerns about the farm now doing more harm than good, with agronomist Ruth Beck stating that "Environmental marketing got ahead of what farmers can actually do". In February 2021, the regenerative agriculture market gained traction after Joe Biden's Secretary of Agriculture Tom Vilsack made reference to it during his Senate Confirmation hearing. The Biden administration wants to utilize $30 billion from the USDA's Commodity Credit Corporations to incentivise farmers to adopt sustainable practices. Vilsack stated in the hearing, "It is a great tool for us to create the kind of structure that will inform future farm bills about what will encourage carbon sequestration, what will encourage precision agriculture, what will encourage soil health and regenerative agricultural practices." After this announcement from the Biden administration, several national and international corporations announced initiatives into regenerative agriculture. During the House of Representatives Committee on Agriculture's first hearing on climate change, Gabe Brown, a proponent of regenerative agriculture, testified about the role of regenerative agriculture in both the economics and sustainability of farming.

In 2021, PepsiCo announced that by 2030 they will work with the farmers in their supply chain to establish regenerative agriculture practices across their approximately 7 million acres. In 2021, Unilever announced an extensive implementation plan to incorporate regenerative agriculture throughout their supply chain. VF Corporation, the parent company of The North Face, Timberland, and Vans, announced in 2021 a partnership with Terra Genesis International to create a supply chain for their rubber that comes from sources utilizing regenerative agriculture. Nestle announced in 2021 a $1.8 billion investment in regenerative agriculture in an effort to reduce their emissions by 95%. Several days before the opening of the 2022 United Nations Climate Change Conference, a report was published, sponsored by some of the biggest agricultural companies. The report was produced by Sustainable Markets Initiative, an organisation of companies trying to become climate friendly, established by King Charles III. According to the report, regenerative agriculture is already implemented on 15% of all cropland. Despite this, the rate of transition is "far too slow" and must be tripled by the year 2030 to prevent the global temperature passing the threshold of 1.5 degrees above preindustrial levels. Agricultural practices must immediately change in order to avoid the damage that would result. One of the authors emphasised that "The interconnection between human health and planetary health is more evident than ever before." The authors proposed a set of measures for accelerating the transition, like creating metrics for measuring how much farming is sustainable, and paying farmers who will change their farming practices to more sustainable ones.

Principles

Several individuals, groups, and organizations have attempted to define the principles of regenerative agriculture. In their review of the existing literature on regenerative agriculture, researchers at Wageningen University. Their analysis of this database found that people using the term regenerative agriculture were using different principles to guide regenerative agriculture efforts. The 4 most consistent principles were found to be, 1) enhancing and improving soil health, 2) optimization of resource management, 3) alleviation of climate change, and 4) improvement of water quality and availability.

Notable Definitions of Principles

The organization The Carbon Underground created a set of principles that have been signed on to by a number of non-profits and corporations including Ben & Jerry's, Annie's, and the Rodale Institute, which was one of the first organization to use the term "Regenerative Agriculture". The principles they've outlined include building soil health and fertility, increase water percolation and retention, increasing biodiversity and ecosystem health, and reducing carbon emissions and current atmospheric CO_2 levels. The group Terra Genesis International, and VF Corporation's partner in their regenerative agriculture initiative, created a set of 4 principles, which include:

- "Progressively improve whole agroecosystems (soil, water and biodiversity)".
- "Create context-specific designs and make holistic decisions that express the essence of each farm".
- "Ensure and develop just and reciprocal relationships amongst all stakeholders".
- "Continually grow and evolve individuals, farms, and communities to express their innate potential".

Instead of focusing on the specifics of food production technologies, human ecologist Philip Loring suggests a food system-level focus on regeneration, arguing that it is the combination of flexibility and diversity in our food systems that supports regenerative ecological practices. Loring argues that, depending on the relative flexibility of people in the food system with respect to the foods they eat and the overall diversity of foods being produced and harvested, food systems can fall into one of four general patterns:

- Regenerative (high diversity, high flexibility), where ecosystems are able to recycle and replenish used energy to usable forms, such as found in many Indigenous food systems.
- Degenerative (High diversity, low flexibility), where people fixate on specific resources and only switch to alternatives once the preferred commodity is exhausted, such as fishing down the food web.

- Coerced (low diversity, low flexibility), where people subsidize prized resources at the expense of the surrounding ecosystem, such as in the Maine Lobster fishery.
- Impoverished (low diversity, high flexibility), where people are willing to be flexible but, because they are living in degraded ecosystems and possibly a poverty trap, cannot allow ecosystems and resources to regenerate.

Loring's typology is based on a principle he calls the Conservation of Change, which states that change must always happen somewhere in ecosystems, and derives from the Second Law of Thermodynamics and Barry Commoner's premise in that, in ecosystems, "there is no free lunch".

Carbon Sequestration: Environmental Impacts

Conventional agricultural practices such as plowing and tilling release carbon dioxide (CO_2) from the soil by exposing organic matter to the surface and thus promoting oxidation. It is estimated that roughly a third of the total anthropogenic inputs of CO_2 to the atmosphere since the industrial revolution have come from the degradation of soil organic matter and that 30–75% of global soil organic matter has been lost since the advent of tillage-based farming. Greenhouse gas (GHG) emissions associated with conventional soil and cropping activities represent 13.7% of anthropogenic emissions, or 1.86 Pg-C y^{-1}. The raising of ruminant livestock also contributes GHGs, representing 11.6% of anthropogenic emissions, or 1.58 Pg-C y^{-1}. Furthermore, runoff and siltation of water bodies associated with conventional farming practices promote eutrophication and emissions of methane.

Regenerative agriculture practices such as no-till farming, rotational grazing, mixed crop rotation, cover cropping, and the application of compost and manure have the potential to reverse this trend. No-till farming reintroduces carbon back into the soil as crop residues are pressed down when seeding. Some studies suggest that adoption of no-till practices could triple soil carbon content in less than 15 years. Additionally, 1 Pg-C y^{-1}, representing roughly a fourth to a third of anthropogenic CO_2 emissions, may be sequestered by converting croplands to no-till systems on a global scale. There is mixed evidence on the carbon sequestration potential of regenerative grazing. A meta-analysis of relevant studies between 1972 and 2016 found that Holistic Planned Grazing had no better effect than continuous grazing on plant cover and biomass, although it may have benefited some areas with higher precipitation. However, some studies have found positive impacts compared to conventional grazing. One study found that regenerative grazing management, particularly adaptive multipaddock (AMP) grazing, has been shown to reduce soil degradation compared to continuous grazing and thus has the potential to mitigate carbon emissions from soil. Another study found that crop rotation and maintenance of permanent cover crops help to reduce soil erosion as well, and in conjunction with AMP grazing, may result in net carbon sequestration.

There is a less developed evidence base comparing regenerative grazing with the absence of livestock on grasslands. Several peer-reviewed studies have found that excluding livestock completely from semi-arid grasslands can lead to significant recovery of vegetation and soil carbon sequestration. A 2021 peer-reviewed paper found that sparsely grazed and natural grasslands account for 80% of the total cumulative carbon sink of the world's grasslands, whereas managed grasslands (i.e. with greater livestock density) have been a net greenhouse gas source over the past decade. A 2011 study found that multi-paddock grazing of the type endorsed by Savory resulted in more soil carbon sequestration than heavy continuous grazing, but very slightly less soil carbon sequestration than "graze exclosure" (excluding grazing livestock from land). Another peer-reviewed paper found that if current pastureland was restored to its former state as wild grasslands, shrublands, and sparse savannas without livestock this could store an estimated 15.2 - 59.9 Gt additional carbon.

The total carbon sequestration potential of regenerative grazing has been debated between advocates and critics. One study suggests that total conversion of livestock raising to AMP grazing practices coupled with conservation cropping has the potential to convert North American farmlands to a carbon sink, sequestering approximately 1.2 Pg-C y^{-1}. Over the next 25–50 years, the cumulative sequestration potential is 30-60 Pg-C. Additions of organic manures and compost further build soil organic carbon, thus contributing to carbon sequestration potential. However, a study by the Food and Climate Research Network in 2017 estimates that, on the basis of meta-study of the scientific literature, the total global soil carbon sequestration potential from grazing management ranges from 0.3-0.8 Gt CO2eq per year, which is equivalent to offsetting a maximum of 4-11% of current total global livestock emissions, and that "Expansion or intensification in the grazing sector as an approach to sequestering more carbon would lead to substantial increases in methane, nitrous oxide and land use change-induced CO2 emissions", leading to an overall increase in emissions. Consistent with this, Project Drawdown (referenced in the film Kiss the Ground) estimates the total carbon sequestration potential of improved managed grazing at 13.72 - 20.92 Gigatons CO2eq between 2020–2050, equal to 0.46-0.70 Gt CO2eq per year. A 2022 peer-reviewed paper estimated the carbon sequestration potential of improved grazing management at a similar level of 0.15-0.70 Gt CO2eq per year. A research made by the Rodale institute suggests that a worldwide transition to regenerative agriculture can soak more than 100% of the CO_2 currently emitted by people.

Biodiversity: Environmental Impacts

Conventional agricultural practices are generally understood to simplify agroecosystems through introduction of monocultures and eradication of diversity in soil microbial communities through chemical fertilization. In natural ecosystems, biodiversity serves to regulate ecosystem function internally, but under conventional agricultural systems, such control is lost and requires increasing levels of external, anthropogenic input. By contrast, regenerative agriculture practices including polycultures, mixed crop rotation, cover cropping, organic soil management, and low- or no-tillage methods have been shown to increase overall species diversity while reducing pest population densities. Additionally, practices that favor organic over inorganic inputs aid in restoring below-ground biodiversity by enhancing the functioning of soil microbial communities. A survey of organic and conventional farms in Europe found that on the whole, species across several taxa were higher in richness and/or abundance on organic farms compared to conventional ones, especially species whose populations have been demonstrably harmed as a direct result of conventional agriculture.

AMP grazing can help improve biodiversity since increased soil organic carbon stocks also promotes a diversity of soil microbial communities. Implementation of AMP in North American prairies, for example, has been correlated with an increase in forage productivity and the restoration of plant species that had previously been decimated by continuous grazing practices. Furthermore, studies of arid and semiarid regions of the world where regenerative grazing has been practiced for a long time following prior periods of continuous grazing have shown a recovery of biodiversity, grass species, and pollinator species. Furthermore, crop diversification ensures that the agroecosystem remains productive when facing lower levels of soil fertility. Higher levels of plant diversity led to increases in numerous factors that contribute to soil fertility, such as soil N, K, Ca, Mg, and C, in CEC and in soil pH.

Soil Health

Soil health is a state of a soil meeting its range of ecosystem functions as appropriate to its environment. In more colloquial terms, the health of soil arises from favorable interactions of all soil components (living and non-living) that belong together, as in microbiota, plants and animals. It is possible that a soil can be healthy in terms of ecosystem functioning but not necessarily serve crop production or human nutrition directly, hence the scientific debate on terms and measurements.

Soil health testing is pursued as an assessment of this status but tends to be confined largely to agronomic objectives. Soil health depends on soil biodiversity (with a robust soil biota), and it can be improved via soil management, especially by care to keep protective living covers on the soil and by natural (carbon-containing) soil amendments. Inorganic fertilizers do not necessarily damage soil health if they are not used in excess, and if they bring about a general improvement of overall plant growth which contributes more carbon-containing residues to the soil.

The term soil health is used to describe the state of a soil in:

- Sustaining plant and animal productivity (agronomic focus);
- Enhancing biodiversity (Soil biodiversity) (ecological focus);
- Maintaining or enhancing water and air quality (environmental/ climate focus); and
- Supporting human health and habitation.
- sequestering carbon

The phrase "soil health" has largely replaced the older "soil quality". The primary difference between the two expressions is that soil quality was focused on individual traits within a functional group, as in "quality of soil for maize production" or "quality of soil for roadbed preparation" and so on. The addition of the word "health" shifted the perception to be integrative, holistic and systematic. The two expressions still overlap considerably. Soil health as an expression derives from organic or "biological farming" movements in Europe, however, well before soil quality was first applied as a discipline around 1990. In 1978, Swiss soil biologist Dr Otto Buess wrote an essay "The Health of Soil and Plants" which largely defines the field even today. The underlying principle in the use of the term "soil health" is that soil is not just an inert, lifeless growing medium, which modern intensive farming tends to represent, rather it is a living, dynamic and ever-so-subtly changing whole environment. It turns out that soils highly fertile from the point of view of crop productivity are also lively from a biological point of view. It is now commonly recognized that soil microbial biomass is large: in temperate grassland soil the bacterial and fungal biomass have been documented to be 1–2 t (2.0 long tons; 2.2 short tons)/hectare and 2–5 t (4.9 long tons; 5.5 short tons)/ha, respectively. Some microbiologists now believe that 80% of soil nutrient functions are essentially controlled by microbes.

Using the human health analogy, a healthy soil can be categorized as one:

- In a state of composite well-being in terms of biological, chemical and physical properties;
- Not diseased or infirmed (i.e. not degraded, nor degrading), nor causing negative off-site impacts;
- With each of its qualities cooperatively functioning such that the soil reaches its full potential and resists degradation; and
- Providing a full range of functions (especially nutrient, carbon and

water cycling) and in such a way that it maintains this capacity into the future.

Conceptualisation

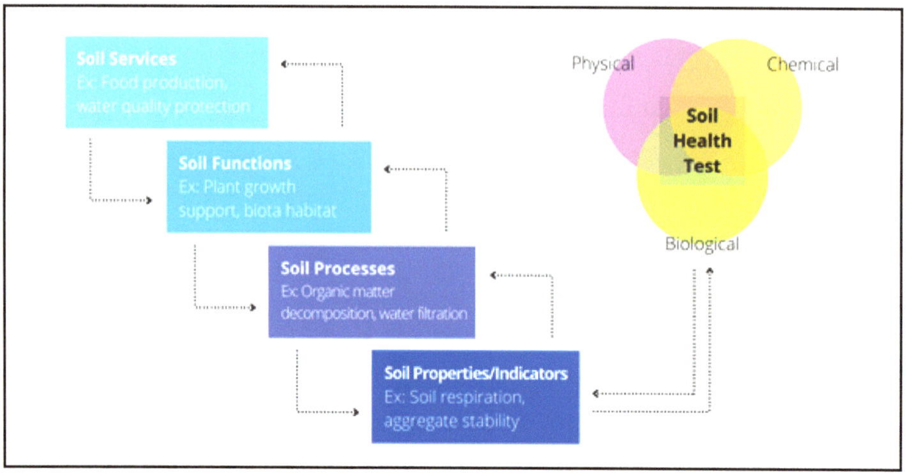

Soil health is the condition of the soil in a defined space and at a defined scale relative to a set of benchmarks that encompass healthy functioning. It would not be appropriate to refer to soil health for soil-roadbed preparation, as in the analogy of soil quality in a functional class. The definition of soil health may vary between users of the term as alternative users may place differing priorities upon the multiple functions of a soil. Therefore, the term soil health can only be understood within the context of the user of the term, and their aspirations of a soil, as well as by the boundary definition of the soil at issue. Finally, intrinsic to the discussion on soil health are many potentially conflicting interpretations, especially ecological landscape assessment vs agronomic objectives, each claiming to have soil health criteria.

Interpretation

Different soils will have different benchmarks of health depending on the "inherited" qualities, and on the geographic circumstance of the soil. The generic aspects defining a healthy soil can be considered as follows:

- "Productive" options are broad;
- Life diversity is broad;
- Absorbency, storing, recycling and processing is high in relation to limits set by climate;
- Water runoff quality is of high standard;
- Low entropy; and
- No damage to or loss of the fundamental components.

This translates to:

- A comprehensive cover of vegetation;
- Carbon levels relatively close to the limits set by soil type and climate;
- Little leakage of nutrients from the ecosystem;
- Biological and agricultural productivity relatively close to the limits set by the soil environment and climate;
- Only geological rates of erosion;
- No accumulation of contaminants; and,

Regenerative Agriculture & Soil Health

Regenerative agriculture (RA) is a holistic approach to farming that emphasizes soil conservation, biodiversity, and sustainable land management. Utilizing various soil health practices, regenerative agriculture "integrates local and indigenous knowledge of landscapes, as well as their management, with established scientific knowledge" while aiming to improve the socioeconomic well-being of a community. Central to RA is the principle that healthy soil is foundational to sustainable agriculture, essentially focusing on feeding the soil rather than feeding each plant. RA serves as an opportunity to directly apply soil health practices to produce crops sustainably. Research highlights that regenerative agriculture enhances nutrient cycling while supporting biodiversity and ecosystem services, which are vital for maintaining soil health. Practices such as cover cropping, crop rotation, no-till farming, integrated pest management, permaculture, and composting support self-sustaining soil ecosystems – further enriching soil fertility while reducing dependence on chemical fertilizers and pesticides, demonstrating that cover crops not only reduce erosion but also improve nutrient cycling. RA's primary contributions to soil health is the enhancement of organic matter and microbial activity. A myriad of practices can be used to increase soil organic content, like cover cropping, composting, and crop rotation to improve soil fertility, water retention, and ability to resist soil erosion. Research supports that soil microbial diversity is critical for maintaining fertility and resilience against the changing climate, and regenerative practices have been shown to enhance and support this biodiversity. Cover crops act as a protective blanket during the winter months, preventing compaction and erosion, while their roots maintain soil structure and nurture microbial diversity. Crop rotation further enriches soil microbiomes by diversifying nutrient and microbial inputs, disrupting pest cycles, and decreasing reliance on chemical inputs. Similarly, no-till farming minimizes physical disturbances to the soil, preserving its structure and improving water infiltration while conserving organic matter and keeping carbon in the soil, and not in the atmosphere. Permaculture is a design philosophy often incorporated into RA due to its focus on sustainable, ecosystem-based farming practices. Permaculture supports soil health by fostering natural nutrient cycles through techniques like companion planting, mulching, and perennial cropping. It emphasizes the creation of agricultural systems that model and mimic natural ecosystems, promoting biodiversity, more efficient resource use, and long-term soil health. These practices minimize soil erosion, enhance organic matter, and encourage beneficial microbial activity.

Regenerative agriculture offers significant economic and community benefits as well, nurturing resilient farming systems that enhance local economies and promote social well-being. Economically, RA reduces input costs by minimizing reliance on chemical fertilizers and pesticides, leading to lower operational expenses and increased profitability for farmers. Enhanced soil health from practices such as cover cropping and composting improves crop yields and market quality, which can provide greater productivity and financial stability. Although, the lack of heavy machinery increases the amount of necessary labor and steepens dependence on workers. Additionally, RA is designed to support community health by improving access to fresh local produce and working to alleviate food insecurity. Through RA, Community Supported Agriculture (CSA) systems can be established to bridge the divides between farmers and consumers, strengthen community ties, and facilitate a direct-market relationship. These practices not only sustain farmers but benefit surrounding communities by promoting sustainable livelihoods and resilience to environmental changes.

RA also addresses climate challenges by promoting carbon sequestration through practices like composting and no-till farming. These methods not only mitigate climate change by lowering atmospheric CO2 levels but also improve soil health, boosting soil productivity and resilience (Mishra et al. 295-309). Increasing soil organic carbon through RA practices has measurable effects on reducing atmospheric CO2 levels while improving soil functionality. The addition of organic material increases levels of soil organic carbon, thereby reducing atmospheric CO2 levels and enhancing soil fertility and productivity.

These practices collectively cultivate a resilient soil ecosystem that supports plant growth, enhances pest and disease resistance, and mitigates greenhouse gas emissions through carbon storage. However, despite its many benefits, RA faces challenges in assessment and widespread adoption. Biological indicators of soil health are often underrepresented in current evaluations due to their complexity and the context-specific knowledge required, as biological indicators of soil health often require context-specific ecological knowledge and are not universally standardized. Addressing these gaps and advancing research into RA's ecological and socioeconomic impacts will be crucial for its broader implementation and success.

Soil Health Gap

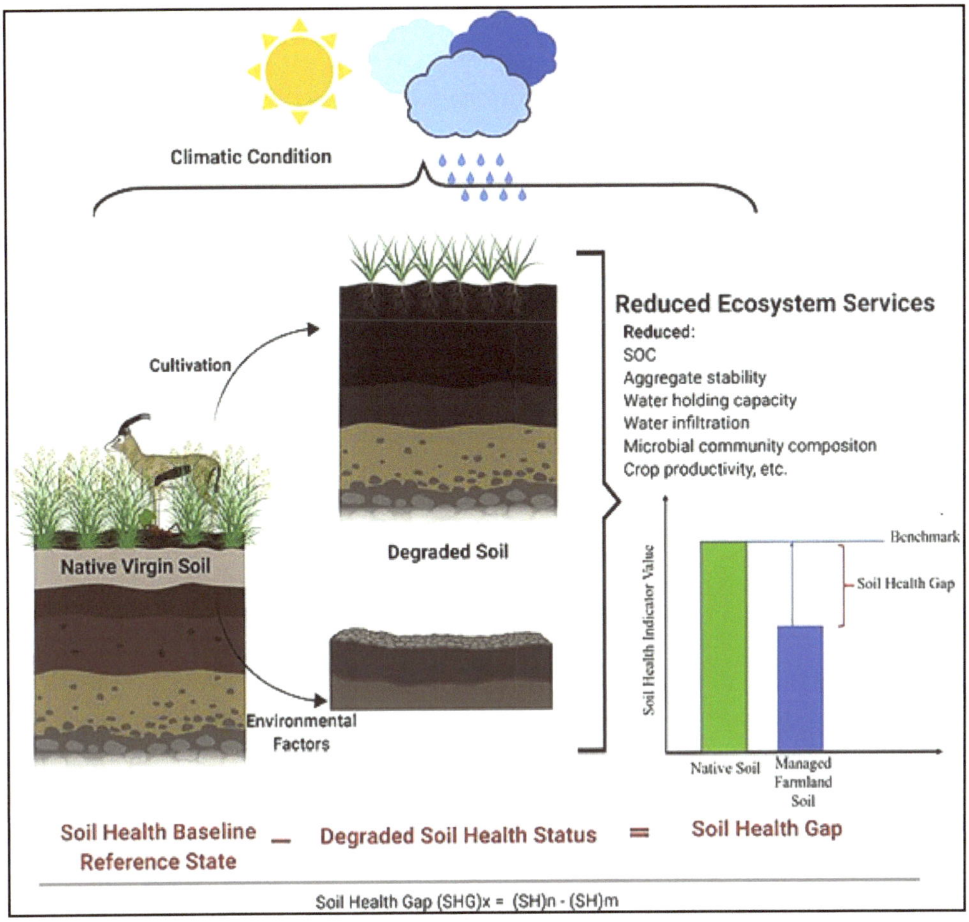

Fig. Concept of Soil Health Gap

The importance of soil for global food security, agro-ecosystem, environment, and human life has exponentially shifted the research trends toward soil health. However, the lack of a site/region-specific benchmark has limited the research toward understanding the effect of different agronomic managements on soil health. In 2020, Maharjan and his team introduced a new term and concept, "Soil Health Gap" and described how native land in a particular region can help in establishing the benchmark to compare the efficacies of different management practices and at the same time, it can be used in understanding quantitative difference in soil health status.

3.3.2 Reducing Food Waste and Loss in the Supply Chain

Food waste and loss in the supply chain represent a significant global challenge, affecting food security, economic stability, and environmental sustainability. The issue arises at various stages, from agricultural production and post-harvest handling to processing, distribution, retail, and consumer levels. Reducing food waste is critical to ensuring that resources such as water, energy, and labor are not wasted, while also mitigating greenhouse gas emissions associated with food decomposition. A holistic approach that includes technological innovations, policy interventions, and behavioral changes is necessary to address this problem effectively.

Reducing food waste and loss in the supply chain requires a multi-faceted approach involving technological advancements, policy interventions, corporate responsibility, and consumer behavior change. Addressing inefficiencies at each stage, from agricultural production to consumer consumption, can significantly lower food waste levels and promote sustainability. By improving food storage, optimizing supply chain logistics, encouraging responsible consumption, and supporting food redistribution efforts, society can work toward a more efficient and equitable food system. Collaborative efforts between governments, businesses, and individuals will be essential in achieving global food waste reduction goals and ensuring a more sustainable future for all.

3.3.3 Circular Approaches to Packaging and Food Processing

The growing concern over environmental sustainability has led to increased interest in circular approaches to packaging and food processing. Traditional packaging and food processing methods often contribute to significant waste generation, resource depletion, and pollution. The linear model of production, which follows a take-make-dispose approach, is no longer sustainable given the rising global demand for food and the increasing burden on waste management systems. A circular economy approach aims to minimize waste, maximize resource efficiency, and create closed-loop systems that promote sustainability in both packaging and food processing.

Circular approaches to packaging and food processing are essential for reducing environmental impact, conserving resources, and promoting long-term sustainability. By prioritizing reusable, recyclable, and biodegradable packaging materials, businesses can reduce waste and support a circular economy. Innovations in food processing, such as repurposing byproducts, improving energy efficiency, and implementing water conservation strategies, contribute to more sustainable food systems. Overcoming challenges related to infrastructure, consumer behavior, and regulatory support requires collective action from governments, businesses, and individuals. Embracing circularity in packaging and food processing will not only reduce waste but also create economic opportunities and enhance global food security for future generations.

The Role of Circular Economy in Packaging

Circular packaging focuses on designing materials that can be reused, recycled, or composted, thereby reducing reliance on virgin resources and minimizing environmental impact. Unlike conventional single-use packaging, circular packaging prioritizes durability, recyclability, and biodegradability. The use of renewable materials, improved recycling systems, and innovative design strategies ensures that packaging waste is reduced and repurposed into new products. A shift toward circular packaging models is essential for reducing plastic pollution, lowering carbon footprints, and conserving natural resources.

Sustainable Packaging Materials and Innovations

The development of sustainable packaging materials is a key component of circular economy strategies. Biodegradable and compostable materials, such as plant-based plastics, paper-based alternatives, and edible packaging, are gaining popularity as eco-friendly solutions. Innovations in packaging design include the use of mycelium-based materials, seaweed-based films, and bio-derived polymers that break down naturally without harming the environment. Additionally, advancements in smart packaging technology, such as sensors that monitor food freshness and reduce spoilage, contribute to waste reduction and improve supply chain efficiency.

Reusable and Refillable Packaging Systems

A crucial aspect of circular packaging is the implementation of reusable and refillable systems. Instead of single-use containers, businesses and consumers are encouraged to adopt refillable packaging models that promote waste reduction and cost savings. Companies are increasingly offering refill stations for beverages, cleaning products, and food staples, allowing customers to bring their own containers. Deposit-return schemes for bottles and containers further encourage the reuse of packaging materials. By prioritizing durable and refillable packaging options, industries can significantly reduce their environmental footprint while maintaining product integrity.

Recycling and Closed-Loop Systems

Recycling plays a vital role in circular packaging by ensuring that materials are continuously repurposed rather than discarded. Effective recycling systems involve proper material sorting, efficient collection mechanisms, and the use of high-quality recycled content in new packaging. Many companies are integrating post-consumer recycled materials into their packaging designs, reducing the demand for virgin plastic and paper. Closed-loop recycling systems, where materials are continuously processed and reintegrated into the production cycle, help achieve long-term sustainability. Governments and businesses must collaborate to improve recycling infrastructure and encourage consumer participation in recycling programs.

Challenges in Implementing Circular Packaging

Despite its benefits, circular packaging faces several challenges. The lack of standardized recycling processes and inadequate waste management infrastructure hinders the widespread adoption of circular packaging solutions. Many regions struggle with limited access to recycling facilities, resulting in packaging waste being sent to landfills or incineration. Consumer behavior and resistance to change also pose obstacles, as individuals may be hesitant to adopt reusable packaging systems. Additionally, the higher initial costs associated with sustainable packaging materials can be a barrier for businesses. Addressing these challenges requires investment in research, regulatory support, and public awareness campaigns to drive the transition toward circular packaging.

Circular Approaches to Food Processing

Food processing plays a crucial role in reducing food waste and optimizing resource use. A circular approach to food processing involves minimizing waste, repurposing byproducts, and utilizing innovative technologies to enhance efficiency. By integrating circular principles into food processing systems, manufacturers can reduce environmental impact while creating value from food waste and surplus materials. Sustainable food processing methods contribute to a more resilient food system and help address global food security challenges.

Reducing Food Waste in Processing and Manufacturing

One of the primary goals of circular food processing is minimizing food waste at the manufacturing stage. Many food processing facilities generate significant waste due to inefficient production practices, quality control rejections, and supply chain inefficiencies. Implementing waste reduction strategies, such as optimizing production planning, improving storage conditions, and repurposing food scraps, helps prevent unnecessary losses. Food manufacturers can also collaborate with food banks and charities to donate surplus products that are still safe for consumption, reducing food waste while supporting communities in need.

Utilizing Food Byproducts and Waste Streams

A key component of circular food processing is the repurposing of food byproducts and waste streams into valuable resources. Many food processing byproducts, such as fruit and vegetable peels, coffee grounds, and dairy whey, contain essential nutrients and bioactive compounds that can be used in various industries. For example, fruit peels can be converted into natural food additives, animal feed, or bio-based packaging materials. Spent grain from brewing processes can be repurposed into high-protein flour for baked goods. By finding innovative ways to use food byproducts, manufacturers can enhance sustainability and create new market opportunities.

Energy Efficiency and Renewable Energy in Food Processing

Energy consumption is a significant factor in food processing, and adopting circular approaches can improve energy efficiency. Many food manufacturers are investing in renewable energy sources, such as solar, wind, and biogas, to power their facilities and reduce dependence on fossil fuels. Additionally, the use of energy-efficient equipment, heat recovery systems, and process optimization techniques helps lower overall energy consumption. Circular food processing emphasizes the integration of renewable energy solutions to minimize the carbon footprint of food production while maintaining efficiency and cost-effectiveness.

Water Conservation and Wastewater Management

Water is a critical resource in food processing, and circular approaches prioritize water conservation and wastewater management. Many food production facilities require large amounts of water for cleaning, processing, and cooling. Implementing water recycling and filtration systems enables manufacturers to reuse water efficiently, reducing overall consumption. Additionally, advanced wastewater treatment technologies allow food processors to recover nutrients and organic matter from wastewater, which can be used as biofertilizers or biogas for energy generation. By adopting circular water management practices, food manufacturers can minimize waste and contribute to sustainable resource use.

The Role of Policy and Regulations in Circular Food Systems

Government policies and regulations play a vital role in promoting circular approaches to packaging and food processing. Many countries have introduced regulations that mandate the reduction of single-use plastics, encourage food waste reduction, and incentivize sustainable packaging alternatives. Extended producer responsibility (EPR) programs require companies to take responsibility for the end-of-life management of their packaging materials. Certification programs, such as organic and eco-labeling, also help consumers identify sustainable products. Strengthening regulatory frameworks and providing financial incentives for circular innovations will accelerate the adoption of sustainable practices across the food industry.

Consumer Engagement and Awareness

Consumer participation is essential for the success of circular approaches to packaging and food processing. Educating consumers about the benefits of sustainable packaging, waste reduction, and responsible consumption helps drive demand for circular solutions. Clear labeling, sustainable product design, and transparent supply chain practices empower consumers to make informed choices. Businesses can also encourage sustainable behaviors through take-back programs, refill stations, and incentives for reusable packaging. By fostering a culture of sustainability, consumer engagement plays a crucial role in supporting the transition to circular food systems.

3.4 CIRCULAR ECONOMY IN TEXTILES AND FASHION

3.4.1 Sustainable Materials and Eco-friendly Fabrics

The fashion and textile industries have long been associated with significant environmental impacts, including excessive water consumption, pollution, and waste generation. With growing awareness of sustainability and the need for responsible consumption, the demand for sustainable materials and eco-friendly fabrics has increased. Sustainable materials are those that are produced, used, and disposed of in ways that minimize harm to the environment, while eco-friendly fabrics focus on reducing carbon footprints, limiting resource depletion, and promoting ethical production.

Sustainable materials and eco-friendly fabrics are essential for reducing the environmental impact of the textile industry. By incorporating organic cotton, hemp, linen, Tencel, recycled fabrics, and plant-based leather alternatives, fashion brands can create clothing that aligns with sustainability principles. Additionally, ethical dyeing techniques and responsible manufacturing practices contribute to a more eco-conscious textile sector. While challenges exist, continued innovation and consumer awareness will help accelerate the shift toward sustainable fashion. By choosing eco-friendly fabrics, individuals and businesses can play a significant role in protecting the planet and promoting ethical production practices for future generations.

The Importance of Sustainable Materials in Textiles

Sustainable materials play a crucial role in reducing the ecological footprint of the textile industry. The production of conventional fabrics, such as cotton and polyester, requires large amounts of water, energy, and chemicals. Traditional textile manufacturing also contributes to microplastic pollution and toxic dye waste that contaminates waterways. Sustainable materials help address these issues by incorporating environmentally friendly practices such as organic farming, closed-loop manufacturing, and biodegradable fibers. By shifting to sustainable materials, the fashion industry can reduce waste, lower carbon emissions, and create longer-lasting products that align with the principles of the circular economy.

Organic Cotton as an Eco-friendly Alternative

Organic cotton is a widely recognized sustainable fabric that offers an environmentally friendly alternative to conventional cotton. Unlike conventional cotton, which relies heavily on synthetic pesticides and fertilizers, organic cotton is grown using natural farming methods that improve soil health and conserve biodiversity. Organic cotton cultivation also uses less water and energy, making it a more sustainable choice. Additionally, organic cotton is free from harmful chemicals, making it safer for consumers and workers alike. By supporting organic cotton production, brands and consumers contribute to a healthier environment and a more ethical textile supply chain.

Hemp: A Highly Sustainable Natural Fiber

Hemp is one of the most sustainable natural fibers available, offering durability, breathability, and minimal environmental impact. It requires significantly less water than cotton and grows rapidly without the need for chemical pesticides or herbicides. Hemp plants also improve soil health by replenishing nutrients and preventing erosion. As a textile, hemp is naturally antibacterial, resistant to UV light, and biodegradable. Due to its strong and versatile nature, hemp fabric is used in clothing, accessories, and even home textiles. Increasing the adoption of hemp fabric can significantly reduce the ecological footprint of the fashion industry.

Linen: A Durable and Low-impact Fabric

Linen, derived from the flax plant, is another sustainable fabric that has been used for centuries. Flax requires minimal water and pesticides to grow, making linen one of the most environmentally friendly fabrics. Additionally, linen fibers are biodegradable and naturally resistant to bacteria and fungi. The durability of linen ensures that garments made from this fabric last longer, reducing the frequency of replacement and waste generation. While linen has traditionally been associated with a coarse texture, modern processing techniques have improved its softness, making it a popular choice for eco-conscious fashion brands.

Tencel and Modal: Sustainable Cellulose-based Fibers

Tencel and Modal are eco-friendly fabrics made from wood pulp sourced from sustainably managed forests. These fibers are produced through closed-loop manufacturing processes, where water and solvents are recycled to minimize waste and pollution. Tencel, known for its softness and moisture-wicking properties, is commonly used in activewear and luxury apparel. Modal, derived from beech trees, is valued for its silky texture and durability. Both fabrics are biodegradable and require less water and energy to produce than conventional cotton or synthetic fabrics. By incorporating Tencel and Modal into clothing lines, brands can promote sustainable fashion while maintaining high-quality textile performance.

Recycled Fabrics: Reducing Waste and Resource Consumption

Recycled fabrics play a critical role in sustainability by repurposing post-consumer waste and reducing the demand for virgin resources. Recycled polyester, made from discarded plastic bottles, helps divert plastic waste from landfills and oceans while reducing reliance on petroleum-based fibers. Similarly, recycled cotton is produced from textile waste, reducing water and energy consumption compared to virgin cotton production. Innovations in textile recycling have also led to the development of upcycled fabrics, where discarded materials are transformed into high-quality textiles without additional chemical processing. By embracing recycled fabrics, the fashion industry can contribute to a more circular and resource-efficient economy.

Bamboo Fabric: A Renewable and Biodegradable Option

Bamboo fabric is often promoted as a sustainable alternative due to its rapid growth rate and ability to thrive without pesticides or fertilizers. Bamboo plantations also absorb large amounts of carbon dioxide, contributing to climate change mitigation.

However, the sustainability of bamboo fabric depends on the processing method. Mechanically processed bamboo, which results in bamboo linen, is the most eco-friendly option, while chemically processed bamboo, often marketed as bamboo rayon, involves intensive chemical treatments that may harm the environment. Consumers should seek certifications such as OEKO-TEX and FSC to ensure that bamboo textiles meet sustainable production standards.

Piñatex and Other Plant-based Leather Alternatives

The leather industry has significant environmental and ethical concerns due to deforestation, water pollution, and animal cruelty. In response, plant-based leather alternatives, such as Piñatex, have emerged as sustainable options. Piñatex is made from pineapple leaf fibers, a byproduct of the fruit industry, making it a zero-waste material. Other alternatives include mushroom leather, apple leather, and cork leather, all of which provide cruelty-free and biodegradable substitutes for animal leather. These plant-based materials mimic the durability and aesthetics of traditional leather while offering a more sustainable and ethical alternative for fashion and accessory production.

The Role of Ethical and Sustainable Dyeing Techniques

Dyeing processes in the textile industry contribute to significant water pollution and chemical waste. Sustainable dyeing techniques, such as plant-based dyes, waterless dyeing, and digital printing, offer eco-friendly alternatives that minimize environmental harm. Natural dyes derived from plants, fruits, and insects provide biodegradable and non-toxic colorants. Waterless dyeing technologies, such as CO_2 dyeing, eliminate the need for excessive water use, reducing wastewater pollution. Digital printing also enables precise color application, minimizing dye waste. By adopting sustainable dyeing techniques, fashion brands can further enhance the sustainability of their textile production.

3.4.2 Clothing Repair, Upcycling, and Recycling Innovations

The fashion industry has long been criticized for its environmental impact, with issues such as textile waste, excessive resource consumption, and pollution becoming increasingly concerning. Fast fashion, characterized by its rapid production cycles and disposable nature, has contributed significantly to the growing problem of clothing waste. In response, sustainable fashion initiatives are gaining momentum, with clothing repair, upcycling, and recycling innovations emerging as viable solutions to reduce textile waste and promote circular economy principles. Clothing repair, upcycling, and recycling innovations offer viable solutions to the environmental challenges posed by the fashion industry. By embracing repair culture, consumers can extend the lifespan of their garments and reduce textile waste. Upcycling transforms discarded clothing into new creations, reducing the demand for virgin resources and encouraging creative reuse. Recycling innovations are improving textile recovery processes, making it possible to regenerate fibers and create a more circular fashion system.

While challenges remain, the increasing focus on sustainability and advancements in textile technology indicate a promising future for eco-friendly fashion. By supporting sustainable practices and making conscious choices, individuals and businesses can contribute to reducing fashion waste and promoting a more responsible and environmentally friendly industry. The shift toward sustainable fashion is not just a trend but a necessary movement that will shape the future of clothing production and consumption for generations to come.

The Importance of Clothing Repair in Sustainable Fashion

Clothing repair is one of the simplest yet most effective ways to reduce waste and promote sustainability. Many garments are discarded due to minor damage, such as loose seams, missing buttons, or small tears, even though they could be easily repaired. Encouraging consumers to mend their clothes rather than dispose of them helps reduce demand for new clothing production and minimizes textile waste. Repairing clothing also preserves the resources invested in the garment's production, including water, energy, and raw materials.

Brands and organizations are now promoting repair culture through initiatives such as repair workshops, online tutorials, and in-store repair services. Some fashion retailers, including Patagonia and Nudie Jeans, offer lifetime repair services to extend the longevity of their products. Additionally, community-driven repair movements, such as Repair Cafés, provide individuals with the tools and knowledge to mend their clothes, fostering a culture of sustainability and self-sufficiency.

Upcycling: Transforming Old Garments into New Creations

Upcycling is an innovative approach to sustainable fashion that involves repurposing old, unwanted, or damaged clothing into new, stylish, and functional pieces. Unlike recycling, which breaks materials down into raw components, upcycling retains the original fabric's integrity, reducing the need for additional energy and resources. This creative process allows designers and consumers to add value to discarded textiles, resulting in unique and high-quality garments.

Upcycling has gained popularity among both independent designers and major fashion brands. Many sustainable fashion labels incorporate upcycled materials into their collections, offering consumers distinctive, eco-friendly clothing options. DIY upcycling has also become a trend, with individuals transforming old jeans into handbags, turning oversized shirts into dresses, or embellishing worn-out clothing with embroidery and patches. The rise of upcycling not only reduces textile waste but also challenges the disposable mindset associated with fast fashion, promoting a more conscious and mindful approach to clothing consumption.

Recycling Innovations in the Fashion Industry

Textile recycling innovations play a crucial role in diverting clothing waste from landfills and reintroducing materials into the production cycle. Traditional textile recycling methods often result in downcycling, where fabrics are converted into lower-value products, such as industrial rags or insulation materials. However, recent advancements in textile recycling technology are enabling more efficient and high-quality recycling processes that allow fibers to be regenerated into new garments.

One of the most significant innovations in textile recycling is chemical recycling, which breaks down synthetic and natural fibers into their original molecular components, enabling the creation of new fabrics without degrading quality. Companies like Worn Again and Renewcell have developed chemical recycling methods that recover cotton and polyester from blended fabrics, addressing one of the major challenges in textile recycling. Mechanical recycling, which involves shredding textiles into fibers for reuse, is also improving, with new techniques enhancing fiber strength and durability.

The Role of Circular Economy in Clothing Repair, Upcycling, and Recycling

A circular economy in fashion focuses on keeping materials in use for as long as possible through repair, reuse, and recycling. Clothing repair, upcycling, and textile recycling are all essential components of this model, helping reduce reliance on virgin resources and minimize waste. Brands that embrace circular design principles create garments with longevity in mind, using durable materials, modular designs, and repairable components. Some companies are adopting take-back programs, where customers can return old clothing for refurbishment, upcycling, or recycling. These initiatives ensure that garments reach their full potential before being discarded. The circular fashion model also encourages collaboration between brands, consumers, and recycling facilities to create a closed-loop system that maximizes resource efficiency and reduces environmental impact.

Consumer Engagement and Education in Sustainable Fashion Practices

Consumer awareness and participation are crucial for the success of clothing repair, upcycling, and recycling initiatives. Many individuals discard clothing out of habit or lack of knowledge about alternative solutions. Educating consumers on the benefits of repairing and repurposing their clothes can foster a shift toward more sustainable fashion habits.

Retailers and fashion brands can play a key role in promoting sustainability by offering repair kits, hosting upcycling workshops, and providing clear recycling instructions. Social media and online platforms have also become powerful tools for spreading awareness, with influencers and sustainability advocates sharing DIY repair and upcycling tutorials. As consumers become more informed, they are more likely to support brands that prioritize sustainability and invest in long-lasting, high-quality clothing.

3.4.3 Circular Fashion Business Models and Consumer Behavior

The global fashion industry is one of the largest contributors to environmental degradation, generating significant waste, pollution, and resource depletion. The rise of fast fashion has exacerbated these issues, promoting a culture of overconsumption and disposable clothing. In response, circular fashion business models have emerged as a sustainable alternative, aiming to close the loop in textile production and consumption. These models focus on extending product lifecycles, reducing waste, and promoting ethical production. Consumer behavior plays a crucial role in determining the success of circular fashion, as shifting mindsets and purchasing habits can drive industry-wide transformation.

Circular fashion business models and consumer behavior are deeply interconnected in shaping the future of the fashion industry. By embracing resale, rental, upcycling, and recycling innovations, brands can reduce waste and create a more sustainable system. Consumer engagement and awareness are key to driving this transition, as purchasing decisions influence industry practices. While challenges exist, ongoing innovation, education, and policy support will pave the way for a more sustainable and circular fashion economy. The shift toward circular fashion is not only necessary for environmental and social sustainability but also presents new opportunities for creativity, economic growth, and responsible consumption.

The Concept of Circular Fashion

Circular fashion is based on the principles of the circular economy, which prioritizes resource efficiency, waste minimization, and product longevity. Unlike the traditional linear model of "take, make, dispose," circular fashion seeks to keep garments in use for as long as possible through repair, reuse, recycling, and responsible disposal. This approach reduces the environmental impact of clothing production while promoting ethical labor practices and responsible consumption.

The circular fashion model relies on several key strategies, including sustainable sourcing, innovative design, product-as-a-service models, resale and rental platforms, and advanced textile recycling technologies. By adopting circular principles, fashion brands can create value while minimizing their environmental footprint, ultimately fostering a more sustainable industry.

Key Circular Fashion Business Models

Several business models have emerged to support the transition toward circular fashion. One of the most prominent is the resale model, where pre-owned clothing is bought, sold, and exchanged through online and physical marketplaces. Platforms like ThredUp, Vestiaire Collective, and The RealReal have popularized secondhand fashion, making it more accessible and appealing to a broader audience. Luxury brands are also embracing resale, recognizing the value of extending the lifecycle of high-quality garments. Another growing model is clothing rental, where consumers can borrow garments for a specific period rather than purchasing them outright. Rental platforms like Rent the Runway and HURR offer high-end fashion options for special occasions or everyday wear, reducing the need for short-term clothing purchases. This model helps reduce waste while providing consumers with variety and access to premium fashion at a lower cost.

Subscription-based fashion services are also gaining traction in the circular economy. Brands such as Nuuly and Le Tote offer clothing subscription plans that allow customers to rotate their wardrobes without accumulating excessive items. These services encourage mindful consumption and reduce the demand for fast fashion. Upcycling and redesign businesses are another vital aspect of circular fashion. Companies that specialize in upcycling transform discarded textiles and garments into new, fashionable pieces. Brands like Eileen Fisher's Renew program and Patagonia's Worn Wear initiative focus on repairing and repurposing clothing, giving old garments new life. These initiatives not only reduce textile waste but also highlight the potential of creative reuse in the industry.

The Role of Consumer Behavior in Circular Fashion

Consumer behavior is a critical factor in the success of circular fashion business models. While many consumers express interest in sustainability, their purchasing decisions are often influenced by factors such as price, convenience, and social norms. Overcoming these barriers requires education, awareness, and incentives that make circular fashion more appealing and accessible.

One significant challenge is shifting consumer perception away from the idea that fashion is disposable. Fast fashion has conditioned many people to view clothing as a short-term purchase, leading to excessive consumption and waste. Encouraging a mindset of quality over quantity can help consumers make more sustainable choices. Brands can promote this shift by emphasizing durability, timeless designs, and the long-term value of their products.

Affordability is another factor influencing consumer adoption of circular fashion. While sustainable and circular fashion brands often have higher price points due to ethical production practices, resale and rental models offer more affordable alternatives. Educating consumers about the true cost of fast fashion, including its environmental and social impact, can encourage them to invest in more sustainable options.

Convenience also plays a role in shaping consumer behavior. Many consumers opt for fast fashion due to its accessibility and ease of purchase. To compete, circular fashion brands must provide seamless online and offline shopping experiences, convenient return policies, and user-friendly platforms for resale and rental services. Technology-driven solutions, such as AI-powered resale platforms and blockchain-based supply chain transparency, can enhance consumer trust and engagement.

Consumer Engagement Strategies for Circular Fashion

Engaging consumers in circular fashion requires innovative strategies that align with their values and lifestyle. Transparency and storytelling are powerful tools that can educate consumers about sustainability and inspire them to participate in circular initiatives. Brands that openly share information about their supply chains, materials, and impact can build trust and foster a loyal customer base.

Incentivizing sustainable behavior is another effective approach. Brands can offer discounts or rewards for customers who return old garments for recycling or participate in clothing swap programs. Loyalty programs that encourage responsible consumption can help drive long-term engagement with circular fashion. Social influence and community engagement also play a significant role in shaping consumer behavior. Collaborating with influencers, sustainability advocates, and fashion bloggers can help spread awareness and normalize circular fashion practices. Hosting events, workshops, and online challenges related to upcycling, repair, and sustainable styling can further encourage consumers to embrace circular fashion.

3.5 CIRCULAR ECONOMY IN ELECTRONICS AND TECHNOLOGY

3.5.1 Designing for Longevity and Repairability

In an era of rapid consumption and disposable products, designing for longevity and repairability has emerged as a critical approach to reducing waste, conserving resources, and promoting sustainability. The concept of longevity in design emphasizes creating products that endure over time, both in terms of durability and relevance. Repairability, on the other hand, ensures that products can be easily maintained, fixed, and restored instead of being discarded. These principles align with the broader goals of a circular economy, where products are kept in use for as long as possible through repair, refurbishment, and reuse. Designing for longevity and repairability is a fundamental aspect of sustainable product development. By prioritizing durable materials, modular design, and accessibility in repair processes, manufacturers can create products that withstand the test of time. While challenges such as planned obsolescence and consumer behavior persist, policy interventions, technological advancements, and increased consumer awareness can drive the transition toward a circular economy. In a world where environmental sustainability is becoming increasingly urgent, embracing longevity and repairability is not just an ethical responsibility but also a necessary step toward a more resilient and resource-efficient future.

The Importance of Longevity in Product Design

Longevity in design refers to the ability of a product to maintain its function, aesthetic appeal, and structural integrity over an extended period. Products designed for longevity resist wear and tear, reducing the frequency of replacement and ultimately decreasing waste. A well-designed, long-lasting product saves consumers money, enhances brand reputation, and minimizes the environmental footprint associated with frequent disposal and manufacturing. Several factors contribute to product longevity, including material selection, structural integrity, and timeless aesthetics. High-quality materials that resist degradation contribute to longer lifespans, reducing the need for frequent replacements. Additionally, designing products with modular components allows for easy upgrades, ensuring continued functionality without complete replacement. Aesthetic longevity is equally important, as products designed with timeless appeal resist short-lived trends and remain desirable for years.

The Role of Repairability in Sustainable Design

Repairability is essential in reducing product obsolescence and extending the lifespan of consumer goods. A product designed for repairability allows users to replace faulty components, perform maintenance, and restore functionality without requiring professional intervention or excessive costs. Unfortunately, many modern products are deliberately designed with planned obsolescence, where components are glued together, sealed, or proprietary, making repair difficult or impossible.

A repairable product incorporates several key features, such as replaceable parts, accessible fasteners, standardized components, and comprehensive repair guides. These elements enable consumers to fix minor issues independently, reducing reliance on manufacturers and expensive repair services. The Right to Repair movement has gained momentum worldwide, advocating for legislation that compels manufacturers to provide access to spare parts, repair manuals, and diagnostic tools, thus empowering consumers to maintain their products.

The Role of Policy and Regulation in Promoting Longevity and Repairability

Government policies and regulations play a crucial role in incentivizing manufacturers to design products with longevity and repairability in mind. Several regions have introduced laws to combat planned obsolescence and ensure that consumers have the right to repair their products. The European Union, for example, has implemented eco-design directives that require household appliances to be repairable, with manufacturers mandated to provide spare parts for a minimum number of years.

Similarly, the Right to Repair movement has gained traction in countries like the United States, Canada, and Australia, pushing for legislation that grants consumers and independent repair shops access to essential repair tools and information. These regulations not only extend product lifespans but also promote a circular economy by keeping products in use for as long as possible.

Additionally, policymakers can support sustainable design through tax incentives and subsidies for companies that prioritize durability and repairability. Extended producer responsibility (EPR) programs, which hold manufacturers accountable for the end-of-life management of their products, can also encourage businesses to design for longevity rather than disposability.

3.5.2 E-Waste Management and Resource Recovery

Electronic waste, commonly known as e-waste, is one of the fastest-growing waste streams in the world. The rapid advancement of technology, combined with the increasing demand for electronic devices, has led to a significant rise in discarded electronic products. E-waste consists of a wide range of items, including smartphones, computers, televisions, batteries, and other electronic appliances. Improper disposal of e-waste poses serious environmental and health hazards due to the presence of hazardous substances such as lead, mercury, and cadmium. However, e-waste also contains valuable materials such as gold, silver, copper, and rare earth metals that can be recovered and reused. Effective e-waste management and resource recovery strategies are essential to minimize environmental impact, reduce landfill waste, and create a more sustainable and circular economy.

E-waste management and resource recovery are critical for reducing environmental harm, conserving valuable materials, and promoting a sustainable future. By implementing effective collection and recycling systems, enforcing regulatory measures, and encouraging responsible consumption, societies can minimize the negative impacts of electronic waste. Manufacturers must take responsibility for designing products that prioritize longevity and recyclability, while consumers must adopt mindful purchasing and disposal habits. With continued advancements in recycling technologies and global cooperation, the challenges of e-waste can be transformed into opportunities for resource efficiency and circular economic growth.

The Growing Problem of E-Waste

The proliferation of electronic devices and their short lifespans contribute to the ever-increasing volume of e-waste. Many electronic products become obsolete within a few years due to rapid technological advancements and consumer preferences for newer models. As a result, vast amounts of discarded electronics end up in landfills or incineration plants, leading to the release of toxic chemicals into the environment. The improper handling of e-waste can contaminate soil and water sources, posing serious risks to human health and ecosystems. Furthermore, the lack of formal recycling systems in many developing countries results in informal e-waste processing, where workers, often under hazardous conditions, extract valuable metals using crude and unsafe methods.

3.5.3 Innovations in Recycling Electronic Components

With the rapid advancement of technology, electronic waste, or e-waste, has become a growing global concern. Millions of electronic devices reach the end of their lifespan each year, resulting in vast amounts of discarded materials. Traditional recycling methods have proven to be inefficient, often leading to environmental hazards and the loss of valuable resources. However, recent innovations in recycling electronic components offer promising solutions to mitigate these challenges. Advanced techniques and new technologies are revolutionizing the way e-waste is processed, making it possible to recover precious metals, rare earth elements, and other valuable materials while minimizing environmental impact. These innovations are crucial in developing a sustainable and circular economy for electronics.

Innovations in recycling electronic components are transforming the way e-waste is managed, making it possible to recover valuable materials efficiently while reducing environmental impact. Advanced sorting technologies, bioleaching, hydrometallurgical and pyrometallurgical processes, and laser-assisted recycling are just a few of the cutting-edge methods that are revolutionizing e-waste recycling. Urban mining, 3D printing with recycled electronics, and eco-friendly PCB designs further contribute to a circular approach to electronic waste management. The integration of artificial intelligence in recycling operations is enhancing efficiency and sustainability. However, for these innovations to be truly effective, consumer awareness and participation must also be prioritized. By embracing these advancements and promoting responsible e-waste disposal, societies can move toward a more sustainable future where electronic waste is no longer a burden but a valuable resource for the circular economy.

Challenges in Recycling Electronic Components

Recycling electronic components is a complex process due to the intricate design of modern electronic devices. Unlike single-material products, electronic waste consists of multiple components made from various materials, including metals, plastics, glass, and hazardous substances. Separating these materials efficiently is a significant challenge. Traditional methods, such as mechanical shredding and incineration, often result in material loss and environmental pollution. Additionally, many electronic devices are designed with non-removable batteries and tightly integrated components, making disassembly difficult. Another challenge is the presence of hazardous substances like lead, mercury, and cadmium, which require specialized handling and processing techniques to prevent environmental contamination.

Advanced Sorting Technologies

One of the key innovations in electronic waste recycling is the development of advanced sorting technologies. Traditional manual sorting is time-consuming and labor-intensive, but new automated systems have improved efficiency and accuracy. Artificial intelligence (AI) and machine learning are now being used to identify and separate different electronic components. High-speed optical sorting systems use cameras and sensors to distinguish between materials based on their composition and structure. Robotic sorting, powered by AI algorithms, can quickly dismantle devices and extract valuable parts with precision. These technologies enable higher recovery rates and reduce the amount of waste sent to landfills.

Bioleaching: A Sustainable Approach

Bioleaching is an innovative and environmentally friendly method for extracting precious metals from electronic waste. This process uses microorganisms, such as bacteria and fungi, to break down metal compounds and release valuable metals like gold, silver, and copper. Unlike traditional chemical leaching, which involves toxic substances like cyanide and strong acids, bioleaching is a sustainable alternative that reduces environmental impact. Research has shown that certain bacteria, such as Acidithiobacillus ferrooxidans, can effectively extract metals from circuit boards and other electronic components. The adoption of bioleaching in e-waste recycling has the potential to revolutionize metal recovery while minimizing pollution and energy consumption.

Hydrometallurgical and Pyrometallurgical Processes

Hydrometallurgy and pyrometallurgy are two advanced techniques used to extract valuable metals from electronic waste. Hydrometallurgical processes involve the use of chemical solutions to dissolve metals from e-waste, allowing them to be recovered through precipitation or electrochemical methods. This technique is particularly useful for extracting precious metals such as gold and platinum. Pyrometallurgical processes, on the other hand, involve high-temperature smelting to separate metals from other materials. This method is effective for recovering base metals like copper and aluminum. Recent advancements in these processes have improved their efficiency and reduced their environmental footprint, making them viable options for large-scale e-waste recycling.

Laser-Assisted Recycling

Laser technology is being explored as a cutting-edge solution for recycling electronic components. Laser-assisted recycling involves using precise laser beams to selectively remove coatings, adhesives, and unwanted materials from electronic devices. This technique allows for the efficient separation of valuable components without damaging them, making it easier to recover reusable parts. Laser technology is also being used to desolder electronic components from circuit boards, enabling their reuse in new products. This innovation reduces the need for energy-intensive mechanical processes and enhances the circularity of electronic components.

Urban Mining: Extracting Value from E-Waste

Urban mining is an emerging concept that focuses on recovering valuable materials from discarded electronic devices rather than relying on traditional mining operations. This approach recognizes e-waste as a rich source of metals and rare earth elements that can be reintroduced into the manufacturing cycle.

By implementing advanced recycling techniques, urban mining reduces the demand for virgin raw materials, which often involve destructive mining practices and environmental degradation. Many companies and research institutions are investing in urban mining technologies to develop efficient methods for extracting metals from e-waste while minimizing waste and pollution.

3D Printing with Recycled Electronics

Additive manufacturing, commonly known as 3D printing, is being integrated into e-waste recycling efforts. Researchers are exploring ways to use recycled electronic components as raw materials for 3D printing applications. Plastics recovered from discarded electronic devices can be processed into filaments for 3D printers, reducing the need for virgin plastic production. Additionally, conductive materials extracted from e-waste are being used to print electronic circuits and components, creating new opportunities for sustainable manufacturing. This innovation promotes resource efficiency and aligns with the principles of the circular economy.

Eco-Friendly Printed Circuit Boards

Printed circuit boards (PCBs) are among the most challenging components to recycle due to their complex composition. However, new developments in eco-friendly PCB manufacturing are making recycling easier. Researchers are designing biodegradable PCBs made from natural fibers and non-toxic resins, which can break down safely at the end of their lifespan. Additionally, modular PCBs are being developed to allow for easy component replacement and disassembly, reducing electronic waste. These innovations support sustainable product design and facilitate more efficient recycling processes.

The Role of Artificial Intelligence in E-Waste Recycling

Artificial intelligence (AI) is playing a crucial role in enhancing e-waste recycling operations. AI-powered systems can analyze large datasets to optimize material recovery processes and predict the most efficient recycling methods. Machine learning algorithms can improve the sorting and classification of electronic components, increasing the accuracy of automated recycling systems. AI is also being used in predictive maintenance for recycling machinery, reducing downtime and improving overall efficiency. The integration of AI in e-waste recycling has the potential to revolutionize the industry by making recycling processes smarter and more sustainable.

Consumer Awareness and the Future of E-Waste Recycling

Innovations in e-waste recycling are not solely dependent on technological advancements; consumer awareness and participation play a vital role in creating a sustainable system. Many consumers remain unaware of proper e-waste disposal methods, leading to improper disposal and loss of valuable materials. Governments, organizations, and manufacturers must invest in awareness campaigns and convenient collection programs to encourage responsible recycling. Incentivizing consumers through take-back programs, trade-in initiatives, and deposit-refund systems can significantly improve e-waste recycling rates. As technology continues to evolve, fostering a culture of sustainability and responsible consumption will be essential in addressing the global e-waste challenge.

CHAPTER 4

Circular Economy Business Models and Strategies

4.1 PRODUCT DESIGN FOR CIRCULARITY

4.1.1 Eco-Design and Sustainable Product Development

Eco-design and sustainable product development are integral to addressing the growing environmental challenges posed by modern industrial production and consumerism. As global awareness of environmental issues increases, companies are under pressure to create products that minimize environmental impact while maintaining functionality and market competitiveness. Eco-design integrates sustainability into every stage of a product's lifecycle, from material selection to end-of-life disposal, ensuring that environmental considerations are at the core of the design and manufacturing processes. Sustainable product development extends beyond eco-design by incorporating broader social and economic factors, promoting responsible production and consumption patterns. Together, these approaches help transition industries toward a circular economy and reduce the ecological footprint of human activities.

Eco-design and sustainable product development are critical to mitigating the environmental impact of industrial production and consumption. By incorporating sustainability principles into product design, companies can reduce waste, improve resource efficiency, and promote a circular economy. The adoption of sustainable materials, energy-efficient manufacturing, and closed-loop systems further enhances the environmental benefits of eco-design. Consumer awareness and participation also play a vital role in driving demand for sustainable products. While challenges exist, ongoing innovations and policy support are fostering a more sustainable approach to product development. By embracing eco-design and sustainability, industries can contribute to a healthier planet and a more responsible global economy.

Principles of Eco-Design

Eco-design is guided by several key principles that ensure a product's sustainability throughout its lifecycle. One of the fundamental aspects of eco-design is resource efficiency, which involves minimizing the use of raw materials and energy in production processes. This principle encourages the selection of renewable, recyclable, and biodegradable materials to reduce environmental degradation. Another critical principle is waste reduction, which focuses on designing products that generate minimal waste during manufacturing and usage. Durability and longevity are also central to eco-design, as they encourage the creation of products that last longer and require fewer replacements, ultimately reducing resource consumption. Additionally, eco-design prioritizes the ease of disassembly and recycling, allowing products to be efficiently broken down into their components for reuse or safe disposal.

Sustainable Material Selection

Choosing sustainable materials is a crucial aspect of eco-design and sustainable product development. The environmental impact of a product is significantly influenced by the materials used in its production. Sustainable materials include biodegradable substances such as natural fibers, plant-based plastics, and compostable packaging, which reduce pollution and landfill waste. Recycled materials, such as reclaimed metals, plastics, and glass, are also widely used to lower the demand for virgin resources and decrease energy consumption in manufacturing. Another innovative approach is the use of bio-based materials, which are derived from renewable resources such as algae, fungi, and agricultural waste. These materials offer a sustainable alternative to traditional synthetic materials while maintaining high-performance characteristics. Additionally, ethical sourcing of materials is vital to ensuring sustainability, as it promotes responsible supply chain practices that minimize environmental and social harm.

Energy Efficiency in Product Development

Energy efficiency is a crucial component of sustainable product development, as energy consumption during manufacturing and product use significantly impacts the environment. Designing energy-efficient products reduces carbon emissions and decreases reliance on fossil fuels. One way to achieve this is by optimizing manufacturing processes to minimize energy waste through advanced production techniques such as 3D printing and automation. Another approach is integrating energy-saving features into products, such as energy-efficient appliances, LED lighting, and low-power electronics. Renewable energy sources, such as solar and wind power, are also being incorporated into product design to promote sustainability. Furthermore, companies are increasingly adopting life cycle assessment (LCA) methodologies to analyze the energy footprint of their products and implement strategies for reducing energy consumption throughout their lifecycle.

Design for Longevity and Reparability

One of the main objectives of eco-design is to create products that are durable, repairable, and upgradeable, reducing the need for frequent replacements and minimizing waste generation. Designing for longevity involves using high-quality materials and robust construction techniques to ensure that products can withstand long-term use. Additionally, modular design approaches enable consumers to replace or upgrade individual components rather than discarding entire products. Reparability is another essential factor in sustainable product development, as it allows users to extend the lifespan of their items by fixing broken parts. Companies are now designing products with easily replaceable components and providing repair manuals and spare parts to encourage maintenance. This shift towards repairability also fosters a repair culture, reducing the dependence on disposable products and lowering overall environmental impact.

Eco-Packaging Solutions

Packaging is a significant contributor to environmental pollution, particularly in industries that rely heavily on plastic materials. Eco-design emphasizes the development of sustainable packaging solutions that minimize waste and resource use. Biodegradable and compostable packaging materials, such as cornstarch-based plastics and mushroom packaging, are becoming popular alternatives to conventional plastic packaging. Minimalist packaging, which reduces unnecessary layers and materials, is another effective strategy for reducing waste. Additionally, reusable and refillable packaging systems are being adopted by companies to decrease single-use packaging consumption. Advances in sustainable packaging technologies, such as water-soluble films and edible packaging, are also driving innovation in the sector. These solutions help reduce plastic pollution while promoting a more sustainable approach to product packaging.

Closed-Loop Manufacturing Systems

Closed-loop manufacturing is a key aspect of sustainable product development that focuses on creating products that can be continuously recycled and repurposed. In a closed-loop system, materials from used products are recovered and reintegrated into new production cycles, minimizing waste and reducing reliance on virgin resources. This approach aligns with the principles of the circular economy, where products are designed to maintain their value and functionality for as long as possible. Many industries are adopting closed-loop manufacturing by implementing take-back programs, where consumers return old products for recycling and refurbishment. This system is particularly effective in the electronics, automotive, and fashion industries, where valuable materials can be reclaimed and reused in new products. By embracing closed-loop manufacturing, companies can significantly reduce their environmental footprint while enhancing resource efficiency.

Sustainable Product Innovation

Innovative approaches to sustainable product development are driving the transition towards greener industries. Companies are exploring alternative production methods, such as biomimicry, which involves designing products based on nature's efficient and sustainable processes. Another emerging trend is the development of multi-functional products that serve multiple purposes, reducing the need for additional resources and materials. Digital technologies, such as artificial intelligence and blockchain, are also playing a role in sustainable product innovation by enabling more efficient supply chain management and transparency in sourcing practices. Additionally, advancements in nanotechnology and material science are leading to the creation of new sustainable materials with improved properties. These innovations are pushing the boundaries of eco-design and demonstrating that sustainability and technological progress can go hand in hand.

Consumer Awareness and Sustainable Consumption

Sustainable product development is not solely dependent on manufacturers; consumer behavior plays a vital role in driving demand for eco-friendly products. Educating consumers about the environmental impact of their purchasing decisions is essential for promoting sustainable consumption patterns. Companies are increasingly providing transparency about the sustainability of their products through eco-labeling and certifications, helping consumers make informed choices. Initiatives such as the right-to-repair movement and zero-waste lifestyles are also encouraging consumers to adopt more responsible consumption habits. Additionally, businesses are leveraging digital platforms to engage consumers in sustainability efforts, offering incentives for recycling and responsible product use. By fostering a culture of conscious consumption, society can collectively contribute to a more sustainable future.

4.1.2 Modular Design for Easy Repair and Upgrading

Modular design is a crucial strategy for enhancing product sustainability, reducing waste, and promoting a circular economy. It involves creating products with interchangeable, self-contained components that can be easily repaired, upgraded, or replaced without discarding the entire product. This approach contrasts with conventional product designs that often lead to premature obsolescence and increased electronic and material waste. By enabling efficient repair and seamless upgrades, modular design extends product lifespans, conserves resources, and reduces environmental impact. It also empowers consumers and businesses to adopt more sustainable practices by making maintenance more accessible and cost-effective. Modular design is a transformative approach that enhances repairability, sustainability, and resource efficiency across various industries. By prioritizing standardized, interchangeable components, modular products enable easy repairs, upgrades, and replacements, significantly reducing waste and promoting longevity. Industries such as electronics, furniture, automotive, and interior design are already embracing modular principles to create more sustainable solutions. However, challenges such as resistance from traditional manufacturing models and standardization issues must be addressed to ensure widespread adoption. Government policies and consumer advocacy are playing a vital role in advancing modular design, reinforcing the importance of repairability and environmental responsibility. As technology continues to evolve, modular design will remain a key driver of sustainable innovation, shaping a future where products are built to last, adapt, and contribute to a more circular economy.

The Principles of Modular Design

Modular design is founded on several key principles that prioritize adaptability, repairability, and sustainability. One of the fundamental principles is standardization, which ensures that different modules within a product are compatible and interchangeable. This simplifies repairs and upgrades by allowing users to swap out faulty or outdated components without requiring specialized tools or technical expertise. Another essential principle is accessibility, which emphasizes designing products with easily removable and replaceable parts. This reduces dependency on professional repair services and empowers users to conduct basic maintenance independently. Durability is also central to modular design, as it promotes the use of high-quality materials and components that can withstand repeated modifications without degradation. Additionally, modular products are designed with minimal use of adhesives and permanent fixtures, making it easier to disassemble and reassemble them when needed.

Benefits of Modular Design for Repairability

One of the most significant advantages of modular design is its contribution to easy repairability. Traditional product designs often integrate multiple functions into a single, non-replaceable unit, making repairs costly and impractical. Modular products, however, allow consumers to replace only the damaged components instead of discarding the entire product. This approach significantly reduces electronic and material waste, particularly in industries such as consumer electronics, where repairable design is often overlooked. Another benefit is cost-effectiveness, as modular products eliminate the need for frequent replacements, ultimately saving consumers money. Modular designs also support a thriving repair economy, enabling independent repair shops and do-it-yourself (DIY) enthusiasts to fix products more efficiently. By making repairs accessible, modular design extends product lifespans and helps reduce landfill waste, aligning with sustainability goals.

Modular Design in Electronics

The electronics industry is one of the biggest beneficiaries of modular design, as it addresses the growing problem of e-waste. Many modern electronic devices, such as smartphones and laptops, are designed with built-in obsolescence, where batteries, screens, and processors are difficult to replace. Modular design counteracts this issue by allowing consumers to swap out individual components, such as batteries, memory modules, and display panels, instead of purchasing entirely new devices. Notable examples include modular smartphones, where users can upgrade specific features like cameras or processors without replacing the entire device. Additionally, modular laptops are becoming more common, offering easily replaceable keyboards, storage drives, and motherboards. This shift not only benefits consumers but also reduces the environmental burden associated with electronic waste disposal and resource extraction.

4.2 CIRCULAR SUPPLY CHAINS

4.2.1 Sustainable Sourcing and Material Efficiency

Sustainable sourcing and material efficiency are critical components of modern sustainability strategies aimed at reducing environmental impact and ensuring the responsible use of natural resources. As industries grow and consumption increases, the demand for raw materials continues to put pressure on ecosystems, leading to resource depletion, environmental degradation, and increased waste. Sustainable sourcing involves procuring materials in a way that minimizes ecological harm, supports ethical labor practices, and promotes long-term resource availability. Material efficiency, on the other hand, focuses on optimizing the use of raw materials, reducing waste, and enhancing product longevity. Together, these approaches contribute to a circular economy by maximizing resource value and minimizing waste generation. Companies and policymakers worldwide are increasingly recognizing the importance of integrating sustainable sourcing and material efficiency into their production and supply chains.

Sustainable sourcing and material efficiency are essential strategies for reducing environmental impact, conserving natural resources, and promoting ethical business practices. By prioritizing responsible procurement and optimizing material usage, industries can create long-lasting products while minimizing waste and pollution. Despite challenges such as high costs, supply chain complexities, and greenwashing, sustainable sourcing offers significant benefits, including environmental conservation, ethical labor practices, and economic resilience. Innovations in material science, digital technologies, and circular economy principles are driving the transition toward more sustainable and resource-efficient production systems. Consumers, policymakers, and businesses all have a role to play in supporting sustainable sourcing and material efficiency, ensuring a future where economic growth aligns with environmental responsibility and social equity.

Principles of Sustainable Sourcing

Sustainable sourcing is based on several fundamental principles that guide businesses in making responsible procurement decisions. One of the core principles is ethical and fair trade practices, ensuring that raw materials are obtained without exploiting labor or violating human rights. Transparency in the supply chain is another critical aspect, as it enables businesses to trace the origin of their materials and ensure compliance with sustainability standards. Environmental responsibility is also central to sustainable sourcing, as companies must prioritize materials that are harvested or extracted using methods that minimize ecological damage, such as deforestation, habitat destruction, and excessive water consumption. Additionally, sustainable sourcing emphasizes the use of renewable and recyclable materials to reduce dependence on finite resources and lower environmental footprints.

Material Efficiency in Manufacturing

Material efficiency focuses on optimizing the use of resources to reduce waste and improve overall productivity. This approach involves designing products that require fewer raw materials while maintaining or improving functionality and durability. One key strategy is lightweighting, which reduces the amount of material needed in product manufacturing without compromising strength or performance. Another essential aspect is material substitution, where companies replace resource-intensive materials with more sustainable alternatives, such as biodegradable plastics, recycled metals, or plant-based fibers. Improved manufacturing techniques, such as precision engineering and additive manufacturing (3D printing), also play a crucial role in reducing material waste by enabling precise and efficient use of raw materials. By integrating material efficiency practices, industries can lower production costs, enhance sustainability, and reduce their overall environmental impact.

4.2.2 Creating Closed-Loop Supply Chains

Closed-loop supply chains (CLSC) are an essential component of the circular economy, designed to minimize waste and maximize resource efficiency by reintegrating used materials back into production cycles. Unlike traditional linear supply chains, which follow a take-make-dispose model, closed-loop supply chains focus on the recovery, refurbishment, and recycling of products at the end of their life cycle. This approach not only reduces environmental impact but also enhances cost savings, supply chain resilience, and sustainability for businesses. With increasing regulatory pressures and consumer demand for eco-friendly products, companies are exploring innovative ways to implement CLSC strategies to create a more sustainable and resource-efficient economic model. Closed-loop supply chains offer a transformative approach to resource management by prioritizing recycling, reuse, and remanufacturing over traditional linear production models. By implementing CLSC strategies, businesses can achieve cost savings, reduce environmental impact, and enhance supply chain resilience. Despite challenges such as logistical complexities, regulatory barriers, and technological limitations, advancements in digital tools, material science, and industry collaboration are driving progress in this field. The future of CLSC will be shaped by innovation, policy support, and consumer engagement, ultimately contributing to a more sustainable and circular economy. Companies that embrace closed-loop principles today will be better positioned for long-term success in an increasingly resource-conscious world.

Principles of Closed-Loop Supply Chains

The foundation of a closed-loop supply chain lies in the principles of resource recovery, waste minimization, and product lifecycle extension. The first key principle is designing products for durability, repairability, and recyclability, ensuring that materials can be easily reintroduced into production after use. The second principle involves efficient collection systems, where companies establish take-back programs, reverse logistics, and collaboration with recycling partners to retrieve used products. The third principle is value retention, where materials are refurbished, remanufactured, or repurposed rather than discarded. By adhering to these principles, businesses can create sustainable supply chains that minimize reliance on virgin resources and reduce landfill waste.

Benefits of Closed-Loop Supply Chains

Implementing a closed-loop supply chain provides several economic, environmental, and social benefits. One of the main advantages is cost reduction, as businesses can lower raw material expenses by reusing recovered materials instead of purchasing new ones. CLSC also helps mitigate risks associated with resource scarcity and price volatility, making supply chains more resilient to fluctuations in material availability. From an environmental perspective, closed-loop systems reduce carbon emissions, landfill waste, and energy consumption by promoting recycling and reuse. Socially, these supply chains create new employment opportunities in refurbishment, remanufacturing, and reverse logistics industries. Additionally, adopting a CLSC model enhances brand reputation, as consumers increasingly favor companies that prioritize sustainability and circular economy principles.

4.2.3 Reverse Logistics and Take-Back Schemes

Reverse logistics and take-back schemes are essential components of sustainable supply chain management, designed to recover, reuse, and recycle products after their initial use. Unlike traditional logistics, which focuses on the forward movement of goods from production to consumers, reverse logistics involves the process of collecting used products, refurbishing them, and reintegrating them into the supply chain. Take-back schemes complement this process by providing structured programs where consumers return used products to manufacturers or retailers for proper disposal, recycling, or reuse. These approaches play a crucial role in reducing environmental impact, conserving resources, and promoting circular economy principles. As businesses and governments increasingly recognize the importance of sustainability, reverse logistics and take-back schemes have become critical strategies for minimizing waste and improving supply chain efficiency.

Reverse logistics and take-back schemes are critical strategies for reducing waste, conserving resources, and promoting circular economy principles. By implementing efficient reverse supply chain processes, businesses can recover valuable materials, reduce costs, and comply with environmental regulations. Despite challenges such as high logistics costs and consumer participation barriers, advancements in technology, regulatory support, and increasing sustainability awareness are driving the adoption of these strategies across industries. As companies continue to innovate and refine their reverse logistics operations, they will play a crucial role in building a more sustainable and resource-efficient future. Organizations that prioritize these initiatives today will be well-positioned for long-term success in an increasingly eco-conscious market.

The Concept of Reverse Logistics

Reverse logistics refers to the set of activities associated with managing product returns, remanufacturing, recycling, and waste disposal in a way that maximizes resource recovery and minimizes environmental harm. It includes the collection, transportation, and processing of used goods, ensuring that materials are efficiently repurposed rather than discarded. Reverse logistics can be applied to various industries, including electronics, automotive, fashion, and packaging. It helps companies comply with environmental regulations, reduce costs associated with raw material procurement, and enhance customer loyalty by offering sustainable return options. With the rise of digital technologies, businesses are increasingly leveraging data analytics, artificial intelligence, and blockchain solutions to optimize reverse logistics processes and improve efficiency.

Importance of Take-Back Schemes

Take-back schemes are structured programs where businesses or retailers collect used products from consumers to facilitate responsible disposal, recycling, or refurbishment. These programs help ensure that products do not end up in landfills but instead enter a secondary lifecycle. Companies in the electronics, fashion, and automotive sectors have implemented take-back initiatives to promote circularity and comply with extended producer responsibility (EPR) regulations. Take-back schemes encourage consumers to participate in sustainability efforts by offering incentives such as discounts on future purchases, trade-in programs, and convenient drop-off locations. These programs not only reduce environmental waste but also allow companies to recover valuable materials and lower production costs by reusing existing resources.

Challenges in Implementing Reverse Logistics and Take-Back Schemes

Despite the advantages of reverse logistics and take-back schemes, businesses face several challenges in their implementation. One major obstacle is the complexity of managing the collection and transportation of used products, especially across different geographic locations. Logistics costs can be high, particularly when dealing with bulky or hazardous materials that require specialized handling. Another challenge is consumer participation, as many customers are unaware of take-back programs or lack incentives to return used products. Additionally, regulatory compliance varies by region, making it difficult for multinational companies to standardize their reverse logistics operations. The lack of advanced recycling infrastructure in some areas further complicates the efficient processing of recovered materials. To address these challenges, companies need to invest in consumer education, collaborate with policymakers, and develop cost-effective logistics solutions that streamline the reverse supply chain.

Key Industries Utilizing Reverse Logistics and Take-Back Schemes

Several industries have successfully integrated reverse logistics and take-back schemes to enhance sustainability. The electronics sector is one of the leading adopters, with companies like Apple and Dell implementing trade-in programs that recover old devices, extract valuable materials, and refurbish components for resale. The automotive industry has also embraced reverse logistics, with manufacturers remanufacturing parts such as engines and transmissions to reduce waste and lower costs. The fashion industry is increasingly focusing on textile recycling and resale programs, with brands like Patagonia and H&M offering incentives for customers to return old garments. The packaging industry has implemented returnable and refillable packaging models to minimize single-use waste. These examples highlight how different sectors are leveraging reverse logistics to achieve environmental and economic benefits.

Role of Technology in Enhancing Reverse Logistics

Technology plays a crucial role in optimizing reverse logistics and improving the efficiency of take-back schemes. Artificial intelligence (AI) and machine learning are being used to predict return patterns, optimize transportation routes, and automate sorting processes. Blockchain technology enhances traceability and transparency in the reverse supply chain, ensuring that recovered materials are processed responsibly. The Internet of Things (IoT) enables smart tracking of returned products, allowing companies to monitor their condition and determine the best reuse or recycling strategies. Robotics and automation are improving disassembly and recycling efficiency, making it easier to recover valuable components from electronic waste and other complex products. As technology continues to evolve, businesses will be able to further refine their reverse logistics strategies and maximize resource recovery.

Policy and Regulatory Framework for Reverse Logistics

Governments and regulatory bodies play a vital role in promoting reverse logistics and take-back schemes through environmental policies and legislation. Extended producer responsibility (EPR) laws require manufacturers to take responsibility for the entire lifecycle of their products, including post-consumer disposal. Many countries have implemented e-waste regulations, mandating companies to establish collection and recycling programs for electronic products. Packaging waste directives encourage businesses to use recyclable materials and implement returnable packaging models. In the European Union, the Circular Economy Action Plan emphasizes the importance of take-back systems and material recovery in achieving sustainability goals. By enforcing stricter regulations and offering incentives for companies to invest in reverse logistics, policymakers can drive greater adoption of circular economy principles across industries.

4.3 BUSINESS MODEL INNOVATION FOR CIRCULAR ECONOMY

4.3.1 Servitization: Shifting from Ownership to Access

Servitization is a transformative business model that shifts the focus from selling products to providing services, enabling customers to access desired functionalities without owning physical assets. This approach aligns with the principles of the circular economy by emphasizing resource efficiency, longevity, and reuse. Companies across various industries, including manufacturing, automotive, and technology, are increasingly adopting servitization strategies to offer subscription-based, rental, or pay-per-use services. By transitioning from ownership to access, businesses can reduce waste, optimize resource utilization, and enhance customer relationships through continuous service engagement. As consumer preferences evolve towards convenience and sustainability, servitization is becoming a key driver of economic and environmental innovation.

Servitization represents a paradigm shift in business models, moving away from traditional product sales towards service-based solutions. By prioritizing access over ownership, companies can create long-term customer relationships, generate recurring revenue, and contribute to sustainability efforts. While challenges such as business model transformation, consumer adoption, and regulatory compliance must be addressed, technological advancements and supportive policies are driving the widespread adoption of servitization. As industries continue to evolve, servitization will play a vital role in promoting resource efficiency, reducing waste, and enhancing economic resilience. Businesses that embrace this shift will be well-positioned to thrive in an increasingly service-oriented and sustainability-conscious marketplace.

Understanding Servitization

Servitization is a business strategy that integrates services with product offerings, creating value beyond traditional sales models. Instead of focusing solely on selling goods, companies provide solutions that include maintenance, upgrades, and performance-based contracts. This shift allows businesses to build long-term relationships with customers while ensuring that products remain in use for extended periods. The servitization model can take various forms, such as product-as-a-service, leasing, or subscription-based access. It enables companies to generate recurring revenue streams, differentiate themselves in competitive markets, and reduce their environmental footprint by designing products for durability and reuse.

Drivers of the Shift to Access-Based Models

Several factors are driving the transition from ownership to access-based business models. One key driver is the changing consumer mindset, with a growing preference for flexible, cost-effective solutions over outright ownership. The rise of the sharing economy, facilitated by digital platforms, has further accelerated this trend. Technological advancements, including the Internet of Things (IoT) and data analytics, have enabled businesses to offer real-time monitoring and predictive maintenance services, enhancing the efficiency of servitized offerings. Additionally, sustainability concerns and regulatory pressures are pushing companies to adopt circular economy principles, making servitization an attractive strategy for reducing waste and improving resource efficiency. Economic considerations, such as cost savings and risk reduction, also play a role, as businesses and consumers seek alternatives to high capital expenditures associated with product ownership.

Industries Embracing Servitization

Servitization has gained traction across various industries, each adapting the model to suit its specific needs. In the manufacturing sector, companies are offering equipment-as-a-service models, where clients pay for usage rather than purchasing machinery outright. This approach ensures optimal performance, reduces downtime, and lowers maintenance costs. The automotive industry has also embraced servitization through car-sharing, subscription services, and fleet management solutions. Companies like Tesla and Volvo offer subscription-based vehicle access, allowing users to enjoy mobility without the financial burden of ownership. In technology, software-as-a-service (SaaS) has revolutionized how businesses and individuals access digital tools, replacing traditional software licensing with cloud-based subscriptions. Even the fashion industry is exploring servitization through clothing rental platforms, reducing waste and promoting circularity. These examples highlight the versatility of servitization across diverse sectors.

Economic and Environmental Benefits of Servitization

Servitization provides significant economic and environmental benefits for both businesses and consumers. From an economic perspective, it enables companies to establish recurring revenue streams, enhancing financial stability and predictability. By extending product lifecycles through maintenance and refurbishment, businesses can reduce manufacturing costs and reliance on raw materials. Consumers benefit from lower upfront costs, increased flexibility, and access to high-quality services without the financial burden of ownership. Environmentally, servitization aligns with circular economy principles by reducing resource consumption, minimizing waste, and promoting product reuse. By designing products for longevity and facilitating take-back schemes, companies can contribute to sustainability goals while maintaining profitability. This model represents a win-win solution that supports both economic growth and environmental responsibility.

The Role of Policy and Regulation in Servitization

Government policies and regulations play a crucial role in facilitating the transition to servitization. Extended producer responsibility (EPR) laws encourage businesses to take accountability for the entire lifecycle of their products, incentivizing the adoption of service-based models. Tax incentives and subsidies for circular business practices can further drive servitization adoption. Standardized regulations on data security and consumer rights ensure that access-based services operate transparently and ethically. In the European Union, initiatives such as the Circular Economy Action Plan promote sustainable business models, including servitization. By implementing supportive policies, governments can accelerate the shift towards a more resource-efficient and sustainable economy.

4.3.2 Platform-Based Circular Business Models

The transition to a circular economy is driving the development of new business models that prioritize sustainability, resource efficiency, and waste reduction. Among these innovative approaches, platform-based circular business models are emerging as powerful tools to facilitate the reuse, sharing, and redistribution of resources. Digital platforms enable businesses and consumers to engage in collaborative consumption, extending product lifecycles and reducing the environmental impact of traditional linear production models. By leveraging technology, these models optimize resource use, create value from waste, and promote sustainable economic growth. The rise of digitalization and data-driven solutions has further accelerated the adoption of platform-based circular business models, making them integral to the circular economy framework.

Platform-based circular business models represent a fundamental shift in how products, resources, and services are exchanged in the economy. By leveraging digital technology and circular economy principles, these models create value while minimizing waste and resource consumption. Despite challenges related to consumer trust, regulation, and infrastructure, the benefits of these models far outweigh the obstacles. Businesses, policymakers, and consumers must work together to accelerate the adoption of platform-based circular solutions. As technology advances and awareness of sustainability grows, these models will play a crucial role in shaping the future of business and environmental stewardship. By embracing platform-based circular business models, societies can move towards a more sustainable and resilient economic system.

Understanding Platform-Based Circular Business Models

Platform-based circular business models utilize digital technologies to connect businesses, consumers, and other stakeholders in an ecosystem where products, materials, and services can be shared, reused, repaired, and recycled. Unlike traditional business models focused on linear supply chains, these platforms create networks that facilitate peer-to-peer exchanges, industrial symbiosis, and remanufacturing processes. By acting as intermediaries, platforms help optimize the flow of goods and services while reducing inefficiencies. These models can take various forms, including sharing economy platforms, digital marketplaces for second-hand goods, and platforms for product-as-a-service offerings. The common thread among them is the integration of circular economy principles with digital connectivity to maximize resource efficiency.

Key Drivers of Platform-Based Circular Business Models

Several factors are driving the adoption of platform-based circular business models. The increasing demand for sustainability and responsible consumption is pushing companies to rethink traditional ownership structures and explore new ways of delivering value. Advances in digital technology, including blockchain, artificial intelligence, and the Internet of Things (IoT), are enabling efficient tracking and management of resources across supply chains. Additionally, consumer behavior is shifting towards access-based consumption models, where people prefer to rent, share, or subscribe to products rather than own them. Regulatory frameworks and government policies promoting circular economy initiatives are further encouraging businesses to embrace platform-based solutions. Economic benefits, such as cost savings and new revenue streams, also contribute to the widespread adoption of these models.

Types of Platform-Based Circular Business Models

There are several types of platform-based circular business models, each designed to address different aspects of sustainability and resource efficiency. Sharing platforms facilitate the use of underutilized assets by enabling peer-to-peer transactions. Examples include car-sharing services, clothing rental platforms, and co-working spaces. Product-as-a-service models provide access to products without requiring ownership, allowing companies to maintain control over product lifecycles and ensure sustainability through maintenance and refurbishment. Digital marketplaces for second-hand goods and refurbished products help extend the usability of items, reducing waste and promoting reuse. Industrial symbiosis platforms connect businesses to exchange byproducts and waste materials, turning one company's waste into another's resource. These models demonstrate the versatility of platform-based approaches in achieving circular economy goals.

Challenges in Implementing Platform-Based Circular Business Models

Despite their advantages, platform-based circular business models face several challenges. One major obstacle is the need for consumer trust and engagement. Users may hesitate to participate in sharing or resale platforms due to concerns about product quality, reliability, and security. Ensuring transparency, certification, and quality assurance mechanisms can help address these concerns. Another challenge is regulatory uncertainty, as many existing policies were designed for traditional linear economies and may not fully support circular business models. Companies must navigate complex legal frameworks related to data protection, product liability, and taxation. Additionally, building and maintaining digital platforms requires significant investment in technology, infrastructure, and user acquisition. Businesses must also consider logistics and reverse supply chain management to effectively handle product returns, refurbishment, and redistribution. Addressing these challenges requires collaboration between stakeholders, policymakers, and technology providers.

The Role of Technology in Platform-Based Circular Business Models

Technology plays a crucial role in enabling and scaling platform-based circular business models. The Internet of Things (IoT) allows businesses to track product usage, monitor condition, and facilitate predictive maintenance, ensuring optimal performance and longevity. Artificial intelligence (AI) enhances platform efficiency by analyzing user behavior, predicting demand, and optimizing resource allocation. Blockchain technology provides transparency and traceability in circular supply chains, ensuring authenticity and reducing fraud in second-hand markets. Cloud computing enables seamless data sharing and integration across digital platforms, supporting scalable and flexible business models. Augmented reality (AR) and virtual reality (VR) can enhance customer experiences by enabling virtual try-ons and digital product previews, reducing unnecessary returns and waste. By leveraging these technological advancements, businesses can enhance the efficiency, security, and appeal of platform-based circular business models.

Economic and Environmental Benefits

Platform-based circular business models offer significant economic and environmental benefits. From an economic perspective, they create new revenue opportunities by monetizing underutilized assets and enabling businesses to generate income from extended product lifecycles. Companies can reduce manufacturing costs by refurbishing and reselling products rather than producing new ones. Consumers benefit from cost savings by accessing high-quality goods at lower prices through rental or resale platforms. Environmentally, these models contribute to waste reduction, lower carbon emissions, and decreased resource extraction. By promoting product reuse and extending lifespans, platform-based circular business models support the transition to a more sustainable and regenerative economy. They also encourage behavioral shifts towards responsible consumption, reducing the demand for disposable goods and fostering a culture of sustainability.

Policy and Regulatory Considerations

The success of platform-based circular business models depends on supportive policy and regulatory frameworks. Governments can incentivize circular economy initiatives through tax benefits, grants, and subsidies for businesses adopting sustainable practices. Extended producer responsibility (EPR) regulations encourage companies to take accountability for the entire lifecycle of their products, promoting the development of platform-based solutions for take-back schemes and refurbishment. Standardized regulations on data protection, liability, and consumer rights are essential to ensure fair and transparent platform operations. Public-private partnerships can facilitate the scaling of these business models by providing infrastructure, research support, and funding opportunities.

Policymakers must work collaboratively with industry stakeholders to create an enabling environment for platform-based circular business models to thrive.

4.3.3 Collaborative Economy and Sharing Platforms

The collaborative economy has emerged as a transformative force in modern business and society, offering alternative ways to access goods and services through shared use rather than individual ownership. This shift is largely facilitated by digital sharing platforms that enable peer-to-peer transactions, fostering a more sustainable and resource-efficient economy. By leveraging technology and social trust, collaborative economy models are disrupting traditional industries while promoting economic inclusion, reducing waste, and maximizing the utility of resources. Sharing platforms play a central role in facilitating collaboration, making it easier for individuals and businesses to exchange products, services, and knowledge in an efficient and mutually beneficial manner.

The collaborative economy and sharing platforms represent a significant shift towards more sustainable, efficient, and inclusive economic models. By facilitating access to goods and services through digital platforms, these models challenge traditional ownership structures and promote responsible consumption. While challenges such as regulatory barriers, trust issues, and digital exclusion persist, ongoing technological advancements and policy interventions can help address these obstacles. As consumer preferences continue to evolve, the collaborative economy will remain a key driver of economic and environmental transformation. Embracing sharing platforms as part of a broader circular economy strategy will contribute to a more resilient and resource-efficient global economy.

Understanding the Collaborative Economy

The collaborative economy, also known as the sharing economy, is based on the principle of shared access to goods and services rather than outright ownership. This economic model harnesses digital platforms to connect individuals, businesses, and communities, enabling them to share resources efficiently. It covers a wide range of sectors, including transportation, accommodation, finance, labor, and consumer goods. By promoting access over ownership, the collaborative economy challenges the traditional consumption patterns that contribute to environmental degradation and resource depletion. Through digital marketplaces and decentralized networks, participants can reduce costs, enhance productivity, and minimize waste, leading to a more sustainable economic model.

The Role of Sharing Platforms

Sharing platforms are the technological enablers of the collaborative economy, providing the necessary infrastructure for participants to connect, transact, and share resources. These platforms facilitate peer-to-peer exchanges, enabling individuals to rent, borrow, or trade assets without relying on traditional businesses. Platforms such as Airbnb, Uber, and TaskRabbit exemplify the power of digital technology in unlocking underutilized assets and optimizing resource distribution. By offering secure payment systems, user reviews, and smart algorithms, sharing platforms enhance trust, transparency, and efficiency, making it easier for people to engage in collaborative consumption. These platforms also support new business models, such as subscription-based access, fractional ownership, and gig economy services, further expanding the reach and impact of the collaborative economy.

Key Drivers of the Collaborative Economy

Several factors contribute to the rapid growth of the collaborative economy. Technological advancements, particularly in mobile applications, cloud computing, and blockchain, have made it easier to facilitate peer-to-peer transactions. Changing consumer preferences, driven by economic constraints and environmental awareness, have encouraged individuals to seek more cost-effective and sustainable alternatives to ownership. Social trust mechanisms, including user ratings and verification systems, have helped overcome barriers related to security and reliability in sharing transactions. Additionally, economic incentives, such as income generation opportunities for individuals and cost savings for consumers, have further accelerated the adoption of collaborative economy models. The rise of remote work and digital nomadism has also played a role in increasing demand for flexible, shared services.

Types of Sharing Platforms

Sharing platforms come in various forms, each catering to different needs and industries. Peer-to-peer (P2P) platforms enable direct exchanges between individuals, allowing them to share assets such as homes, vehicles, and tools. Business-to-consumer (B2C) sharing platforms, on the other hand, involve businesses offering shared access to products and services, such as car rental or coworking spaces. Crowd-based platforms facilitate collective financing and investment, as seen in crowdfunding and peer-to-peer lending services. Knowledge-sharing platforms connect individuals for skill exchange, online tutoring, and professional networking. These diverse models highlight the versatility of the collaborative economy and its ability to disrupt multiple industries while fostering more sustainable consumption patterns.

Economic and Environmental Benefits

The collaborative economy presents significant economic and environmental benefits. By enabling the efficient use of underutilized assets, sharing platforms reduce costs for consumers and create new revenue streams for asset owners.

This model promotes economic inclusion by providing income opportunities to a broader population, including freelancers, small businesses, and independent service providers. Environmentally, the collaborative economy reduces resource consumption and waste generation by promoting reuse, sharing, and extending product lifespans. By minimizing the need for excessive production and transportation, sharing platforms help lower carbon emissions and alleviate pressure on natural resources. The reduction in disposable consumerism also contributes to a more circular and regenerative economic system.

4.4 CIRCULAR ECONOMY AND DIGITAL TRANSFORMATION

4.4.1 The Role of IoT, Blockchain, and Big Data in Circular Economy

The global economy is shifting towards sustainability, aiming to reduce waste and enhance resource efficiency. The circular economy model, which promotes reuse, recycling, and regeneration of materials, has emerged as a viable alternative to the traditional linear economy. This transition is being facilitated by technological advancements such as the Internet of Things (IoT), blockchain, and big data. These technologies play a crucial role in improving resource optimization, enhancing transparency, and driving sustainability.

The transition to a circular economy is crucial for achieving long-term sustainability, and technologies such as IoT, blockchain, and big data play a vital role in this transformation. IoT enhances real-time resource tracking and waste management, blockchain ensures transparency and trust in supply chains, and big data provides insights for optimizing resource utilization. By integrating these technologies, businesses and governments can build efficient and sustainable economic models that minimize waste and promote circularity. While challenges exist, continued innovation and policy support will drive the adoption of these technologies, paving the way for a more sustainable future.

Internet of Things (IoT) and Circular Economy

The IoT has revolutionized various industries by enabling smart, interconnected systems that enhance efficiency and reduce waste. In the circular economy, IoT plays a pivotal role in resource tracking, predictive maintenance, and smart manufacturing. Sensors embedded in products and infrastructure provide real-time data that help monitor resource consumption and optimize usage. One of the key applications of IoT in the circular economy is smart waste management. IoT-enabled waste bins can track waste levels and optimize collection routes, reducing fuel consumption and emissions. Additionally, IoT sensors help in sorting waste more effectively, ensuring that materials are recycled efficiently. In manufacturing, IoT allows companies to monitor the lifecycle of materials, enabling predictive maintenance that reduces downtime and extends the life of machinery. By using

IoT-driven solutions, industries can implement closed-loop production systems where materials are reused, refurbished, or recycled with minimal waste.

Furthermore, IoT helps in sustainable product design. Companies can use sensor data to understand product performance and durability, leading to improved designs that facilitate recyclability and reusability. IoT also enhances supply chain transparency by tracking the movement of goods, ensuring responsible sourcing, and reducing inefficiencies in logistics. These applications contribute significantly to the circular economy by promoting sustainability and reducing environmental impact.

Blockchain Technology and Circular Economy

Blockchain technology, known for its decentralized and immutable ledger system, is a powerful tool in ensuring transparency and trust in the circular economy. By providing a secure and verifiable record of transactions, blockchain enhances traceability and accountability across supply chains, reducing fraud and promoting ethical sourcing.

One of the major applications of blockchain in the circular economy is in material traceability. Many industries struggle with verifying the origin and sustainability of raw materials. Blockchain allows companies to record every stage of a product's lifecycle, from sourcing to disposal, ensuring that materials are ethically and sustainably managed. This is particularly beneficial in industries such as fashion and electronics, where supply chain opacity often leads to unethical practices and resource inefficiency.

Another critical role of blockchain is in enabling product-as-a-service models. Instead of selling products outright, companies can lease or provide services, ensuring that products are returned, refurbished, and reused. Blockchain smart contracts facilitate these transactions by automating agreements, ensuring compliance, and reducing the risk of fraud. This model not only minimizes waste but also fosters a more sustainable consumption pattern.

Blockchain also improves waste management by creating secure and transparent records of waste collection, recycling, and disposal. Governments and organizations can use blockchain-based platforms to incentivize responsible waste management practices, ensuring that materials are properly recycled or repurposed. The technology also supports digital tokens and reward systems that encourage consumers to participate in recycling programs, thus fostering a culture of sustainability. Moreover, blockchain enhances circular economy financing. Traditional financing models often struggle to support sustainable initiatives due to a lack of transparency and trust. Blockchain enables innovative funding mechanisms such as tokenization of assets, crowdfunding for sustainable projects, and peer-to-peer lending, making it easier for circular economy initiatives to access capital.

Big Data and Circular Economy

Big data analytics is another transformative technology that supports the circular economy by providing valuable insights into resource utilization, consumer behavior, and environmental impact. By analyzing large datasets, businesses and policymakers can make informed decisions that optimize resource use, improve efficiency, and reduce waste.

One of the primary applications of big data in the circular economy is demand forecasting. Companies can analyze consumer purchasing patterns and product lifecycles to predict future demand accurately. This enables businesses to produce only what is needed, reducing overproduction and minimizing waste. Predictive analytics also help in inventory management, ensuring that raw materials are used efficiently and that surplus materials are repurposed instead of discarded.

Big data is also instrumental in optimizing logistics and supply chain operations. By analyzing transportation and distribution data, companies can minimize fuel consumption, reduce emissions, and lower operational costs. Data-driven supply chain management allows for real-time tracking of materials and products, ensuring that they are efficiently utilized and returned to the production cycle whenever possible.

Another significant role of big data is in monitoring environmental impact. Advanced analytics help businesses assess their carbon footprint, water usage, and energy consumption, enabling them to implement sustainability measures effectively. By leveraging big data, organizations can develop eco-friendly strategies, such as switching to renewable energy sources, optimizing water usage, and reducing emissions through process improvements.

Big data also supports circular economy initiatives by enhancing product lifecycle analysis. By collecting and analyzing data on product usage, durability, and recyclability, companies can design products that align with circular economy principles. This ensures that materials are reused, refurbished, or recycled efficiently, reducing the environmental impact of production and consumption.

Integrating IoT, Blockchain, and Big Data for a Circular Economy

While IoT, blockchain, and big data each contribute to the circular economy individually, their integration creates a more robust and efficient system. By combining these technologies, businesses and governments can build smart, data-driven circular economy models that maximize resource efficiency and minimize waste. For example, IoT sensors can collect real-time data on resource usage, which is then analyzed using big data analytics to identify inefficiencies and suggest improvements. Blockchain ensures the transparency and security of these data transactions, providing a trusted record of sustainability efforts. This integration enables automated and efficient management of resources, improving circularity in industries such as manufacturing, retail, and waste management.

A practical example of this integration can be seen in smart city initiatives. Cities can deploy IoT-enabled waste bins that track and report waste levels in real-time. The data collected is then analyzed using big data to optimize waste collection schedules, reducing fuel consumption and emissions. Blockchain can be used to record waste disposal transactions, ensuring accountability and incentivizing proper waste management practices. This holistic approach results in a more sustainable and efficient urban environment.

Challenges and Future Prospects

Despite the significant benefits of IoT, blockchain, and big data in the circular economy, several challenges hinder their widespread adoption. One of the main challenges is the high implementation cost. Deploying IoT sensors, developing blockchain systems, and analyzing large datasets require significant investment in infrastructure and expertise. Additionally, integrating these technologies with existing systems can be complex and time-consuming. Data privacy and security are also critical concerns. IoT devices generate vast amounts of data, raising concerns about unauthorized access and data breaches. Blockchain, while secure, requires significant energy consumption for transaction verification, posing sustainability challenges. Addressing these issues through regulatory frameworks and technological advancements is essential for ensuring the successful implementation of these technologies in the circular economy.Looking ahead, continued advancements in artificial intelligence (AI) and machine learning (ML) are expected to further enhance the capabilities of IoT, blockchain, and big data in the circular economy. AI-driven analytics can provide deeper insights into resource efficiency, while ML algorithms can optimize predictive maintenance and demand forecasting. Additionally, improvements in blockchain technology, such as energy-efficient consensus mechanisms, will make it more sustainable and scalable.

4.4.2 Digitalization of Reverse Supply Chains

The global economy is increasingly focusing on sustainability and efficient resource utilization, leading to a greater emphasis on reverse supply chains. Unlike traditional supply chains that primarily focus on moving products from manufacturers to consumers, reverse supply chains deal with the return, recycling, refurbishment, and remanufacturing of products. Digitalization has revolutionized this process by incorporating advanced technologies such as the Internet of

Things (IoT), blockchain, artificial intelligence (AI), and big data analytics. These technologies enhance transparency, efficiency, and sustainability, making reverse logistics more effective and economically viable.

The digitalization of reverse supply chains is revolutionizing the way businesses manage product returns, refurbishment, and recycling. Technologies such as IoT, blockchain, AI, and big data analytics enhance transparency, efficiency, and sustainability, making reverse logistics more effective. By integrating these digital solutions, companies can optimize resource utilization, reduce waste, and comply with environmental regulations. Despite challenges such as high implementation costs and data security concerns, the future of digitalized reverse supply chains is promising. As technological advancements continue to evolve, businesses that embrace digital transformation will gain a competitive advantage in the sustainable economy of the future.

The Concept of Reverse Supply Chains

Reverse supply chains are critical for reducing waste and maximizing the value of returned products. This process involves various stages, including collection, inspection, sorting, refurbishing, and reintroducing products into the market or recycling their materials. The digitalization of these processes improves efficiency, reduces costs, and ensures compliance with environmental regulations.

One of the primary drivers of reverse supply chains is the increasing consumer demand for sustainable practices. Companies across industries are adopting circular economy models, where products are designed for multiple lifecycles instead of single-use consumption. Digital technologies facilitate this transition by optimizing the collection and processing of returned goods, thereby extending product life cycles and reducing environmental impact.

Role of IoT in Digitalizing Reverse Supply Chains

The Internet of Things (IoT) plays a crucial role in improving visibility and efficiency in reverse supply chains. IoT-enabled sensors and tracking devices provide real-time data on product location, condition, and status, allowing businesses to monitor returned products more effectively. This technology enhances the efficiency of collection and transportation processes, reducing delays and operational costs.

IoT-powered smart bins and collection points enable automated sorting of returned products based on their material composition, ensuring that reusable and recyclable components are separated efficiently. Additionally, IoT-based predictive maintenance helps businesses determine when a product is nearing the end of its lifecycle, allowing for proactive planning of refurbishment or recycling processes.

In the retail industry, IoT is used to streamline return management. Smart packaging and RFID tags enable businesses to verify product authenticity, condition, and warranty status before accepting returns. This reduces fraud and improves customer satisfaction by ensuring a seamless return experience.

Blockchain for Transparency and Traceability

Blockchain technology enhances trust and accountability in reverse supply chains by providing an immutable record of transactions and product movements. Transparency is a key challenge in reverse logistics, as multiple stakeholders, including consumers, retailers, and recyclers, are involved in handling returned products. Blockchain ensures that all participants have access to accurate and verifiable information, reducing disputes and inefficiencies.

One of the major applications of blockchain in reverse supply chains is product authentication. Counterfeit and fraudulent returns pose significant challenges to businesses. By using blockchain, companies can create digital certificates of authenticity for products, ensuring that only genuine returns are processed. This technology also helps track the origin and history of returned goods, facilitating informed decisions on whether to refurbish, resell, or recycle them.

Smart contracts on blockchain platforms automate the return and reimbursement process, eliminating delays and reducing administrative costs. These self-executing contracts enforce predefined conditions, ensuring that refunds or exchanges are processed only when specific criteria, such as product condition and warranty validation, are met. Blockchain also enhances compliance with environmental regulations by maintaining a verifiable record of recycling and disposal activities. Governments and regulatory bodies can use blockchain-based data to monitor waste management practices and ensure adherence to sustainability goals.

Artificial Intelligence and Machine Learning in Reverse Logistics

Artificial intelligence (AI) and machine learning (ML) significantly enhance decision-making and process optimization in reverse supply chains. These technologies analyze large volumes of data to predict return patterns, identify defects in products, and optimize refurbishment processes.

AI-powered image recognition systems are used in warehouses and return centers to assess the condition of returned products automatically. This reduces manual inspection efforts and accelerates processing times. Machine learning algorithms also improve demand forecasting for refurbished or remanufactured products, ensuring that businesses allocate resources efficiently. AI-driven chatbots and virtual assistants improve customer interactions in the return process. These systems handle return requests, guide customers through troubleshooting steps, and suggest alternative solutions such as repairs instead of replacements. By enhancing customer support, AI reduces unnecessary returns and improves overall supply chain efficiency.

Furthermore, AI enhances inventory management in reverse supply chains. By analyzing historical return data, businesses can anticipate seasonal fluctuations in product returns and adjust storage capacity accordingly. This prevents overstocking or underutilization of resources, leading to cost savings and operational efficiency.

Big Data Analytics for Process Optimization

Big data analytics plays a crucial role in transforming reverse supply chains by providing actionable insights into return trends, customer behavior, and operational bottlenecks. Businesses collect and analyze vast amounts of data from various sources, including IoT sensors, customer reviews, and transaction records, to enhance decision-making. One key application of big data in reverse logistics is return pattern analysis. By identifying the most frequently returned products and the reasons behind these returns, companies can improve product design, reduce defects, and enhance quality control measures. This minimizes the volume of returns and improves customer satisfaction.

Predictive analytics helps businesses anticipate future returns and adjust their reverse logistics operations accordingly. For instance, retailers can forecast peak return periods, such as post-holiday seasons, and allocate additional resources to handle increased return volumes efficiently. Big data also supports sustainability initiatives by optimizing recycling and waste management processes. Companies can analyze material composition data to determine the most efficient recycling methods, reducing waste and promoting circular economy practices.

Integration of Digital Technologies for Seamless Reverse Logistics

The true potential of digitalization in reverse supply chains is realized when IoT, blockchain, AI, and big data analytics are integrated into a unified system. A seamless digital ecosystem ensures real-time tracking, automated processing, and data-driven decision-making, enhancing efficiency and sustainability.

For example, a smart return management system can use IoT sensors to track product location, AI to assess its condition, blockchain to verify authenticity, and big data analytics to optimize refurbishment or recycling decisions. This integrated approach reduces operational complexities, minimizes costs, and improves customer experience.

Moreover, cloud-based platforms facilitate collaboration among stakeholders, including manufacturers, retailers, logistics providers, and recyclers. By sharing real-time data on returned products, these stakeholders can coordinate their efforts to maximize resource recovery and minimize waste.

Challenges and Future Outlook

Despite the benefits of digitalizing reverse supply chains, several challenges must be addressed for widespread adoption. One of the primary challenges is the high initial investment required for implementing digital technologies. Businesses need to invest in IoT infrastructure, AI-powered analytics systems, and blockchain networks, which may pose financial constraints for small and medium enterprises.

Data privacy and security concerns also present challenges, as reverse logistics involves handling sensitive customer information. Ensuring robust cybersecurity measures and compliance with data protection regulations is essential to maintain consumer trust and prevent data breaches.

Additionally, the complexity of integrating multiple digital technologies requires skilled personnel and strategic planning. Businesses must invest in training employees and developing expertise in emerging technologies to maximize the benefits of digitalization.

Looking ahead, advancements in artificial intelligence, automation, and cloud computing will further enhance the efficiency of reverse supply chains. The adoption of circular economy principles will drive greater investments in digital technologies, making reverse logistics more sustainable and cost-effective. As businesses and governments prioritize sustainability, digitalization will play a crucial role in transforming reverse supply chains into a key enabler of resource efficiency and environmental conservation.

4.4.3 Data-Driven Decision Making in Circular Systems

The transition from a linear economy to a circular economy is crucial for achieving sustainability and resource efficiency. Circular systems aim to minimize waste, maximize resource utilization, and promote recycling, refurbishment, and remanufacturing. However, effective implementation of circular strategies requires accurate, real-time, and actionable insights. This is where data-driven decision-making plays a pivotal role. By leveraging big data analytics, artificial intelligence (AI), machine learning (ML), and the Internet of Things (IoT), businesses and policymakers can optimize resource flows, enhance supply chain transparency, and ensure sustainable production and consumption.

Data-driven decision-making in circular systems enables organizations to predict demand, optimize material usage, and enhance operational efficiency. This approach not only reduces environmental impact but also increases economic viability. By integrating digital technologies with circular principles, businesses can make informed decisions that drive sustainability, reduce costs, and improve long-term competitiveness.

Data-driven decision-making is revolutionizing circular systems by enabling businesses and policymakers to optimize resource usage, reduce waste, and enhance sustainability. Technologies such as big data analytics, IoT, AI, and blockchain provide critical insights that improve efficiency, transparency, and accountability. By leveraging these digital solutions, organizations can implement innovative circular business models that promote economic growth while minimizing environmental impact. While challenges such as data integration and cybersecurity must be addressed, the future of data-driven circular systems holds immense potential for creating a more sustainable and resource-efficient world.

The Role of Big Data in Circular Systems

Big data plays a fundamental role in transforming circular economy initiatives by providing critical insights into resource flows, product life cycles, and consumer behavior. The ability to collect, process, and analyze vast amounts of data enables companies to identify inefficiencies and optimize processes across various stages of the product lifecycle.

One of the most significant applications of big data in circular systems is predictive analytics. Companies can use historical and real-time data to forecast material demand, assess product durability, and anticipate potential waste generation. This enables businesses to make proactive decisions, such as adjusting production volumes, improving product design for longevity, and implementing more effective recycling strategies. Additionally, big data enhances reverse logistics by streamlining the collection, sorting, and redistribution of used materials. Companies can analyze return patterns to optimize reverse supply chains, ensuring that products and materials are efficiently reintegrated into the production cycle. This minimizes waste and reduces costs associated with disposal and raw material procurement.

Furthermore, big data allows for better tracking of materials and products through digital twin technology. By creating virtual replicas of physical assets, businesses can monitor product performance, maintenance needs, and end-of-life considerations, ensuring that resources are utilized to their fullest potential.

The Impact of IoT on Circular Decision Making

The Internet of Things (IoT) is another critical enabler of data-driven decision-making in circular systems. IoT devices, such as smart sensors and RFID tags, provide real-time monitoring of resources, products, and waste streams, facilitating more efficient and sustainable operations. IoT-powered smart manufacturing allows businesses to track energy consumption, monitor equipment performance, and reduce material waste. By analyzing sensor data, companies can implement predictive maintenance, reducing downtime and extending the lifespan of machinery. This approach minimizes resource depletion and ensures that industrial assets operate at peak efficiency.

In waste management, IoT technology enhances material recovery and recycling efforts. Smart waste bins equipped with sensors can detect fill levels and optimize collection schedules, reducing fuel consumption and emissions from transportation. Additionally, automated sorting systems powered by IoT improve the accuracy of material separation, increasing the efficiency of recycling processes.

IoT also plays a vital role in product lifecycle management. Businesses can use connected devices to track products throughout their lifecycle, enabling better decisions on reuse, refurbishment, and remanufacturing. This enhances circularity by ensuring that products are not discarded prematurely and are reintegrated into the economy whenever possible.

Artificial Intelligence and Machine Learning in Circular Systems

Artificial intelligence (AI) and machine learning (ML) enhance decision-making in circular systems by identifying patterns, optimizing operations, and enabling real-time decision-making. These technologies process large datasets and provide actionable insights that drive sustainability and efficiency. AI-powered optimization models help businesses reduce waste and improve material efficiency. For example, AI algorithms can analyze production data to identify areas where material usage can be minimized or substituted with recycled content. This leads to more sustainable manufacturing practices and cost savings. Machine learning also plays a significant role in demand forecasting. By analyzing market trends, consumer preferences, and historical sales data, businesses can predict demand fluctuations and adjust production accordingly. This prevents overproduction, reduces excess inventory, and minimizes resource wastage. Another critical application of AI in circular systems is automated quality assessment. Machine learning algorithms can analyze product conditions and determine whether they should be repaired, refurbished, or recycled. This ensures that valuable resources are not wasted and are utilized in the most efficient manner. Moreover, AI facilitates circular business models such as product-as-a-service (PaaS). By analyzing user behavior and usage patterns, companies can offer subscription-based models, where products are returned, upgraded, and reused instead of being discarded. This approach not only reduces waste but also creates new revenue streams for businesses.

Blockchain for Transparency and Accountability

Blockchain technology plays a crucial role in ensuring transparency, traceability, and accountability in circular systems. By providing an immutable and decentralized ledger, blockchain enhances trust among stakeholders and reduces inefficiencies in material tracking and supply chain management. One of the primary applications of blockchain in circular systems is supply chain transparency. Companies can use blockchain to create a verifiable record of material sourcing, product lifecycle, and end-of-life disposal. This ensures that products meet sustainability standards and enables consumers to make informed purchasing decisions.

Smart contracts on blockchain platforms automate transactions in circular supply chains. For example, blockchain-based smart contracts can facilitate leasing agreements, ensuring that products are returned for refurbishment or recycling after use. This eliminates manual interventions, reduces administrative costs, and enhances circularity. Blockchain also enhances waste management by providing a transparent record of waste collection, processing, and recycling activities. This helps regulatory bodies monitor compliance with sustainability policies and ensures that waste is managed responsibly.

Data-Driven Circular Business Models

Data-driven decision-making enables the development of innovative circular business models that promote sustainability and economic viability. These models leverage digital technologies to optimize resource flows and create new value propositions. One such model is predictive maintenance, where businesses use IoT and AI to anticipate equipment failures and schedule maintenance proactively. This extends the lifespan of machinery, reduces operational costs, and minimizes resource consumption. Another emerging model is the sharing economy, where digital platforms facilitate the sharing of products and services, reducing the need for new production. Companies like ride-sharing and equipment rental services use data analytics to optimize resource allocation and reduce environmental impact. Additionally, data-driven insights enable closed-loop supply chains, where manufacturers take responsibility for end-of-life product management. By analyzing return patterns and material recovery rates, businesses can design products that are easier to disassemble, repair, and recycle, ensuring a more sustainable production cycle.

Challenges and Future Outlook

Despite the numerous benefits of data-driven decision-making in circular systems, several challenges must be addressed for widespread adoption. One of the primary challenges is data integration. Many businesses operate in silos, making it difficult to collect and share data across the supply chain. Establishing standardized data-sharing protocols is essential for effective circular decision-making. Another challenge is the high cost of implementing digital technologies. Investing in IoT infrastructure, AI algorithms, and blockchain systems requires substantial financial resources. Governments and organizations must develop policies and incentives to support businesses in adopting these technologies.Data security and privacy concerns also pose significant challenges. With the increasing reliance on digital platforms, protecting sensitive business and consumer data is critical. Companies must implement robust cybersecurity measures to prevent data breaches and ensure regulatory compliance. Looking ahead, advancements in digital twin technology, AI-driven automation, and decentralized data-sharing platforms will further enhance circular decision-making. The continued integration of these technologies will drive greater efficiency, reduce waste, and accelerate the transition toward a more sustainable economy.

4.5 FINANCING AND INVESTMENT IN CIRCULAR ECONOMY

4.5.1 Circular Economy as a Driver of Green Investment

The global transition to a sustainable economy has placed increasing emphasis on green investments as a means to address environmental challenges while fostering economic growth. One of the most effective frameworks for achieving sustainability is the circular economy, which focuses on reducing waste, maximizing resource efficiency, and promoting the reuse and recycling of materials. Unlike the traditional linear economy, which follows a "take, make, dispose" model, the circular economy ensures that products and materials remain in use for as long as possible. This shift not only reduces environmental impact but also creates new investment opportunities in sustainable industries, clean technologies, and resource-efficient business models.

Green investment refers to the allocation of financial resources towards projects and initiatives that promote environmental sustainability. The circular economy provides a strong foundation for green investment by offering profitable and scalable solutions for waste reduction, renewable energy adoption, and sustainable production practices. Through data-driven insights, technological innovations, and regulatory support, businesses and investors can leverage the circular economy to drive long-term economic and environmental benefits.

The circular economy is emerging as a powerful driver of green investment, offering sustainable solutions that balance economic growth with environmental responsibility. By promoting resource efficiency, waste reduction, and innovative business models, the circular economy attracts investors seeking long-term value creation. The integration of advanced technologies, government incentives, and sustainable finance initiatives further enhances the potential of circular investments. While challenges exist, the ongoing evolution of circular strategies will create new opportunities for investors to contribute to a greener, more resilient global economy.

The Intersection of Circular Economy and Green Investment

Green investment and the circular economy are deeply interconnected, as both prioritize sustainability, resource conservation, and environmental responsibility.

The transition to circular economic models requires substantial financial backing to develop new technologies, build sustainable infrastructure, and support businesses in adopting circular practices. Investors are increasingly recognizing the financial viability of circular economy initiatives, as they provide long-term value creation while mitigating risks associated with resource depletion and environmental degradation. The rise of environmental, social, and governance (ESG) criteria in investment decision-making has further accelerated interest in circular economy projects. Investors are now considering companies' sustainability performance before allocating capital. Businesses that adopt circular principles are viewed as lower-risk and more resilient to future regulatory changes, making them attractive investment opportunities. By channeling capital into circular economy initiatives, investors contribute to building a more sustainable and resource-efficient global economy.

Key Sectors Driving Green Investment through the Circular Economy

Several key sectors are driving green investment by integrating circular economy principles into their operations. These sectors offer lucrative opportunities for investors seeking to fund sustainable and profitable ventures.

One of the primary sectors benefiting from circular investment is the renewable energy industry. Solar, wind, and bioenergy projects are gaining traction as they provide clean and renewable alternatives to fossil fuels. The circular economy enhances these investments by promoting the recycling and repurposing of materials used in renewable energy infrastructure, such as solar panels and wind turbines. This extends their lifecycle and reduces waste, further aligning with sustainable investment goals.

The waste management and recycling industry is another major recipient of green investment. With increasing global waste generation, businesses that focus on innovative recycling technologies, waste-to-energy solutions, and biodegradable alternatives are attracting substantial capital. The circular economy promotes closed-loop systems where materials are continuously reused, reducing dependency on raw materials and minimizing landfill waste. Investors recognize the economic and environmental benefits of these initiatives, leading to significant funding in the sector. The manufacturing and industrial sector is also embracing circular economy principles to reduce waste and improve resource efficiency. Companies investing in eco-friendly production methods, sustainable packaging, and remanufacturing processes are drawing interest from green investors. By adopting circular strategies such as product-as-a-service models and extended producer responsibility (EPR) schemes, manufacturers are reducing costs, enhancing brand reputation, and meeting evolving consumer demand for sustainable products.

The Role of Technology in Advancing Circular Green Investment

Technological advancements play a crucial role in making circular economy investments more viable and scalable. Innovations such as artificial intelligence (AI), the Internet of Things (IoT), blockchain, and big data analytics enable businesses to optimize resource use, track material flows, and enhance supply chain transparency. These technologies provide investors with accurate data and measurable outcomes, increasing confidence in the profitability and sustainability of circular economy projects. AI and machine learning facilitate predictive analytics, allowing businesses to forecast material demand, optimize production, and reduce waste. This helps investors assess the long-term viability of circular business models. IoT-powered smart sensors enable real-time monitoring of resource consumption, making it easier to implement sustainable practices in manufacturing, logistics, and waste management.

Blockchain technology enhances supply chain traceability, ensuring that materials used in circular economy initiatives are ethically sourced and properly recycled. This transparency boosts investor confidence by reducing risks associated with fraud, greenwashing, and regulatory non-compliance. Big data analytics further supports green investment by identifying trends, evaluating sustainability performance, and optimizing investment portfolios to align with circular economy principles.

Government Policies and Regulatory Support for Circular Investments

Government policies and regulatory frameworks play a significant role in driving green investment in the circular economy. Many countries are implementing incentives, tax breaks, and subsidies to encourage businesses to adopt circular practices. These policies make circular economy projects more financially attractive to investors and accelerate the transition towards sustainability.

Carbon pricing mechanisms, extended producer responsibility (EPR) regulations, and landfill taxes are among the key policy measures that encourage companies to invest in circular solutions. By imposing costs on environmentally harmful practices and rewarding sustainable initiatives, governments create a favorable environment for green investments. Public-private partnerships (PPPs) are also instrumental in financing large-scale circular economy projects. Collaborative efforts between governments, private investors, and non-governmental organizations (NGOs) facilitate the development of circular infrastructure, research and development (R&D) in sustainable technologies, and the scaling of circular business models.

Additionally, financial institutions are increasingly incorporating circular economy considerations into their investment criteria. Banks and asset management firms are launching sustainable finance initiatives, including green bonds and impact investing funds, to support businesses aligned with circular principles. These financial instruments provide much-needed capital for circular economy projects while generating competitive returns for investors.

The Economic Benefits of Circular Green Investments

Green investments in circular economy projects offer numerous economic advantages, making them a compelling choice for investors. One of the most significant benefits is resource efficiency, which leads to cost savings and increased profitability. Companies that adopt circular strategies reduce material consumption, minimize waste disposal costs, and improve supply chain resilience.

Job creation is another positive outcome of circular economy investments. The transition to a circular economy generates employment opportunities in recycling, remanufacturing, sustainable product design, and waste management. These jobs contribute to economic growth while fostering environmental sustainability.

Circular investments also enhance business competitiveness and brand reputation. Consumers are becoming increasingly conscious of environmental impact, and companies that embrace sustainability gain a competitive edge in the market. By aligning with consumer preferences, businesses attract more customers and build long-term brand loyalty.

Furthermore, green investments in circular projects mitigate financial risks associated with resource scarcity, regulatory changes, and climate-related disruptions. Companies that proactively implement circular practices are better positioned to adapt to future challenges, ensuring long-term financial stability.

Challenges and Future Prospects of Circular Economy Investments

Despite the numerous benefits, investing in circular economy projects comes with challenges. One of the primary obstacles is the high initial cost of transitioning to circular business models. Companies often require significant capital to redesign products, implement new technologies, and develop sustainable supply chains. Investors may be hesitant to commit funds without clear short-term returns. Another challenge is the lack of standardized metrics for measuring circular economy performance. Unlike traditional financial indicators, circular metrics such as material recovery rates, waste reduction, and lifecycle assessments require new frameworks and methodologies. Establishing industry-wide standards will be crucial for attracting more investors to circular initiatives.

Despite these challenges, the future of circular economy investments is promising. As sustainability continues to gain global importance, investors will increasingly prioritize projects that align with circular principles. The expansion of sustainable finance mechanisms, technological advancements, and supportive regulatory policies will further accelerate the growth of circular green investments.

4.5.2 Circular Business Case Development and Financial Metrics

The transition to a circular economy requires businesses to rethink traditional economic models and develop strategies that prioritize sustainability, resource efficiency, and long-term value creation. Circular business case development involves assessing the financial viability of circular economy initiatives, identifying key value drivers, and aligning business objectives with environmental and social goals. Unlike linear business models that rely on continuous resource extraction and waste generation, circular business models focus on keeping materials and products in use for as long as possible, maximizing their value while minimizing environmental impact.

Circular business case development and financial metrics are essential for demonstrating the economic viability of circular economy initiatives. By leveraging financial indicators such as ROI, TCO, LCA, and resource efficiency metrics, businesses can attract investment, optimize resource use, and enhance long-term profitability. The integration of digital technologies further strengthens financial decision-making, enabling data-driven insights and improved transparency. While challenges exist, the growing emphasis on sustainability, regulatory support, and technological innovation will drive the evolution of circular finance, positioning circular business models as a key driver of sustainable economic growth.

Key Components of Circular Business Case Development

Developing a robust circular business case requires a comprehensive approach that considers economic, environmental, and social factors. The first step involves identifying opportunities for circularity within the business model. This includes evaluating product design, supply chain operations, resource recovery mechanisms, and waste reduction strategies. Companies must analyze how circular practices such as recycling, remanufacturing, and product-as-a-service models can create new revenue streams and improve operational efficiency.

A strong business case must also assess market demand for circular products and services. Consumer preferences are shifting towards sustainability, and businesses that incorporate circularity into their value proposition can gain a competitive advantage. Additionally, companies must analyze regulatory frameworks and industry standards that promote circular economy practices, ensuring compliance while leveraging policy incentives.

Risk assessment is another critical component of circular business case development. Transitioning to a circular model requires upfront investment in infrastructure, technology, and process reengineering. Businesses must evaluate financial, operational, and market risks associated with circular initiatives and develop mitigation strategies. Collaborations with supply chain partners, investment in digital technologies, and government support can help minimize risks and enhance business resilience.

Financial Metrics for Evaluating Circular Business Models

To attract investors and measure the success of circular initiatives, businesses must use appropriate financial metrics. Traditional financial indicators, while important, may not fully capture the long-term value and sustainability benefits of circular economy models. Integrating circular-specific financial metrics provides a more comprehensive evaluation of business performance.

Return on Investment (ROI) is one of the most widely used financial metrics for assessing circular initiatives. It measures the profitability of an investment relative to its cost. Circular projects such as waste reduction programs, recycling infrastructure, and remanufacturing processes often require initial capital investment but yield long-term cost savings and revenue generation. By calculating ROI, businesses can determine the financial viability of their circular strategies.

Total Cost of Ownership (TCO) is another essential metric, particularly for circular business models that emphasize product longevity and resource efficiency. TCO evaluates the total cost associated with a product or service throughout its lifecycle, including acquisition, maintenance, operation, and end-of-life disposal. Businesses adopting circular principles can reduce TCO by designing durable products, implementing repair and refurbishment programs, and extending product lifespans.

Lifecycle Cost Analysis (LCA) provides a holistic view of costs and benefits associated with circular initiatives. Unlike traditional cost analysis, LCA considers environmental and social costs alongside financial expenses. It enables businesses to compare circular and linear approaches, demonstrating the economic and sustainability advantages of circular strategies. Investors and stakeholders increasingly value LCA as a decision-making tool for assessing long-term impact.

Revenue from Circular Business Models is a key indicator of financial success. Companies transitioning to circular economy principles can generate new revenue streams through leasing, sharing, and product-as-a-service models. By offering products on a subscription basis rather than a one-time sale, businesses create steady revenue flows while reducing resource consumption. Tracking revenue from circular business models helps measure the scalability and profitability of circular strategies. Material and Resource Efficiency Metrics assess how effectively a business utilizes resources in its operations. Metrics such as material circularity indicators (MCI), waste diversion rates, and resource productivity measure the extent to which companies reduce raw material consumption and optimize resource use. Higher efficiency levels translate into cost savings, reduced environmental impact, and improved financial performance.

Carbon and Environmental Footprint Reduction is a financial and sustainability metric that evaluates the economic benefits of reducing emissions, waste, and pollution. Businesses investing in circular solutions such as closed-loop recycling, energy-efficient production, and carbon-neutral logistics can lower operational costs while enhancing brand reputation and regulatory compliance.

The Role of Digital Technologies in Circular Finance

Digital technologies are transforming the financial evaluation and implementation of circular business models. Big data analytics, artificial intelligence (AI), blockchain, and the Internet of Things (IoT) enable businesses to collect and analyze data on resource flows, product lifecycle performance, and environmental impact. These insights support data-driven decision-making and improve the accuracy of financial forecasting for circular investments.

Blockchain technology enhances transparency and accountability in circular finance. By providing secure, tamper-proof records of material sourcing, product usage, and end-of-life processing, blockchain builds investor confidence in circular projects. Smart contracts on blockchain platforms facilitate automated transactions in circular supply chains, reducing administrative costs and enhancing financial efficiency. IoT-powered smart sensors enable real-time monitoring of asset performance, material consumption, and waste generation. Businesses can use IoT data to optimize resource allocation, prevent overproduction, and reduce costs associated with inefficiencies. AI-driven predictive analytics further enhances circular finance by identifying trends, forecasting demand, and optimizing inventory management.

Challenges in Circular Business Case Development and Financial Metrics

Despite the growing recognition of circular business opportunities, several challenges remain in developing strong business cases and financial assessments. One of the primary challenges is the difficulty in quantifying long-term environmental and social benefits in financial terms. Many circular initiatives yield returns over an extended period, making short-term financial assessments less reflective of true value creation.

Another challenge is the lack of standardized financial metrics for circular business models. While traditional financial indicators remain relevant, there is a need for industry-wide adoption of circular-specific metrics. The absence of standardized measurement frameworks makes it challenging for investors to compare different circular initiatives and assess their financial performance effectively.

Regulatory uncertainty also poses a challenge for circular business case development. While governments are increasingly promoting circular economy policies, regulatory landscapes vary across regions and industries. Businesses must navigate evolving regulations and compliance requirements while making long-term investment decisions.

Future Outlook for Circular Finance and Business Case Development

The future of circular business case development and financial metrics is promising, as sustainability becomes a core driver of economic growth. The increasing adoption of ESG investment principles, sustainable finance initiatives, and digital technologies will accelerate the integration of circular economy models into mainstream business practices.

Financial institutions and policymakers are expected to play a crucial role in advancing circular finance. Banks, asset managers, and investment funds are launching green bonds, impact investing funds, and sustainability-linked loans to support circular economy projects. Governments are also introducing tax incentives, grants, and subsidies to encourage businesses to adopt circular strategies. Technological advancements will continue to refine circular financial metrics, enabling more accurate assessment of economic, environmental, and social performance. AI-driven financial modeling, real-time data analytics, and blockchain-based financial transactions will enhance transparency, risk management, and investment decision-making in circular business models.

4.5.3 Circular Economy Funds and Venture Capital

The transition to a circular economy requires substantial financial investments to develop sustainable business models, innovative technologies, and resource-efficient production systems. As traditional linear economic models give way to circular strategies focused on reuse, recycling, and sustainable resource management, the role of finance becomes increasingly critical. Circular economy funds and venture capital investments play a pivotal role in accelerating this transition by providing the necessary capital for businesses that prioritize sustainability, waste reduction, and regenerative economic practices. Circular economy funds are specialized investment vehicles dedicated to financing projects that align with circular principles. These funds support businesses involved in sustainable product design, material recovery, renewable energy, and closed-loop manufacturing systems. Similarly, venture capital (VC) firms are recognizing the potential of circular economy startups, providing early-stage funding to innovative companies that develop technologies and business models aimed at minimizing environmental impact.

Circular economy funds and venture capital investments are critical drivers of the transition to a sustainable economic system. By financing businesses that prioritize resource efficiency, waste reduction, and innovative circular solutions, these investment mechanisms contribute to long-term environmental and financial sustainability. Despite challenges such as regulatory uncertainties and difficulties in measuring financial returns, the growing momentum behind ESG investing and technological advancements will accelerate the adoption of circular finance. As circular economy principles become mainstream, the financial sector will play an increasingly influential role in shaping a more sustainable and resilient global economy.

The Role of Circular Economy Funds

Circular economy funds are designed to support companies that integrate sustainability into their operations. These funds invest in businesses across various sectors, including renewable energy, waste management, sustainable agriculture, and eco-friendly manufacturing. The primary goal of these funds is to generate financial returns while promoting environmental and social benefits. Institutional investors, including pension funds, asset managers, and sovereign wealth funds, are increasingly allocating capital to circular economy funds. This shift is driven by growing awareness of climate change risks, regulatory pressures, and consumer demand for sustainable products.

By investing in circular economy funds, these institutions contribute to the development of a more resilient and resource-efficient economy. Governments and development banks also play a crucial role in establishing circular economy funds. Public-private partnerships (PPPs) are often used to de-risk investments in circular projects, making them more attractive to private investors. Policy incentives, such as tax breaks and subsidies, further encourage the growth of circular economy funds, fostering a financial ecosystem that supports sustainable development.

Venture Capital and the Circular Economy

Venture capital is instrumental in funding early-stage circular economy startups that develop innovative solutions for resource efficiency and waste reduction. VC firms provide funding to high-potential startups with scalable business models that align with circular economy principles. These investments enable startups to commercialize their technologies, expand market reach, and refine their business strategies. Circular economy startups attract VC investment across various domains. In the materials sector, companies are developing biodegradable alternatives to plastics, closed-loop recycling technologies, and advanced material recovery solutions. In the energy sector, startups focus on renewable energy storage, decentralized energy systems, and waste-to-energy technologies. The sharing economy is another key area, with VC-backed companies offering product-as-a-service and leasing models that reduce consumption and extend product lifecycles.

Venture capital investors recognize the financial potential of circular business models due to their ability to drive cost savings, regulatory compliance, and consumer demand for sustainable alternatives. However, investing in circular economy startups comes with risks, including regulatory uncertainties, high initial costs, and longer return-on-investment periods. To mitigate these risks, VC firms often collaborate with industry experts, sustainability consultants, and government agencies to support startups in navigating market challenges.

Investment Trends in Circular Economy Funds and Venture Capital

The demand for circular economy investments is growing rapidly, driven by the global shift toward sustainability and responsible investing. Environmental, social, and governance (ESG) criteria are influencing investment decisions, with investors prioritizing businesses that demonstrate strong sustainability performance. As a result, new financial instruments and investment strategies are emerging to support the circular economy. Green bonds and sustainability-linked loans are becoming popular funding mechanisms for circular economy projects. These financial instruments provide businesses with access to capital while ensuring accountability in achieving sustainability targets. Private equity firms are also entering the circular economy space, acquiring companies with circular business models and providing them with growth capital.

Corporate venture capital (CVC) is another significant trend in circular economy investments. Large corporations are investing in startups that align with their sustainability goals, fostering innovation and accelerating the adoption of circular strategies. Companies in industries such as consumer goods, automotive, and technology are leveraging CVC to integrate circular solutions into their supply chains and product offerings.

Challenges in Financing the Circular Economy

Despite the increasing interest in circular economy investments, several challenges hinder the widespread adoption of circular finance. One of the primary barriers is the difficulty in quantifying the financial returns of circular business models. Unlike traditional linear businesses, circular economy ventures often require longer timeframes to generate profits, making them less attractive to short-term investors. The lack of standardized metrics for assessing circular investments poses another challenge. Investors need clear, quantifiable indicators to evaluate the financial performance and impact of circular initiatives. The development of standardized circular economy performance metrics will be crucial in addressing this issue and attracting more investment.

Regulatory uncertainty is also a concern for investors in circular economy projects. While governments worldwide are implementing policies to promote circularity, regulatory frameworks vary across regions and industries. Investors must navigate complex compliance requirements and anticipate policy changes that could affect the financial viability of circular initiatives.

The Future of Circular Economy Funds and Venture Capital

The future of circular economy finance is promising, with continued growth in investment opportunities and evolving financial mechanisms. The expansion of impact investing and ESG-focused funds will drive further capital into circular economy initiatives, aligning financial objectives with sustainability goals. Technology will play a key role in shaping the future of circular investments. Advances in artificial intelligence (AI), blockchain, and big data analytics will enhance transparency, risk assessment, and financial modeling for circular projects. These technologies will provide investors with real-time insights into resource flows, carbon footprints, and supply chain efficiency, enabling more informed investment decisions.

Collaboration among financial institutions, governments, and businesses will be essential for scaling circular economy investments. Public-private partnerships, blended finance models, and policy incentives will help bridge the funding gap and create a more supportive investment environment for circular initiatives.

CHAPTER

5

Circular Economy and Waste Management

5.1 REDUCING WASTE AND MAXIMIZING RESOURCE RECOVERY

5.1.1 The Circular Waste Hierarchy

Waste (management) hierarchy is a tool used in the evaluation of processes that protect the environment alongside resource and energy consumption from most favourable to least favourable actions. The hierarchy establishes preferred program priorities based on sustainability. To be sustainable, waste management cannot be solved only with technical end-of-pipe solutions and an integrated approach is necessary. The waste management hierarchy indicates an order of preference for action to reduce and manage waste, and is usually presented diagrammatically in the form of a pyramid. The hierarchy captures the progression of a material or product through successive stages of waste management, and represents the latter part of the life-cycle for each product. The aim of the waste hierarchy is to extract the maximum practical benefits from products and to generate the minimum amount of waste. The proper application of the waste hierarchy can have several benefits. It can help prevent emissions of greenhouse gases, reduce pollutants, save energy, conserve resources, create jobs and stimulate the development of green technologies.

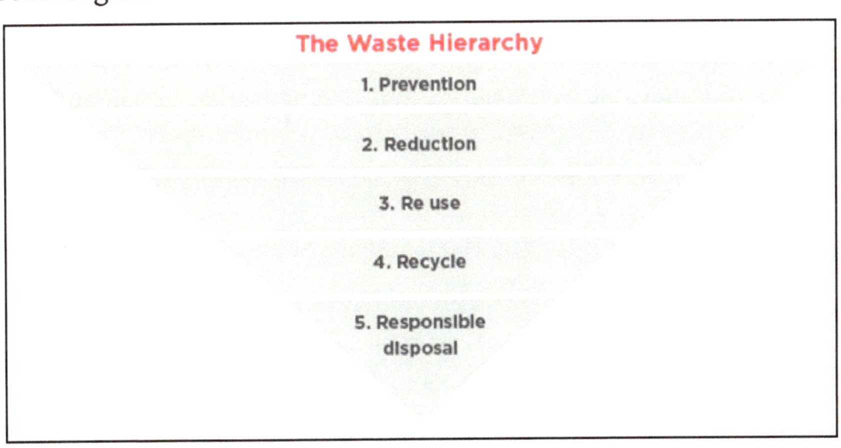

Fig: The Waste Management Hierarchy Starts from Prevention and Reduction Actions

Life-Cycle Thinking

All products and services have environmental impacts, from the extraction of raw materials for production to manufacture, distribution, use and disposal. Following the waste hierarchy will generally lead to the most resource-efficient and environmentally sound choice but in some cases refining decisions within the hierarchy or departing from it can lead to better environmental outcomes.

Life cycle thinking and assessment can be used to support decision-making in the area of waste management and to identify the best environmental options. It can help policy makers understand the benefits and trade-offs they have to face when making decisions on waste management strategies. Life-cycle assessment provides an approach to ensure that the best outcome for the environment can be identified and put in place. It involves looking at all stages of a product's life to find where improvements can be made to reduce environmental impacts and improve the use or reuse of resources. A key goal is to avoid actions that shift negative impacts from one stage to another. Life cycle thinking can be applied to the five stages of the waste management hierarchy. For example, life-cycle analysis has shown that it is often better for the environment to replace an old washing machine, despite the waste generated, than to continue to use an older machine which is less energy-efficient. This is because a washing machine's greatest environmental impact is during its use phase. Buying an energy-efficient machine and using low-temperature detergent reduce environmental impacts.

The European Union Waste Framework Directive has introduced the concept of life-cycle thinking into waste policies. This duality approach gives a broader view of all environmental aspects and ensures any action has an overall benefit compared to other options. The actions to deal with waste along the hierarchy should be compatible with other environmental initiatives.

Challenges for Local and Regional Authorities

The task of implementing the waste hierarchy in waste management practices within a country may be delegated to the different levels of government (national, regional, local) and to other possible factors including industry, private companies and households. Local and regional authorities can be particularly challenged by the following issues when applying the waste hierarchy approach.

- A coherent waste management strategy must be set up
- Separate collection and sorting systems for many different waste streams need to be established.
- Adequate treatment and disposal facilities must be established.
- An effective horizontal co-operation between local authorities and

municipalities and a vertical co-operation between the different levels of government, local to regional and when beneficial, also at the national level need to established

- Finding financing for the establishing or upgrading of expensive sustainable waste management infrastructure to address the needs of managing waste
- A lack of data available on waste management strategies must be overcome and monitoring requirements must be met to implement the waste programs
- The enforcement and control of business plans and practices be established and applied to maximize benefits to the environment and human health
- A lack of administrative capacity at the regional and local level. The lack of finances, information, and technical expertise must be overcome for effective implementation and success of the waste management policies.

Source Reduction

Source reduction involves efforts to reduce hazardous waste and other materials by modifying industrial production. Source reduction methods involve changes in manufacturing technology, raw material inputs, and product formulation. At times, the term "pollution prevention" may refer to source reduction. Another method of source reduction is to increase incentives for recycling. Many communities in the United States are implementing variable-rate pricing for waste disposal (also known as Pay As You Throw - PAYT) which has been effective in reducing the size of the municipal waste stream. Source reduction is typically measured by efficiencies and cutbacks in waste. Toxics use reduction is a more controversial approach to source reduction that targets and measures reductions in the upstream use of toxic materials. Toxic use reduction emphasizes the more preventive aspects of source reduction but, due to its emphasis on toxic chemical inputs, has been opposed more vigorously by chemical manufacturers. Toxic use reduction programs have been set up by legislation in some states, e.g., Massachusetts, New Jersey, and Oregon. The 3 R's represent the 'Waste Hierarchy' which lists the best ways of managing waste from the most to the least desirable. Many of the things we currently throw away could be reused again with just a little thought and imagination.

5.1.2 Reducing Landfill Use and Promoting Recycling

The rapid increase in global waste generation has led to serious environmental, social, and economic challenges. Landfills, traditionally used for waste disposal, pose significant risks, including soil and water contamination, greenhouse gas emissions, and habitat destruction. The overreliance on landfills as a waste management solution is unsustainable and demands urgent action. Reducing landfill use and promoting recycling are critical strategies for mitigating environmental damage, conserving natural resources, and fostering a more sustainable economy.

Reducing landfill use and promoting recycling are fundamental components of a sustainable future. By implementing waste reduction strategies, investing in recycling infrastructure, and fostering policy frameworks that support circular economy principles, societies can minimize environmental impact and create economic opportunities. Businesses, governments, and communities must collaborate to drive systemic change in waste management. With collective efforts, it is possible to transition towards a world where resources are used efficiently, waste is minimized, and landfill dependency is significantly reduced.

The Environmental and Economic Impacts of Landfills

Landfills contribute to severe environmental degradation. Decomposing waste generates methane, a potent greenhouse gas that significantly contributes to climate change. Additionally, landfill leachate, a toxic liquid formed from waste decomposition, can seep into soil and water bodies, polluting groundwater and harming ecosystems. The space required for landfills leads to deforestation and habitat destruction, further exacerbating biodiversity loss. Economically, landfills impose high costs on municipalities and taxpayers. Land acquisition, maintenance, and waste transportation expenses strain public budgets. The long-term environmental consequences, including land devaluation and health-related costs due to pollution, further increase financial burdens. In contrast, investing in recycling infrastructure and waste reduction initiatives presents cost-effective alternatives that generate employment, reduce environmental risks, and create new business opportunities in the green economy.

Strategies for Reducing Landfill Use

Reducing landfill use requires a multi-faceted approach involving waste reduction at the source, improved waste sorting, and enhanced recycling processes. One of the most effective strategies is implementing policies that encourage sustainable consumption and production. Governments can introduce regulations such as extended producer responsibility (EPR), where manufacturers are held accountable for the end-of-life disposal of their products. By designing products for durability, repairability, and recyclability, businesses can significantly reduce waste sent to landfills. Public awareness campaigns play a vital role in reducing landfill waste. Educating consumers on responsible waste disposal, composting, and sustainable consumption habits can lead to behavioral changes that decrease waste generation.

Incentive programs, such as deposit-refund schemes for beverage containers, encourage consumers to return used products for recycling rather than discarding them in landfills. Waste segregation is another essential strategy. Separating organic waste from recyclable materials reduces landfill waste and facilitates more efficient recycling. Organic waste can be composted or converted into biogas, reducing methane emissions while producing valuable resources. Investing in advanced sorting technologies, such as automated waste separation systems, enhances recycling efficiency and minimizes contamination in recyclable streams.

The Role of Recycling in Sustainable Waste Management

Recycling is a fundamental pillar of sustainable waste management. It conserves natural resources, reduces energy consumption, and minimizes pollution. Recycling materials such as paper, plastic, glass, and metals reduces the need for raw material extraction, preserving ecosystems and decreasing carbon emissions associated with manufacturing processes. For example, recycling aluminum saves up to 95% of the energy required to produce new aluminum from raw materials.

Developing strong recycling infrastructure is crucial for increasing recycling rates. Governments and private enterprises must invest in modern recycling facilities, collection systems, and processing technologies to maximize material recovery. Implementing standardized labeling on packaging and providing accessible recycling bins in public spaces further enhances participation in recycling programs. Technological advancements are also improving recycling capabilities. Innovations in chemical recycling enable the breakdown of plastics into their original components, making them reusable for high-quality manufacturing. AI-powered sorting systems improve material separation accuracy, increasing the efficiency of recycling plants. Research into biodegradable and compostable materials provides alternative solutions that minimize landfill dependency.

Policy and Regulatory Approaches to Waste Reduction and Recycling

Governments play a crucial role in reducing landfill use and promoting recycling through policy interventions. Legislation that sets recycling targets and landfill diversion goals compels businesses and individuals to adopt sustainable waste management practices. For example, many European countries have implemented strict landfill bans on recyclable materials, leading to significant increases in recycling rates.

Tax incentives and subsidies for recycling initiatives encourage businesses to invest in sustainable waste management solutions. Governments can also implement pay-as-you-throw (PAYT) systems, where households and businesses are charged based on the amount of waste they generate. This approach incentivizes waste reduction and encourages more responsible disposal practices.

International collaboration is essential in addressing waste management challenges. Global agreements, such as the Basel Convention on the Control of Transboundary Movements of Hazardous Wastes, regulate the international trade of waste and promote environmentally sound recycling practices. By working together, countries can share best practices, develop innovative recycling technologies, and establish circular economy frameworks that reduce landfill use worldwide.

The Role of Businesses in Promoting Recycling and Waste Reduction

Businesses have a significant responsibility in minimizing waste and promoting recycling. Corporations can implement circular business models that prioritize material recovery and product reuse. For instance, some companies have adopted take-back programs, where consumers return used products for recycling or refurbishing.

Sustainable packaging solutions reduce landfill waste and enhance brand reputation. Many companies are transitioning to biodegradable packaging, reusable containers, and minimalistic packaging designs to decrease material waste. Additionally, adopting closed-loop manufacturing systems, where waste materials are reintegrated into production processes, reduces reliance on raw materials and minimizes landfill contributions.

Collaboration between businesses and recycling organizations strengthens recycling efforts. By forming partnerships with waste management companies, manufacturers can ensure that their products are effectively recycled at the end of their lifecycle. Investing in research and development of alternative materials and efficient recycling processes further enhances waste reduction efforts.

Community Engagement and Grassroots Initiatives

Community involvement is vital in achieving waste reduction and recycling goals. Grassroots initiatives, such as zero-waste movements and local recycling programs, empower individuals to take responsibility for their waste. Community-led recycling centers and composting programs provide accessible solutions for waste diversion.

Schools and educational institutions play an essential role in promoting recycling awareness. Incorporating sustainability education into school curricula instills environmentally responsible habits from an early age. Hands-on activities, such as school recycling programs and waste audits, engage students in practical waste management solutions.

Non-governmental organizations (NGOs) and environmental advocacy groups contribute to landfill reduction by lobbying for policy changes, organizing clean-up drives, and educating communities about waste management. By fostering a culture of sustainability, these initiatives create long-term positive impacts on waste reduction efforts.

The Future of Waste Management: Moving Towards a Circular Economy

The future of waste management lies in embracing a circular economy approach, where resources are continuously reused, repurposed, and recycled. Advancements in waste-to-energy technologies, sustainable material innovations, and digital waste tracking systems will further improve waste reduction efforts. Governments, businesses, and individuals must work together to implement holistic waste management strategies that prioritize recycling and minimize landfill use. Consumer behavior will continue to shape waste management trends. As sustainability becomes a more prominent factor in purchasing decisions, businesses will be compelled to adopt circular economy principles. The expansion of sustainable product certifications and eco-labeling will guide consumers in making environmentally responsible choices. Investment in green technologies and infrastructure will be essential in scaling up recycling capabilities. Emerging industries, such as e-waste recycling and bio-based material production, present new opportunities for economic growth while addressing waste challenges. Public and private sector collaboration will be key in driving innovation and ensuring the successful transition to a zero-waste future.

5.2 CIRCULAR ECONOMY IN WASTE-TO-ENERGY AND WASTE MANAGEMENT

5.2.1 Energy Recovery from Waste Materials

Waste-to-energy (WtE) or energy-from-waste (EfW) refers to a series of processes designed to convert waste materials into usable forms of energy, typically electricity or heat. As a form of energy recovery, WtE plays a crucial role in both waste management and sustainable energy production by reducing the volume of waste in landfills and providing an alternative energy source.

The most common method of WtE is direct combustion of waste to produce heat, which can then be used to generate electricity via steam turbines. This method is widely employed in many countries and offers a dual benefit: it disposes of waste while generating energy, making it an efficient process for both waste reduction and energy production.

In addition to combustion, other WtE technologies focus on converting waste into fuel sources. For example, gasification and pyrolysis are processes that thermochemically decompose organic materials in the absence of oxygen to produce syngas, a synthetic gas primarily composed of hydrogen, carbon monoxide, and small amounts of carbon dioxide. This syngas can be converted into methane, methanol, ethanol, or even synthetic fuels, which can be used in various industrial processes or as alternative fuels in transportation.

Furthermore, anaerobic digestion, a biological process, converts organic waste into biogas (mainly methane and carbon dioxide) through microbial action. This biogas can be harnessed for energy production or processed into biomethane, which can serve as a substitute for natural gas.

The WtE process contributes to circular economy principles by transforming waste products into valuable resources, reducing dependency on fossil fuels, and mitigating greenhouse gas emissions. However, challenges remain, particularly in ensuring that emissions from WtE plants, such as dioxins and furans, are properly managed to minimize environmental impact. Advanced pollution control technologies are essential to address these concerns and ensure WtE remains a viable, environmentally sound solution.

WtE technologies present a significant opportunity to manage waste sustainably while contributing to global energy demands. They represent an essential component of integrated waste management strategies and a shift toward renewable energy systems. As technology advances, WtE may play an increasingly critical role in both reducing landfill use and enhancing energy security.

Methods

Incineration

Incineration, the combustion of organic material such as waste with energy recovery, is the most common WtE implementation. All new WtE plants in OECD countries incinerating waste (residual MSW, commercial, industrial or RDF) must meet strict emission standards, including those on nitrogen oxides (NO_x), sulphur dioxide (SO_2), heavy metals and dioxins. Hence, modern incineration plants are vastly different from old types, some of which neither recovered energy nor materials. Modern incinerators reduce the volume of the original waste by 95-96 percent, depending upon composition and degree of recovery of materials such as metals from the ash for recycling.

Incinerators may emit fine particulate, heavy metals, trace dioxin and acid gas, even though these emissions are relatively low from modern incinerators. Other concerns include proper management of residues: toxic fly ash, which must be handled in hazardous waste disposal installation as well as incinerator bottom ash (IBA), which must be reused properly.

Critics argue that incinerators destroy valuable resources and they may reduce incentives for recycling. The question, however, is an open one, as European countries which recycle the most (up to 70%) also incinerate to avoid landfilling.

Incinerators have electric efficiencies of 14-28%. In order to avoid losing the rest of the energy, it can be used for e.g. district heating (cogeneration). The total efficiencies of cogeneration incinerators are typically higher than 80% (based on the lower heating value of the waste).

The method of incineration to convert municipal solid waste (MSW) is a relatively old method of WtE generation. Incineration generally entails burning waste (residual MSW, commercial, industrial and RDF) to boil water which powers steam generators that generate electric energy and heat to be used in homes, businesses, institutions and industries. One problem associated is the potential for pollutants to enter the atmosphere with the flue gases from the boiler. These pollutants can be acidic and in the 1980s were reported to cause environmental degradation by turning rain into acid rain. Modern incinerators incorporate carefully engineered primary and secondary burn chambers, and controlled burners designed to burn completely with the lowest possible emissions, eliminating, in some cases, the need for lime scrubbers and electro-static precipitators on smokestacks. By passing the smoke through the basic lime scrubbers, any acids that might be in the smoke are neutralized which prevents the acid from reaching the atmosphere and hurting the environment. Many other devices, such as fabric filters, reactors, and catalysts destroy or capture other regulated pollutants.

According to the New York Times, modern incineration plants are so clean that "many times more dioxin is now released from home fireplaces and backyard barbecues than from incineration". According to the German Environmental Ministry, "because of stringent regulations, waste incineration plants are no longer significant in terms of emissions of dioxins, dust, and heavy metals".

Compared with other waste to energy technologies, incineration seems to be the most attractive due to its higher power production efficiency, lower investment costs, and lower emission rates. Additionally, incineration yields the highest amount of electricity with the highest capacity to lessen pile of wastes in landfills through direct combustion.

Fuel from Plastics

One process that is used to convert plastic into fuel is pyrolysis, the thermal decomposition of materials at high temperatures in an inert atmosphere. It involves change of chemical composition and is mainly used for treatment of organic materials. In large scale production, plastic waste is ground and melted and then pyrolyzed.

Catalytic converters help in the process. The vapours are condensed with oil or fuel and accumulated in settling tanks and filtered. Fuel is obtained after homogenation and can be used for automobiles and machinery. It is commonly termed as thermofuel or energy from plastic. A new process uses a two-part catalyst, cobalt and zeolite, to convert plastics into propane. It works on polyethylene and polypropylene and the propane yield is approximately 80%.

Other

There are a number of other new and emerging technologies that are able to produce energy from waste and other fuels without direct combustion. Many of these technologies have the potential to produce more electric power from the same amount of fuel than would be possible by direct combustion. This is mainly due to the separation of corrosive components (ash) from the converted fuel, thereby allowing higher combustion temperatures in e.g. boilers, gas turbines, internal combustion engines, fuel cells. Some advanced technologies are able to efficiently convert the energy in the feedstocks into liquid or gaseous fuels, using heat but in the absence of oxygen, without actual combustion, by using a combination of thermal technologies.

Typically, they are cleaner, as the feedstock is separated prior to treatment to remove the unwanted components:

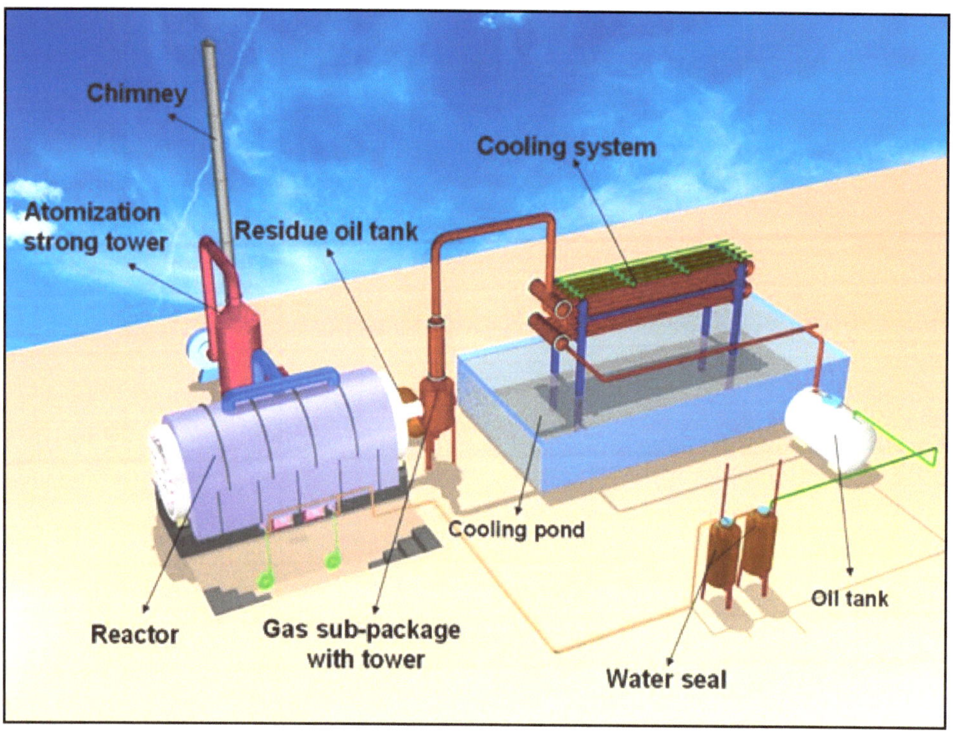

Fig: Pyrolysis Plant

Thermal treatment technologies include:

- Gasification: produces combustible gas, hydrogen, synthetic fuels

- Thermal depolymerization: produces synthetic crude oil, which can be further refined
- Pyrolysis: produces combustible tar/bio-oil and chars
- Plasma arc gasification or plasma gasification process (PGP): produces rich syngas including hydrogen and carbon monoxide usable for fuel cells or generating electricity to drive the plasma arch, usable vitrified silicate and metal ingots, salt and sulphur

Non-thermal technologies:

- Anaerobic digestion: Biogas rich in methane
- Fermentation production: examples are ethanol, lactic acid, hydrogen
- Mechanical biological treatment (MBT)
  - MBT + Anaerobic digestion
  - MBT to Refuse derived fuel

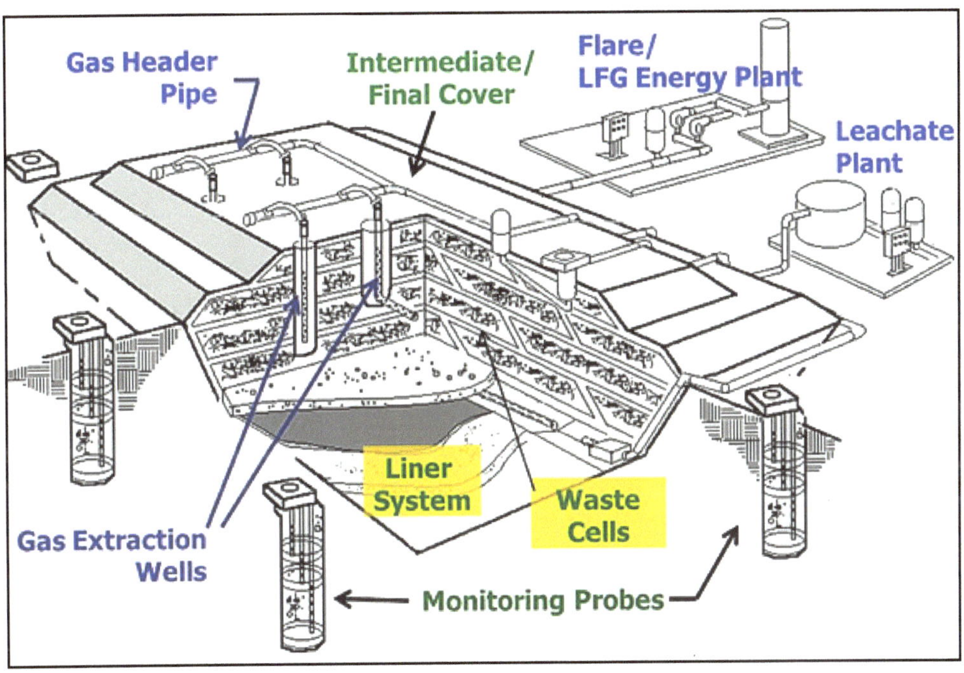

Fig: Landfill Gas Collection

Global Developments

During the 2001–2007 period, the waste-to-energy capacity increased by about four million metric tons per year. Japan and China each built several plants based on direct smelting or on fluidized bed combustion of solid waste. In China there were about 434 waste-to-energy plants in early 2016. Japan is the largest user in thermal treatment of municipal solid waste in the world, with 40 million tons.

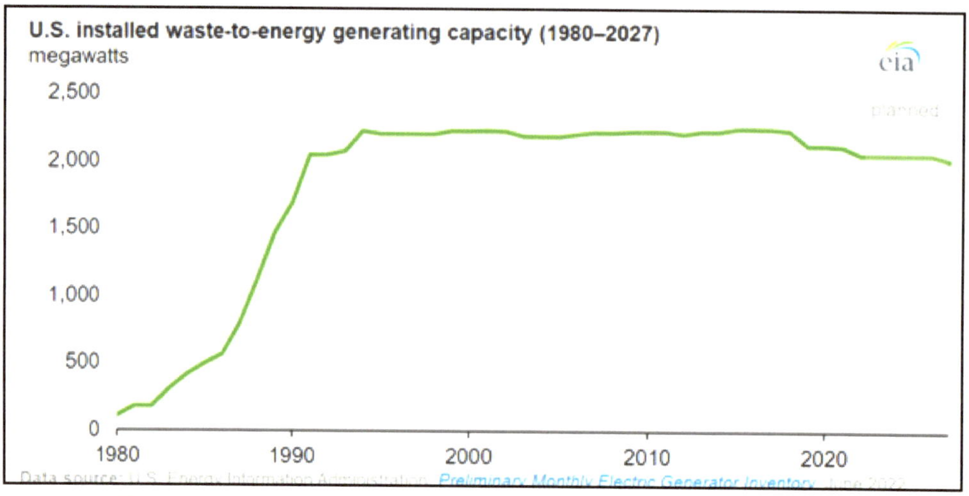

Fig: Waste-to-energy generating capacity in the United States

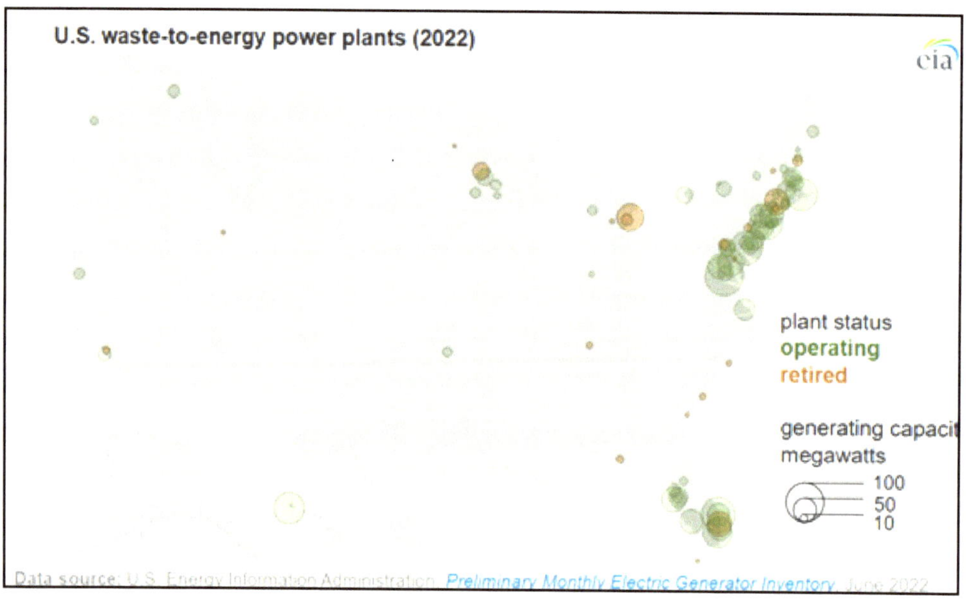

Fig: Waste-to-energy plants in the United States

Some of the newest plants use stoker technology and others use the advanced oxygen enrichment technology. Several treatment plants exist worldwide using relatively novel processes such as direct smelting, the Ebara fluidization process and the Thermoselect JFE gasification and melting technology process.

As of June 2014, Indonesia had a total of 93.5 MW installed capacity of waste-to-energy, with a pipeline of projects in different preparation phases together amounting to another 373MW of capacity.

Biofuel Energy Corporation of Denver, Colorado, opened two new biofuel plants in Wood River, Nebraska, and Fairmont, Minnesota, in July 2008. These plants use distillation to make ethanol for use in motor vehicles and other engines. Both plants are currently reported to be working at over 90% capacity.

Fulcrum BioEnergy, which started in 2007 in Pleasanton, California, built a WtE plant near Reno, NV to convert waste to sustainable aviation fuel (SAF). The plant was in commissioning from 2022 to May 2024 under the name Sierra BioFuels. Fulcrum predicted that the plant would produce approximately 10.5 million gallons per year of Fischer-Tropsch products from nearly 200,000 tons per year of MSW. The total exported product amounted to just 350 gallons of syncrude which were transported to Marathon Petroleum's refinery for conversion into jet fuel. The plant had issues including damage from unexpected generation of nitric acid and deposits of a concrete-like substance up to 10 feet thick in its gasification system. In 2024 Fulcrum BioEnergy ceased operations at the plant after defaulting on $290 million bonds issued through the Nevada Department of Business and Industry used to fund the plant's construction.

Waste-to-energy technology includes fermentation, which can take biomass and create ethanol, using waste cellulosic or organic material. In the fermentation process, the sugar in the waste is converted to carbon dioxide and alcohol, in the same general process that is used to make wine. Normally fermentation occurs with no air present.

Esterification can also be done using waste-to-energy technologies, and the result of this process is biodiesel. The cost-effectiveness of esterification will depend on the feedstock being used, and all the other relevant factors such as transportation distance, amount of oil present in the feedstock, and others. Gasification and pyrolysis by now can reach gross thermal conversion efficiencies (fuel to gas) up to 75%, however, a complete combustion is superior in terms of fuel conversion efficiency. Some pyrolysis processes need an outside heat source which may be supplied by the gasification process, making the combined process self-sustaining.

Carbon Dioxide Emissions

In thermal WtE technologies, nearly all of the carbon content in the waste is emitted as carbon dioxide (CO_2) to the atmosphere (when including final combustion of the products from pyrolysis and gasification; except when producing biochar for fertilizer). Municipal solid waste (MSW) contain approximately the same mass fraction of carbon as CO_2 itself (27%), so treatment of 1 metric ton (1.1 short tons) of MSW produce approximately 1 metric ton (1.1 short tons) of CO_2.

In the event that the waste was landfilled, 1 metric ton (1.1 short tons) of MSW would produce approximately 62 cubic metres (2,200 cu ft) methane via the anaerobic decomposition of the biodegradable part of the waste. This amount of methane has more than twice the global warming potential than the 1 metric ton (1.1 short tons) of CO_2, which would have been produced by combustion. In some countries, large amounts of landfill gas are collected. However, there is still the global warming potential of the landfill gas being emitted to atmosphere. For example, in the US in 1999 landfill gas emission was approximately 32% higher than the amount of CO_2 that would have been emitted by combustion.

In addition, nearly all biodegradable waste is biomass. That is, it has biological origin. This material has been formed by plants using atmospheric CO_2 typically within the last growing season. If these plants are regrown the CO_2 emitted from their combustion will be taken out from the atmosphere once more.

Such considerations are the main reason why several countries administrate WtE of the biomass part of waste as renewable energy. The rest—mainly plastics and other oil and gas derived products—is generally treated as non-renewables.

The CO_2 emissions from plastic waste-to-energy systems are higher than those from current fossil fuel-based power systems per unit of power generated, even after considering the contribution of carbon capture and storage. Power generation using plastic waste will significantly increase by 2050. Carbon must be separated during energy recovery processes. Otherwise, the fight against global warming would fail due to plastic waste.

Determination of the Biomass Fraction

MSW to a large extent is of biological origin (biogenic), e.g. paper, cardboard, wood, cloth, food scraps. Typically half of the energy content in MSW is from biogenic material. Consequently, this energy is often recognised as renewable energy according to the waste input. Several methods have been developed by the European CEN 343 working group to determine the biomass fraction of waste fuels, such as Refuse Derived Fuel/Solid Recovered Fuel. The initial two methods developed (CEN/TS 15440) were the manual sorting method and the selective dissolution method. A detailed systematic comparison of these two methods was published in 2010. Since each method suffered from limitations in properly characterizing the biomass fraction, two alternative methods have been developed.

The first method uses the principles of radiocarbon dating. A technical review (CEN/TR 15591:2007) outlining the carbon 14 method was published in 2007. A technical standard of the carbon dating method (CEN/TS 15747:2008) is published in 2008. In the United States, there is already an equivalent carbon 14 method under the standard method ASTM D6866.

The second method (so-called balance method) employs existing data on materials composition and operating conditions of the WtE plant and calculates the most probable result based on a mathematical-statistical model. Currently the balance method is installed at three Austrian and eight Danish incinerators.

A comparison between both methods carried out at three full-scale incinerators in Switzerland showed that both methods came to the same results.

Carbon 14 dating can determine with precision the biomass fraction of waste, and also determine the biomass calorific value. Determining the calorific value is important for green certificate programs such as the Renewable Obligation Certificate program in the United Kingdom. These programs award certificates based on the energy produced from biomass. Several research papers, including the one commissioned by the Renewable Energy Association in the UK, have been published that demonstrate how the carbon 14 result can be used to calculate the biomass calorific value. The UK gas and electricity markets authority, Ofgem, released a statement in 2011 accepting the use of Carbon 14 as a way to determine the biomass energy content of waste feedstock under their administration of the Renewables Obligation. Their Fuel Measurement and Sampling (FMS) questionnaire describes the information they look for when considering such proposals.

5.2.2 Technological Innovations in Waste Sorting and Recycling

The global increase in waste production presents significant environmental challenges, necessitating the development of efficient waste sorting and recycling systems. Traditional waste management methods struggle to cope with the volume and complexity of modern waste streams, leading to inefficient recycling rates and excessive landfill use. Technological innovations in waste sorting and recycling are transforming the industry by improving efficiency, reducing contamination, and enhancing material recovery. Advanced technologies such as artificial intelligence, robotics, chemical recycling, and blockchain-based waste tracking are playing a crucial role in optimizing waste management processes and contributing to a more sustainable circular economy.

Technological innovations in waste sorting and recycling are revolutionizing the way societies manage waste. AI-driven sorting systems, robotics, chemical recycling, IoT-enabled waste management, blockchain-based tracking, and big data analytics are enhancing efficiency, reducing environmental impact, and supporting the transition to a circular economy. While challenges remain, continued investment and collaboration will drive the adoption of these technologies, leading to more sustainable and effective waste management systems. By embracing innovation, societies can move closer to achieving zero waste and a more resource-efficient future.

The Role of Artificial Intelligence in Waste Sorting

Artificial intelligence (AI) is revolutionizing waste sorting by automating and optimizing the separation of different materials. AI-powered sorting systems use machine learning algorithms and computer vision to identify and classify waste based on material composition, color, and shape. High-speed cameras and sensors capture images of waste items as they move along conveyor belts, while AI algorithms analyze the data to sort materials into appropriate categories.

AI-driven sorting systems improve accuracy and efficiency in waste management facilities by reducing manual labor and minimizing contamination in recyclable streams. These systems can differentiate between various types of plastics, metals, glass, and paper with high precision, ensuring that valuable materials are properly recycled. Additionally, AI can be used to predict waste generation patterns and optimize collection routes, reducing operational costs and environmental impact.

Robotics and Automation in Recycling Facilities

Robotics is another key innovation enhancing waste sorting and recycling processes. Automated robotic arms equipped with AI-driven sensors and suction grippers can rapidly identify and pick recyclable materials from mixed waste streams. These robotic systems work faster and more accurately than human workers, increasing sorting efficiency and reducing health risks associated with manual waste handling. Advancements in robotic technology enable recycling facilities to adapt to changing waste compositions. Robots equipped with deep learning capabilities continuously improve their sorting accuracy by learning from new data. Some recycling plants have integrated fully automated systems where AI-powered robots perform the entire sorting process, eliminating the need for manual intervention.

In addition to waste sorting, automation is being used in the processing of recycled materials. Automated shredders, compactors, and pelletizers transform waste into reusable raw materials, streamlining the recycling supply chain. These innovations enhance the overall efficiency of recycling plants and improve the quality of recycled products.

Chemical Recycling for Enhanced Material Recovery

Chemical recycling is an emerging technology that addresses the limitations of traditional mechanical recycling. Unlike mechanical recycling, which degrades material quality over multiple cycles, chemical recycling breaks down waste into its molecular components, enabling the production of high-quality recycled materials.

Chemical recycling technologies, such as pyrolysis and depolymerization, convert plastic waste into raw chemicals and fuels. These processes allow plastics that are traditionally difficult to recycle, such as multilayer packaging and mixed polymer waste, to be transformed into valuable resources. The ability to recover materials at the molecular level reduces dependence on virgin raw materials and supports the development of a circular economy.

Despite its potential, chemical recycling faces challenges such as high energy consumption and scalability issues. Ongoing research and investment in renewable energy sources aim to make chemical recycling more sustainable and economically viable. As technology advances, chemical recycling is expected to play a crucial role in reducing plastic waste and increasing recycling rates worldwide.

Smart Waste Bins and IoT-Enabled Waste Management

The Internet of Things (IoT) is transforming waste management by enabling real-time monitoring and optimization of waste collection and sorting processes. Smart waste bins equipped with sensors and connectivity features provide data on fill levels, waste composition, and disposal patterns. This information helps municipalities and waste management companies optimize collection schedules, reducing fuel consumption and operational costs. IoT-enabled waste management systems integrate with AI and data analytics to improve efficiency. Predictive analytics can forecast waste generation trends, allowing cities to allocate resources more effectively. Additionally, smart bins with automated sorting capabilities encourage proper waste disposal by guiding users to separate recyclables from general waste. IoT technology also enhances transparency in the recycling process. By tracking waste from its source to recycling facilities, stakeholders can ensure compliance with sustainability regulations and improve the accountability of waste management systems. These innovations contribute to higher recycling rates and reduced landfill use.

Blockchain for Transparent and Efficient Recycling

Blockchain technology is emerging as a solution for tracking and verifying recycling efforts. By creating decentralized and tamper-proof records, blockchain enhances transparency and accountability in waste management. Waste tracking systems based on blockchain provide real-time data on material flows, ensuring that recyclables reach the appropriate processing facilities. One application of blockchain in recycling is the implementation of digital recycling incentives. Individuals and businesses that recycle can earn digital tokens or credits, which can be exchanged for rewards or used to offset waste management costs. These incentive programs encourage greater participation in recycling initiatives and promote a culture of sustainability. Blockchain also facilitates circular supply chain management by enabling manufacturers to trace the origin of recycled materials. This ensures the integrity of recycled content in new products and helps companies meet sustainability commitments. As blockchain adoption increases, its integration with waste management systems is expected to enhance efficiency and foster trust among stakeholders.

The Role of Big Data in Waste Management Optimization

Big data analytics is transforming waste management by providing actionable insights into waste generation, sorting, and recycling trends. By analyzing large volumes of data, waste management companies can identify inefficiencies, optimize logistics, and improve material recovery rates.

Data-driven waste sorting systems leverage machine learning to refine classification algorithms and enhance sorting accuracy. Real-time data monitoring enables facilities to detect contamination in recycling streams and take corrective actions promptly. Additionally, big data analytics supports policy development by providing governments with evidence-based recommendations for waste reduction and recycling strategies. Predictive modeling based on big data helps municipalities anticipate waste generation patterns and plan infrastructure investments accordingly. By leveraging data-driven decision-making, cities can design smarter waste management systems that minimize environmental impact and improve resource efficiency.

Challenges and Future Prospects

While technological innovations in waste sorting and recycling offer numerous benefits, challenges remain in their widespread adoption. High implementation costs, technical complexities, and the need for regulatory support can hinder the deployment of advanced waste management technologies. Additionally, public awareness and participation in recycling programs play a crucial role in ensuring the success of these innovations.

The future of waste sorting and recycling lies in continued technological advancements and increased collaboration among stakeholders. Governments, businesses, and research institutions must invest in research and development to improve the scalability and efficiency of emerging technologies. Policies that incentivize innovation and sustainable waste management practices will further accelerate progress in the field.

Advancements in nanotechnology, biodegradable materials, and artificial intelligence are expected to drive the next wave of innovation in waste recycling. The integration of smart technologies with circular economy principles will create a more sustainable waste management system, reducing landfill dependency and maximizing resource recovery.

5.3 PLASTIC WASTE AND CIRCULAR ECONOMY SOLUTIONS

5.3.1 Reducing Single-Use Plastics

Single-use plastics have become one of the most pressing environmental issues of the modern era. These disposable plastic products, including straws, cutlery, shopping bags, and food packaging, contribute significantly to global pollution. Their widespread use, combined with their resistance to degradation, leads to the accumulation of plastic waste in landfills, oceans, and natural ecosystems. Addressing this crisis requires urgent action through policy changes, consumer behavior shifts, corporate responsibility, and innovative alternatives. Reducing single-use plastics is essential to protect the environment, conserve resources, and mitigate the adverse effects of plastic pollution on human health and biodiversity.

Reducing single-use plastics is an urgent environmental priority that requires action at multiple levels. Government regulations, corporate sustainability initiatives, technological advancements, and individual behavior changes all play essential roles in mitigating plastic pollution. While challenges remain, continued progress in innovation and policy development offers hope for a future with reduced plastic dependency. Through collective efforts, society can move toward sustainable waste management practices and a healthier planet free from the burden of single-use plastics.

The Environmental Impact of Single-Use Plastics

The environmental consequences of single-use plastics are severe. These plastics take hundreds of years to decompose, breaking down into microplastics that infiltrate soil, water, and even the food chain. Marine ecosystems suffer extensively from plastic pollution, as discarded plastics are ingested by marine animals, leading to injuries, poisoning, and death. Birds, fish, and mammals often mistake plastic debris for food, which results in fatal consequences due to blockages or chemical contamination.

Beyond marine pollution, the production and disposal of single-use plastics contribute to greenhouse gas emissions. The extraction and refinement of fossil fuels for plastic production require significant energy, releasing carbon dioxide and other pollutants into the atmosphere. Additionally, plastic waste incineration further exacerbates air pollution, posing health risks to surrounding communities. Reducing single-use plastics is crucial for addressing climate change and protecting environmental integrity.

Policy and Legislation to Reduce Single-Use Plastics

Governments around the world have begun implementing policies to limit single-use plastics and encourage sustainable alternatives. Bans on plastic bags, straws, and cutlery have been introduced in various countries, compelling businesses and consumers to transition to reusable or biodegradable options. Regulatory measures such as extended producer responsibility (EPR) require manufacturers to take accountability for the lifecycle of their plastic products, ensuring proper waste management and recycling.

Taxation on plastic products is another strategy used to reduce consumption. By imposing levies on plastic packaging and disposable items, policymakers can incentivize businesses to invest in sustainable materials. Some governments have also introduced deposit-return schemes for plastic bottles, encouraging consumers to return used containers for recycling.

International agreements play a vital role in tackling the plastic crisis. The United Nations has proposed global frameworks for plastic waste reduction, fostering collaboration among nations to develop effective solutions. These policies, combined with corporate sustainability commitments, are critical to driving long-term reductions in single-use plastics.

Corporate Responsibility and Sustainable Alternatives

Businesses play a significant role in the transition away from single-use plastics. Many corporations are adopting eco-friendly practices by eliminating unnecessary plastic packaging and investing in biodegradable or compostable materials. Some companies have replaced plastic straws and cutlery with alternatives made from bamboo, metal, or paper, reducing the environmental impact of disposable products. The shift towards reusable packaging is gaining traction in industries such as food and beverage, cosmetics, and retail. Brands are increasingly offering refillable containers and encouraging customers to bring their own reusable bags, bottles, and cups. By prioritizing sustainable supply chains and circular economy principles, businesses can significantly reduce plastic waste.

Innovation in material science is also contributing to plastic reduction efforts. Researchers are developing biodegradable plastics derived from natural sources such as cornstarch, seaweed, and fungi. These materials decompose more rapidly than traditional plastics, minimizing long-term environmental harm. However, the widespread adoption of biodegradable alternatives requires investment in composting infrastructure and waste management systems to ensure proper disposal.

Consumer Behavior and the Role of Individuals

Consumer awareness and behavior play a crucial role in reducing single-use plastics. Simple lifestyle changes, such as carrying reusable bags, water bottles, and coffee cups, significantly decrease plastic waste. Individuals can also opt for products with minimal or plastic-free packaging and support brands committed to sustainability. Educational campaigns and social movements have been instrumental in promoting plastic-free lifestyles. Grassroots organizations and environmental activists raise awareness about the harmful effects of plastics and advocate for responsible consumption. Social media platforms amplify these messages, inspiring collective action against plastic pollution.

Consumer pressure has led to policy changes and corporate accountability, demonstrating the power of informed purchasing decisions. By choosing sustainable alternatives and supporting businesses that prioritize plastic reduction, individuals contribute to the broader effort of mitigating plastic pollution.

The Role of Technology and Innovation in Plastic Reduction

Technological advancements offer promising solutions to reduce plastic dependency. Waste-to-energy technologies convert plastic waste into renewable energy sources, reducing landfill accumulation and fossil fuel reliance. Recycling innovations, such as chemical recycling and AI-powered sorting systems, enhance material recovery and improve the efficiency of plastic waste management.

Smart packaging solutions are being developed to minimize waste while preserving product quality. Edible packaging made from seaweed or starch-based films provides an alternative to plastic wrappers, particularly in the food industry. Water-soluble packaging materials dissolve in water without leaving harmful residues, offering a sustainable option for single-use applications.

Blockchain technology is also being explored to track and authenticate recycled materials, ensuring transparency in supply chains. By integrating digital solutions into waste management systems, stakeholders can enhance plastic recovery efforts and promote circular economy practices.

Challenges and Barriers to Plastic Reduction

Despite progress in plastic reduction initiatives, challenges remain in achieving large-scale change. The affordability and convenience of single-use plastics continue to drive consumption, particularly in developing countries where alternatives may be expensive or inaccessible. The lack of robust waste management infrastructure further exacerbates plastic pollution, as many regions struggle to implement effective recycling programs.

Resistance from industries reliant on plastic production presents another obstacle. The petrochemical sector, which profits from plastic manufacturing, often lobbies against regulatory measures aimed at reducing plastic use. Overcoming these barriers requires strong policy enforcement, financial incentives for sustainable alternatives, and public-private collaboration to drive systemic change.

Misinformation about biodegradable plastics also poses a challenge. Some biodegradable materials require specific conditions to break down properly, and without appropriate composting facilities, they may persist in the environment like conventional plastics. Clear labeling and consumer education are essential to ensure the responsible disposal of eco-friendly materials.

The Future of Single-Use Plastic Reduction

The future of single-use plastic reduction depends on continued innovation, policy development, and consumer participation. Governments must strengthen regulatory frameworks to limit plastic production and promote circular economy models. Businesses should accelerate their commitment to sustainable practices, while technological advancements will further improve waste management solutions. Public awareness campaigns will remain vital in driving behavioral change. Educational initiatives in schools, media, and community programs can instill sustainable habits from an early age. Collaboration among governments, industries, and environmental organizations is necessary to create scalable solutions that effectively reduce plastic waste. The transition to a plastic-free society requires collective effort. By adopting sustainable practices, supporting policy reforms, and investing in alternative materials, global communities can significantly reduce single-use plastics and protect the planet for future generations.

5.3.2 Innovations in Biodegradable Plastics and Packaging

The rise in plastic pollution has led to significant environmental concerns, prompting researchers and industries to seek sustainable alternatives. Biodegradable plastics and innovative packaging solutions offer a promising approach to reducing waste and minimizing the ecological footprint of plastic materials. These advancements in biodegradable plastics aim to replace conventional petroleum-based plastics, which persist in the environment for centuries.

Innovations in biodegradable plastics and packaging offer a viable path toward reducing plastic pollution and promoting sustainability. The development of plant-based, water-soluble, and nanotechnology-enhanced packaging materials demonstrates the potential of these alternatives in various industries. While challenges such as waste management infrastructure and production costs remain, continued research and policy support will drive the adoption of biodegradable plastics on a larger scale. By embracing these innovations, society can move towards a more circular economy, reducing environmental impact and preserving natural resources for future generations.

Understanding Biodegradable Plastics

Biodegradable plastics are designed to break down naturally into water, carbon dioxide, and biomass when exposed to specific environmental conditions. Unlike traditional plastics, which accumulate in landfills and oceans, biodegradable plastics decompose through microbial activity, reducing long-term environmental harm. These plastics are often derived from renewable sources such as corn starch, sugarcane, and cellulose, making them a viable alternative to fossil fuel-based plastics. There are different types of biodegradable plastics, including polylactic acid (PLA), polyhydroxyalkanoates (PHA), and polybutylene adipate terephthalate (PBAT). PLA is one of the most commonly used biodegradable plastics, often found in food packaging and disposable cutlery. PHA, produced by bacterial fermentation, is known for its high biodegradability in marine and soil environments. PBAT, a flexible and compostable plastic, is frequently used in agricultural films and compostable bags. The effectiveness of these materials depends on proper disposal methods, as industrial composting facilities are often required to ensure complete degradation.

Innovations in Biodegradable Packaging Materials

Recent advancements in biodegradable packaging materials have focused on enhancing durability, functionality, and sustainability. Researchers are exploring novel biopolymers and plant-based materials to create packaging that decomposes efficiently without compromising performance. Edible packaging made from seaweed, starch, and gelatin is gaining traction as a sustainable alternative to single-use plastic wrappers. These materials not only reduce plastic waste but also provide additional nutritional benefits. Another breakthrough in biodegradable packaging is the development of water-soluble films. These films, made from polyvinyl alcohol (PVA) and other biodegradable compounds, dissolve in water without leaving toxic residues. They are increasingly used in detergent pods, food packaging, and medical applications. Additionally, mushroom-based packaging, created from mycelium, offers a durable and compostable alternative to Styrofoam. Mycelium packaging is grown from agricultural waste and decomposes naturally within weeks, making it an environmentally friendly option for protective packaging.

Advancements in nanotechnology have also contributed to biodegradable packaging innovations. Nanocellulose, a lightweight and biodegradable material derived from plant fibers, is being used to enhance the barrier properties of packaging materials. This innovation improves moisture resistance and extends the shelf life of perishable products, reducing food waste while maintaining sustainability.

Challenges in the Adoption of Biodegradable Plastics

Despite the promising potential of biodegradable plastics, several challenges hinder their widespread adoption. One of the primary concerns is the lack of proper waste management infrastructure. Many biodegradable plastics require industrial composting facilities to decompose fully, but such facilities are not widely available. When these materials end up in regular landfills or oceans, their degradation process slows significantly, diminishing their environmental benefits.

Another challenge is the cost of production. Biodegradable plastics are generally more expensive to manufacture than traditional plastics due to the high costs of raw materials and processing technologies. This price difference makes it difficult for biodegradable plastics to compete with conventional plastic products, limiting their accessibility and market penetration. Misinformation and labeling issues also pose challenges. Many consumers mistakenly believe that biodegradable plastics will degrade naturally in any environment, leading to improper disposal practices. Clear labeling and public awareness campaigns are essential to educate consumers on the correct disposal methods and the environmental impact of biodegradable plastics.

The Future of Biodegradable Plastics and Packaging

The future of biodegradable plastics and packaging lies in continued research and technological advancements. Scientists are working on developing next-generation bioplastics that degrade more efficiently in natural environments. Innovations such as enzyme-infused plastics, which accelerate decomposition, and microbial-engineered plastics, which break down more rapidly, are promising solutions for addressing plastic pollution.

Governments and industries are also playing a crucial role in promoting biodegradable packaging. Policy interventions, such as bans on single-use plastics and incentives for sustainable packaging alternatives, are encouraging businesses to adopt biodegradable solutions. Companies in the food, cosmetics, and retail industries are increasingly investing in eco-friendly packaging to meet consumer demand for sustainability.

Collaboration between researchers, policymakers, and industries will be essential in scaling up biodegradable plastic solutions. By improving production efficiency, expanding composting infrastructure, and enhancing material properties, biodegradable plastics can become a mainstream alternative to conventional plastics, contributing to a cleaner and more sustainable planet.

5.4 CIRCULAR ECONOMY IN E-WASTE MANAGEMENT

5.4.1 Recycling of Rare Earth Metals and Electronics Components

Rare earth metals are critical elements used in a wide range of technological applications, including smartphones, electric vehicles, wind turbines, and medical devices. These metals, such as neodymium, dysprosium, and terbium, are essential for producing high-performance magnets, batteries, and advanced electronics. However, their extraction and processing have significant environmental and geopolitical challenges. Recycling rare earth metals from electronic waste offers a sustainable solution to reduce dependency on mining, mitigate environmental impacts, and secure a stable supply of these valuable resources.

Recycling rare earth metals and electronic components is a crucial step in addressing resource scarcity, environmental degradation, and supply chain vulnerabilities. While challenges exist, technological advancements, policy interventions, and industry initiatives are driving progress toward a more sustainable approach to rare earth metal recovery. By integrating innovative recycling methods, expanding infrastructure, and promoting responsible consumption, societies can reduce dependence on mining and contribute to a circular economy. As global demand for rare earth metals continues to grow, investing in efficient recycling solutions will be essential for building a resilient and sustainable future.

The Importance of Rare Earth Metal Recycling

The demand for rare earth metals is rapidly increasing due to technological advancements and the transition to green energy solutions. However, their extraction is concentrated in a few countries, leading to supply chain vulnerabilities. Mining rare earth metals requires extensive land use, energy consumption, and chemical processing, which contribute to soil degradation, water pollution, and greenhouse gas emissions. Recycling these materials from end-of-life electronic devices can significantly reduce the ecological footprint of rare earth metal production while addressing supply shortages and geopolitical risks.

Recovering rare earth metals from discarded electronics also helps in reducing electronic waste, which has become a growing environmental concern. Millions of tons of e-waste are generated annually, much of which ends up in landfills or is improperly disposed of, leading to hazardous chemical leaching and pollution. By implementing efficient recycling systems, valuable materials can be reclaimed and reintegrated into the production cycle, promoting a circular economy.

Challenges in Recycling Rare Earth Metals

Despite the benefits, recycling rare earth metals presents significant challenges. One of the primary obstacles is the complexity of extracting these elements from electronic waste. Rare earth metals are often used in small quantities and embedded in complex components, making their recovery technically demanding and costly. Traditional recycling methods, such as shredding and smelting, are not effective in separating these metals without significant material loss.

Another challenge is the lack of standardized collection and recycling infrastructure. Many electronic devices are not designed for easy disassembly, and the absence of efficient take-back programs leads to low recycling rates. Consumers often discard old electronics without proper disposal, further complicating the recovery process. Additionally, the economic viability of rare earth metal recycling remains a concern, as the costs associated with extraction and refinement often exceed those of primary mining.

Innovations in Rare Earth Metal Recycling

Recent advancements in recycling technologies are improving the efficiency and feasibility of rare earth metal recovery. Hydrometallurgical processes, which use chemical leaching to extract metals, have shown promise in separating rare earth elements from electronic waste with minimal environmental impact. Researchers are also exploring bioleaching techniques, where microorganisms break down materials to release rare earth metals, offering an eco-friendly alternative to traditional extraction methods.

Solvent extraction and electrochemical separation are other emerging methods that enhance the purity and recovery rate of rare earth metals. These techniques enable the selective separation of specific elements, reducing contamination and improving material reuse. Additionally, closed-loop recycling systems, where manufacturers design products with easy recyclability in mind, are gaining attention as a strategy to enhance material recovery. Artificial intelligence and machine learning are also being integrated into recycling operations to optimize sorting and material identification. Automated dismantling and robotics-assisted processing improve efficiency, ensuring that valuable components are recovered with precision. These innovations are paving the way for a more sustainable and economically viable approach to rare earth metal recycling.

The Role of Policy and Industry Initiatives

Governments and industries play a crucial role in promoting rare earth metal recycling through policy measures and corporate responsibility programs. Regulatory frameworks that mandate e-waste collection, recycling targets, and extended producer responsibility (EPR) are essential for increasing recycling rates. Countries such as the European Union, Japan, and the United States have implemented policies that encourage rare earth metal recovery through strict e-waste management regulations. Industry leaders are also investing in closed-loop supply chains to reduce dependence on newly mined materials. Tech companies, automotive manufacturers, and renewable energy firms are exploring partnerships with recycling facilities to recover critical metals from end-of-life products. Some businesses have introduced buyback and refurbishment programs to extend product life cycles and facilitate material recovery. International cooperation is also necessary to address global supply chain challenges. Rare earth metal recycling requires cross-border collaboration to ensure efficient collection, processing, and redistribution. Initiatives that promote knowledge sharing, research funding, and sustainable sourcing agreements can accelerate progress in establishing a robust recycling ecosystem.

Future Prospects of Rare Earth Metal Recycling

The future of rare earth metal recycling depends on continued innovation, policy support, and consumer participation. Advancements in green chemistry and sustainable extraction techniques will further enhance the efficiency and environmental impact of recycling processes. Developing scalable and cost-effective solutions is crucial to making rare earth metal recycling a mainstream practice.

Consumer awareness and participation are also key factors in driving change. Encouraging responsible disposal and e-waste collection through education campaigns and incentive programs can improve recycling rates. By fostering a circular economy mindset, societies can reduce waste generation and make better use of existing resources.

Incorporating design-for-recycling principles into product development will also shape the future of rare earth metal recovery. Electronics and battery manufacturers must prioritize modular and easily recyclable designs to facilitate material extraction. By aligning technological advancements with sustainable practices, the industry can transition toward a more resource-efficient future.

5.4.2 The Role of Extended Producer Responsibility (EPR) in E-Waste

Extended Producer Responsibility (EPR) is a crucial policy approach that holds manufacturers accountable for the entire lifecycle of their products, particularly in managing electronic waste (e-waste). With the rapid increase in electronic consumption and technological advancements, the accumulation of e-waste has become a significant environmental challenge. EPR is designed to shift the responsibility of waste management from consumers and governments to producers, ensuring that manufacturers take an active role in the collection, recycling, and proper disposal of their products.

One of the key aspects of EPR is the financial and operational responsibility placed on manufacturers. They are required to set up collection mechanisms, fund recycling programs, and comply with regulations to prevent illegal dumping of e-waste. This not only reduces the burden on municipal waste management systems but also promotes a circular economy by encouraging resource recovery and reducing the need for raw material extraction. Countries with well-established EPR frameworks, such as those in the European Union, have witnessed higher e-waste collection rates and increased investment in recycling infrastructure. Such policies also create economic opportunities by fostering industries involved in refurbishing, repairing, and recycling electronic products.

EPR also plays a vital role in mitigating environmental and health hazards associated with e-waste. Electronic products contain toxic elements such as lead, mercury, and cadmium, which can contaminate soil and water if not disposed of properly. Through strict regulations and incentives, EPR encourages producers to eliminate hazardous substances from their products and adopt safer disposal methods. Additionally, consumers benefit from improved recycling accessibility, as manufacturers often provide take-back schemes and drop-off points for old electronics. This not only enhances responsible consumer behavior but also strengthens the efficiency of waste management systems.

Despite its benefits, the successful implementation of EPR faces challenges, including regulatory loopholes, inadequate enforcement, and varying levels of compliance among producers. In many developing countries, informal recycling sectors handle a significant portion of e-waste, often under unsafe conditions. To address these issues, governments need to strengthen EPR policies through stringent monitoring, incentives for compliance, and public awareness campaigns. Collaboration between policymakers, manufacturers, and consumers is essential to ensure the effectiveness of EPR in tackling the global e-waste crisis. By holding producers accountable and promoting sustainable practices, EPR serves as a powerful tool in achieving environmental sustainability and responsible electronic waste management.

5.5 CIRCULAR ECONOMY IN FOOD WASTE REDUCTION

5.5.1 Reducing Food Waste in Households and Retail

Food waste is a significant global issue that affects both households and the retail sector. It contributes to environmental degradation, economic losses, and food insecurity. Reducing food waste requires a combination of awareness, responsible consumption, and efficient supply chain management. Households and retailers play a crucial role in addressing this challenge by adopting strategies that minimize waste and promote sustainability.

Reducing food waste in households and retail requires a collective effort from consumers, businesses, and policymakers. By implementing practical strategies such as proper meal planning, storage, and responsible purchasing, households can significantly minimize waste. Retailers, on the other hand, can adopt better inventory practices, promote the sale of near-expiry products, and support food donation initiatives. Addressing food waste not only helps reduce environmental impact but also ensures that food resources are used efficiently to benefit society as a whole.

Causes of Food Waste in Households

Food waste at the household level often results from over-purchasing, improper storage, and a lack of meal planning. Consumers frequently buy more food than they can consume before it spoils, leading to unnecessary waste. Misinterpretation of expiration labels such as "best before" and "use by" also contributes to discarding food that is still safe to eat. Additionally, improper storage conditions can cause food to spoil prematurely, reducing its shelf life. Cultural habits, such as serving large portions and not utilizing leftovers, further exacerbate the problem.

Strategies to Reduce Household Food Waste

To reduce food waste, households can adopt simple yet effective strategies such as meal planning, proper storage, and mindful consumption. Planning meals in advance helps avoid impulse purchases and ensures that all ingredients are used efficiently. Storing food correctly, such as keeping perishable items at the right temperature and using airtight containers, extends freshness. Understanding food labels can prevent unnecessary disposal of edible products. Additionally, repurposing leftovers into new meals and donating surplus food to local food banks can significantly minimize waste. Raising awareness about the impact of food waste and encouraging responsible consumer behavior is essential in addressing this issue.

Food Waste in the Retail Sector

Retail businesses also contribute significantly to food waste due to overstocking, cosmetic standards, and inefficient inventory management. Supermarkets often discard products that are close to their expiration date, even if they are still safe for consumption. Strict aesthetic requirements for fruits and vegetables lead to the rejection of perfectly edible but slightly imperfect produce. Overstocking shelves to create an impression of abundance often results in unsold food being discarded. These practices not only lead to financial losses for retailers but also contribute to environmental harm.

Solutions for Retailers to Minimize Food Waste

Retailers can implement several strategies to reduce food waste, including improved inventory management, discounting near-expiry products, and donating surplus food. Using data analytics to track demand patterns helps retailers stock appropriate quantities and avoid over-purchasing. Offering discounts on items nearing their expiration date encourages consumers to buy them before they go to waste. Partnering with food banks and organizations that redistribute excess food to those in need is another effective way to reduce waste. Additionally, embracing "ugly produce" campaigns and educating consumers on the importance of buying imperfect but edible fruits and vegetables can help reduce waste at the source.

5.5.2 Innovative Technologies for Food Recovery and Recycling

Food waste is a growing global challenge, with millions of tons discarded every year, contributing to environmental degradation and food insecurity. Innovative technologies for food recovery and recycling offer sustainable solutions to minimize waste and repurpose surplus food. These advancements help optimize food distribution, convert waste into valuable resources, and promote a circular economy.

Innovative technologies for food recovery and recycling are essential in tackling the global food waste crisis. Smart tracking systems, digital food redistribution platforms, bioconversion methods, and upcycling initiatives contribute to a more sustainable food system. By adopting these technologies, businesses and consumers can reduce waste, conserve resources, and support environmental sustainability. The integration of technology in food recovery and recycling not only minimizes waste but also drives economic growth and strengthens food security worldwide.

Smart Food Tracking and Waste Prevention

One of the most effective ways to reduce food waste is through smart food tracking technologies that help monitor inventory and expiration dates. Artificial intelligence (AI) and the Internet of Things (IoT) enable real-time tracking of food products in households, restaurants, and retail stores. Smart refrigerators and mobile apps provide alerts when food is nearing expiration, encouraging timely consumption. Supermarkets and food service providers use AI-powered inventory systems to forecast demand accurately, preventing overstocking and ensuring that perishable goods are sold before they spoil. These technologies enhance efficiency and reduce unnecessary food waste at various points in the supply chain.

Food Recovery and Redistribution Platforms

Digital platforms play a crucial role in food recovery by connecting surplus food with those in need. Mobile applications and online networks facilitate the donation of excess food from restaurants, supermarkets, and households to food banks and charities. Apps like Too Good To Go and Olio allow consumers and businesses to sell or give away food at reduced prices rather than discarding it. Blockchain technology enhances food traceability, ensuring that recovered food meets safety standards and reaches beneficiaries efficiently. By streamlining food donation processes, technology bridges the gap between surplus food and food insecurity.

Bioconversion and Composting Innovations

Advancements in bioconversion and composting technologies enable the transformation of food waste into valuable byproducts. Anaerobic digestion systems break down organic waste to produce biogas, which can be used as a renewable energy source. Insect-based bioconversion, where food waste is fed to black soldier fly larvae, produces high-protein animal feed and organic fertilizer. Smart composting machines accelerate the decomposition process, turning food scraps into nutrient-rich compost for agricultural use. These innovations support waste reduction while contributing to sustainable energy production and soil enrichment.

Food Waste Upcycling and Alternative Products

Upcycling technologies repurpose food waste into new products, reducing environmental impact and creating economic opportunities. Food manufacturers use surplus ingredients to develop innovative products such as protein powders, plant-based snacks, and beverages. Fruit and vegetable peels are processed into natural food additives, while coffee grounds and bread waste are converted into bio-based materials. Startups and research institutions are exploring ways to extract valuable compounds from food waste for use in cosmetics, pharmaceuticals, and packaging materials. These innovations demonstrate how food waste can be transformed into sustainable and marketable solutions.

5.5.3 The Role of Circular Business Models in Reducing Food Loss

Food loss is a major global concern that affects food security, environmental sustainability, and economic stability. Traditional linear business models, which follow a "take-make-dispose" approach, contribute significantly to food waste at various stages of the supply chain. Circular business models, on the other hand, focus on resource efficiency, waste minimization, and the continual use of food products and byproducts.

The adoption of circular business models is a powerful strategy for reducing food loss and promoting sustainability in the food industry. By focusing on supply chain efficiency, food recovery, upcycling, and consumer engagement, businesses can create a closed-loop system that minimizes waste and maximizes resource use. These models not only benefit the environment but also enhance economic resilience and food security. As more companies embrace circular practices, the food industry moves closer to a future where food loss is significantly reduced, and resources are used more responsibly.

Sustainable Supply Chain Management

One of the key aspects of circular business models is the implementation of sustainable supply chain practices that minimize food loss at the production, distribution, and retail levels. Businesses are adopting precision agriculture techniques, such as AI-driven crop monitoring and smart irrigation, to optimize food production and prevent unnecessary losses. Improved storage and transportation technologies, including cold chain logistics and smart packaging, help extend the shelf life of perishable goods. Companies also collaborate with farmers to develop innovative harvesting methods that reduce losses in the field. By prioritizing efficiency in the supply chain, circular models ensure that food resources are utilized effectively.

Food Recovery and Redistribution Initiatives

Circular business models promote food recovery and redistribution as a strategy to prevent surplus food from being wasted. Many companies partner with food banks, social enterprises, and redistribution platforms to donate excess food to those in need. Digital applications facilitate the connection between food producers, retailers, and consumers, ensuring that edible food is repurposed instead of discarded. Restaurants and supermarkets are adopting dynamic pricing strategies, where near-expiry products are sold at discounted rates to encourage consumption. These initiatives not only reduce food loss but also contribute to social responsibility by addressing hunger and food insecurity.

Upcycling Food Waste into New Products

A core principle of circular business models is upcycling food waste into valuable products. Food manufacturers and startups are repurposing surplus ingredients to create innovative food items, such as protein powders from fruit peels, vegetable-based snacks, and sustainable beverages. Breweries use leftover bread to produce beer, while coffee companies repurpose used coffee grounds for skincare and bio-based packaging. By transforming food waste into marketable products, businesses reduce environmental impact while generating new revenue streams. Upcycling supports a circular food economy by ensuring that food byproducts are continuously utilized rather than discarded.

The Role of Consumer Engagement and Education

Circular business models emphasize consumer participation in reducing food loss through awareness and behavioral change. Businesses are investing in educational campaigns that inform consumers about proper food storage, expiration labels, and sustainable consumption habits. Some companies provide incentives for customers who return food packaging, participate in composting programs, or purchase imperfect produce. Subscription-based meal kits help consumers plan meals efficiently, minimizing food waste at home. By actively engaging consumers, businesses create a culture of sustainability that reinforces circular economy principles.

CHAPTER 6

Policy and Regulatory Frameworks for Circular Economy

6.1 GOVERNMENT POLICIES AND CIRCULAR ECONOMY PROMOTION

6.1.1 National Circular Economy Strategies

A circular economy is an economic system designed to minimize waste, maximize resource efficiency, and promote sustainability by keeping products and materials in use for as long as possible. Many countries are adopting national circular economy strategies to transition from traditional linear economic models, which follow a "take-make-dispose" pattern, to more regenerative and resource-efficient systems. These strategies aim to reduce environmental impact, strengthen economic resilience, and foster innovation in waste management, production, and consumption.

National circular economy strategies are vital for creating a sustainable future by reducing waste, optimizing resource use, and promoting economic resilience. Through policy frameworks, technological innovation, sustainable consumption initiatives, and collaborative efforts, governments can drive the transition towards circularity. As more nations adopt and refine their circular economy strategies, the global economy moves closer to a system where environmental sustainability and economic prosperity go hand in hand.

Policy Frameworks and Legislative Support

Governments play a crucial role in shaping circular economy strategies through policy frameworks and regulations that encourage sustainable practices. Many countries have introduced national action plans, legal mandates, and incentives to promote circularity in industries such as manufacturing, agriculture, and construction. The European Union's Circular Economy Action Plan sets ambitious targets for waste reduction, sustainable product design, and recycling initiatives. China's Circular Economy Promotion Law emphasizes resource efficiency in industrial processes, while Japan's Sound Material-Cycle Society policy focuses on waste prevention and material reuse. Strong regulatory frameworks ensure that businesses and consumers actively participate in circular economy initiatives.

Innovation and Industrial Transformation

National circular economy strategies emphasize technological innovation and industrial transformation to reduce resource consumption and waste generation. Governments invest in research and development to support eco-friendly production processes, bio-based materials, and smart waste management systems. Advanced recycling technologies, such as chemical recycling and bioconversion, enhance material recovery and extend product lifecycles. Industrial symbiosis, where waste from one industry becomes a resource for another, fosters collaboration and minimizes environmental impact. Countries with strong innovation ecosystems encourage businesses to integrate circularity into their operations, driving economic growth while reducing waste.

Sustainable Consumption and Waste Reduction

Promoting sustainable consumption is a key aspect of national circular economy strategies. Governments implement awareness campaigns, educational programs, and incentive-based policies to encourage responsible consumer behavior. Initiatives such as extended producer responsibility (EPR) ensure that manufacturers take accountability for the lifecycle of their products, including recycling and disposal. Bans on single-use plastics, deposit-return schemes for beverage containers, and food waste reduction programs help minimize waste at the consumer level. By fostering a culture of sustainability, national strategies empower individuals to make environmentally conscious choices.

Public-Private Partnerships and Global Collaboration

Collaboration between governments, businesses, and international organizations is essential for the success of circular economy strategies. Many countries establish public-private partnerships to accelerate circular initiatives, promote sustainable investments, and develop infrastructure for waste management and recycling. Global cooperation through platforms such as the United Nations' Sustainable Development Goals (SDGs) and the Ellen MacArthur Foundation strengthens knowledge-sharing and policy alignment across nations. By working together, countries can address global challenges such as resource depletion, climate change, and pollution through circular economy principles.

6.1.2 Regulatory Instruments: Incentives, Taxation, and Standards

Regulatory instruments play a crucial role in shaping economic and environmental policies by influencing business practices, consumer behavior, and market dynamics. Among these instruments, incentives, taxation, and standards are widely used to promote sustainability, economic growth, and social well-being. Governments implement these measures to encourage compliance, drive innovation, and balance economic development with environmental responsibility.

Regulatory instruments such as incentives, taxation, and standards are key tools for promoting sustainable economic practices and responsible environmental management. By offering financial support, imposing taxes on harmful activities, and setting compliance standards, governments can influence market behavior and drive the transition towards sustainability. Effective policy integration and enforcement ensure that these instruments contribute to long-term economic resilience and environmental protection. As regulatory frameworks continue to evolve, they will play an increasingly vital role in shaping a sustainable and equitable future.

Incentives for Sustainable Practices

Incentives are financial and policy-driven tools designed to encourage businesses and individuals to adopt environmentally friendly and socially responsible practices. Governments offer subsidies, grants, and tax credits to companies investing in renewable energy, clean technologies, and circular economy initiatives. Incentive programs also support research and development in sectors such as green manufacturing, sustainable agriculture, and waste management. For consumers, incentives like rebates on electric vehicles, solar panels, and energy-efficient appliances promote sustainable choices. By lowering the financial barriers to sustainability, incentives encourage widespread adoption of eco-friendly innovations and responsible consumption.

Taxation as a Regulatory Tool

Taxation is a powerful regulatory instrument used to discourage harmful practices while generating revenue for public investments. Environmental taxes, such as carbon taxes and plastic waste levies, impose financial penalties on businesses and individuals contributing to pollution and resource depletion. These taxes create economic pressure to shift towards cleaner alternatives and sustainable operations. Additionally, differential tax policies, such as lower tax rates for green businesses or higher tariffs on non-recyclable materials, help drive sustainable market behavior. Tax incentives for businesses that implement circular economy principles further reinforce responsible production and resource efficiency.

Standards and Compliance Regulations

Standards are essential in ensuring product quality, safety, and sustainability across industries. Governments and international organizations establish regulatory standards that set minimum requirements for environmental impact, energy efficiency, and waste management. Certification programs, such as ISO environmental management standards and LEED green building certifications, provide benchmarks for compliance and industry best practices. Strict regulations on emissions, water usage, and hazardous waste disposal help maintain environmental integrity. By enforcing these standards, regulators ensure that businesses adhere to sustainable practices while fostering consumer trust and confidence in certified products and services.

The Role of Policy Integration and Enforcement

The effectiveness of regulatory instruments depends on their integration within broader policy frameworks and their enforcement mechanisms. Governments must align incentives, taxation policies, and standards with national and international sustainability goals. Strong monitoring systems, transparent reporting, and penalties for non-compliance are essential to ensuring accountability. Public-private partnerships can enhance regulatory effectiveness by combining government oversight with industry expertise and technological advancements. When properly enforced, regulatory instruments create a balanced system that promotes economic competitiveness while safeguarding environmental and social interests.

6.1.3 The Role of Public Procurement in Supporting Circularity

Public procurement is a powerful tool for promoting sustainability and circular economy principles. Governments and public institutions are among the largest consumers of goods and services, and their purchasing decisions have a significant impact on market trends, resource use, and waste generation. By adopting circular procurement practices, public authorities can drive demand for sustainable products, reduce environmental impact, and encourage businesses to integrate circular economy strategies. Public procurement policies that prioritize resource efficiency, waste reduction, and product longevity can accelerate the transition to a circular economy. Public procurement is a critical mechanism for advancing circular economy objectives by shaping market demand, promoting innovation, and reducing resource consumption. Through sustainable procurement policies, governments can lead by example and create incentives for businesses to adopt circular practices. By integrating circularity into procurement processes, public institutions contribute to environmental sustainability, economic resilience, and long-term resource efficiency. As more governments embrace circular public procurement, it will play an increasingly vital role in building a sustainable future.

Sustainable Procurement Policies and Guidelines

Many governments have introduced sustainable procurement policies to incorporate circularity into purchasing decisions. These policies set criteria that favor products and services with minimal environmental impact, extended lifecycles, and high recyclability. Procurement guidelines often require suppliers to use recycled materials, adopt eco-friendly packaging, and implement take-back schemes for used products. Additionally, public contracts may prioritize services over product ownership, such as leasing models for electronics and office equipment, to extend product lifespan and reduce waste. By embedding circular economy principles in procurement guidelines, governments ensure that sustainability is a key factor in decision-making.

Promoting Innovation and Green Markets

Circular public procurement creates market incentives for businesses to develop innovative and sustainable solutions. When governments prioritize circular products and services, companies are encouraged to invest in eco-friendly production methods, modular design, and material recovery processes. This drives competition in green markets, leading to the development of new business models that support circularity, such as remanufacturing and repair services. Small and medium-sized enterprises (SMEs) that specialize in circular economy solutions also benefit from access to public contracts, fostering economic growth in sustainable industries. By using procurement as a strategic tool, governments can stimulate innovation and expand green markets.

Reducing Waste and Resource Consumption

Public procurement plays a crucial role in minimizing waste generation and optimizing resource use. By prioritizing durable, repairable, and recyclable products, government agencies can significantly reduce landfill waste and pollution. Circular procurement practices in sectors such as construction, transportation, and office supplies ensure that resources are used efficiently. For example, public infrastructure projects can mandate the use of recycled materials, energy-efficient technologies, and modular construction techniques that allow for easy disassembly and reuse. Similarly, procuring refurbished IT equipment instead of new devices helps conserve raw materials and lowers electronic waste. These strategies contribute to a more resource-efficient public sector while setting an example for private businesses and consumers.

The Role of Policy and Collaboration

Effective implementation of circular public procurement requires strong policy support and collaboration between government agencies, businesses, and international organizations. Policies must establish clear circularity criteria, provide training for procurement officials, and set measurable sustainability targets. Collaborative efforts between public and private sectors can help develop best practices, share knowledge, and identify scalable solutions. Additionally, international cooperation on procurement standards and certification systems can enhance the global impact of circular economy initiatives. By fostering policy coherence and multi-stakeholder engagement, governments can maximize the benefits of circular procurement.

6.2 INTERNATIONAL FRAMEWORKS AND INITIATIVES

6.2.1 The European Union Circular Economy Action Plan

The European Union (EU) Circular Economy Action Plan is a strategic framework aimed at transitioning the EU towards a more sustainable and resource-efficient economic model. Recognizing the environmental and economic challenges posed by the traditional linear economy, which follows a "take-make-dispose" pattern, the EU introduced this action plan to promote circularity in production, consumption, and waste management.

The European Union Circular Economy Action Plan is a comprehensive strategy that drives the transition toward a more sustainable and resource-efficient economy. Through targeted policies, legal frameworks, and financial incentives, the plan promotes circularity across various sectors while reducing waste and environmental impact. By fostering innovation, responsible consumption, and international cooperation, the EU is setting a global benchmark for circular economy practices. As the plan continues to evolve, it will play a crucial role in achieving long-term sustainability and economic resilience in Europe and beyond.

Key Objectives and Focus Areas

The Circular Economy Action Plan is designed to reduce waste, extend product lifecycles, and enhance the circularity of industries. It focuses on promoting sustainable product design, ensuring that goods are durable, repairable, and recyclable. The plan also emphasizes responsible consumption by providing consumers with better information on product sustainability, including labeling and repairability scores. Additionally, the framework encourages waste prevention strategies, improved recycling systems, and the reduction of landfill dependence. These objectives align with the EU's broader climate goals, including carbon neutrality and resource conservation.

Sector-Specific Strategies

The action plan targets key sectors with high environmental impact, such as electronics, textiles, packaging, construction, and food systems. For electronics, the EU promotes the "right to repair" policies, ensuring that consumers can fix and extend the lifespan of devices rather than discarding them. In the textiles industry, the plan supports sustainable material use, eco-friendly production, and clothing recycling programs. Packaging waste is addressed through stricter regulations on single-use plastics and the promotion of reusable and biodegradable materials. The construction sector benefits from circularity measures that encourage the reuse of materials and energy-efficient designs. By focusing on these industries, the EU aims to create systemic changes that support a circular economy.

Legal and Financial Measures

To ensure effective implementation, the EU Circular Economy Action Plan is backed by legislation, funding programs, and incentives. The European Green Deal and the Sustainable Products Initiative provide legal frameworks that enforce circular economy principles. Financial support is available through the Horizon Europe research program and the European Investment Bank, which fund projects that develop circular innovations and sustainable business models. Extended producer responsibility (EPR) regulations require manufacturers to take accountability for their products' entire lifecycle, from production to disposal. These measures encourage businesses to integrate circular economy principles into their operations while ensuring compliance with EU sustainability goals.

Global Leadership and Cooperation

The EU's Circular Economy Action Plan also serves as a model for global sustainability efforts. Through international partnerships, trade agreements, and policy dialogues, the EU advocates for circular economy principles beyond its borders. Collaboration with international organizations, such as the United Nations and the World Trade Organization, helps spread best practices and align sustainability standards worldwide. By positioning itself as a leader in circular economy initiatives, the EU influences global markets and encourages other nations to adopt similar policies.

6.2.2 The Ellen MacArthur Foundation and Global Circular Economy Networks

The Ellen MacArthur Foundation is a leading organization dedicated to accelerating the global transition to a circular economy. Since its establishment in 2010, the foundation has played a critical role in advocating for circular economy principles, influencing policymakers, businesses, and industries worldwide. By fostering collaboration, research, and innovation, the foundation has helped shape a growing global network of circular economy initiatives. Through strategic partnerships and knowledge-sharing platforms, it continues to drive systemic change toward sustainable resource management, waste reduction, and regenerative economic practices. The Ellen MacArthur Foundation has been instrumental in shaping the global circular economy movement by promoting innovative business models, fostering international collaboration, and driving systemic change. Through research, advocacy, and strategic partnerships, it continues to influence industries, policymakers, and consumers toward sustainable practices. As global circular economy networks expand, the foundation's role remains crucial in advancing resource efficiency, waste reduction, and economic resilience. Its efforts provide a blueprint for achieving a more regenerative and sustainable future on a global scale.

The Ellen MacArthur Foundation's Role in Circular Economy Advancement

The foundation serves as a thought leader in circular economy strategies by providing research, frameworks, and guidelines that support businesses and governments in adopting circular practices. One of its key contributions is the development of the "butterfly diagram," which illustrates how biological and technical materials can be effectively cycled through the economy with minimal waste.

It has also introduced the concept of "designing out waste," which emphasizes the importance of creating products that are reusable, repairable, and recyclable. By working with corporations, startups, and policymakers, the foundation helps integrate circular economy principles into industrial processes, supply chains, and consumer behavior.

Global Circular Economy Networks and Collaboration

The Ellen MacArthur Foundation plays a pivotal role in connecting businesses, governments, and international organizations through global circular economy networks. Its Circular Economy 100 (CE100) program brings together companies, policymakers, and innovators to share best practices, develop solutions, and scale circular business models. The foundation collaborates with the United Nations, the World Economic Forum, and the European Commission to influence regulatory policies and integrate circular economy principles into global trade and sustainability frameworks. Through these networks, knowledge-sharing and coordinated action accelerate the adoption of circular strategies across industries and regions.

Impact on Key Sectors and Business Models

The foundation's initiatives have had a significant impact on industries such as plastics, fashion, food, and manufacturing. The New Plastics Economy initiative, launched by the foundation, aims to eliminate plastic waste by promoting circular design, reusable packaging systems, and alternative materials. In the fashion industry, the Make Fashion Circular program works with brands to improve textile durability, recyclability, and sustainability. The foundation also advocates for regenerative food systems that reduce waste, optimize resource use, and support biodiversity. By influencing business models and supply chain practices, it fosters circularity across multiple sectors, encouraging a shift away from traditional linear economic approaches.

Education and Advocacy for Circular Economy Adoption

A core aspect of the foundation's mission is to educate businesses, governments, and the public about circular economy principles. It provides open-access reports, case studies, and online learning resources to help organizations understand and implement circular strategies. Partnerships with universities and academic institutions further support research and curriculum development focused on circular economy innovation. Public advocacy campaigns raise awareness about sustainability issues, influencing consumer behavior and policy discussions on waste management, resource efficiency, and economic resilience. Through education and outreach, the foundation ensures that circular economy principles reach a broad and diverse audience.

6.2.3 The Role of the UN and International Trade Bodies

The UN and international trade bodies are key drivers of economic policy, sustainability, and global trade governance. Through multilateral agreements, policy frameworks, and economic cooperation, these organizations ensure that trade and economic growth align with environmental and social goals. By promoting sustainable trade practices, supporting circular economy transitions, and fostering international collaboration, they play an essential role in shaping the future of global commerce. As the world faces increasing environmental and economic challenges, the continued efforts of these organizations will be critical in building a more inclusive, sustainable, and resilient global economy.

The United Nations and Sustainable Economic Development

The UN serves as a key global institution for setting sustainability and economic development goals through initiatives such as the Sustainable Development Goals (SDGs) and the Paris Agreement. Organizations within the UN, such as the United Nations Conference on Trade and Development (UNCTAD) and the United Nations Environment Programme (UNEP), develop policies that guide nations toward economic strategies that balance growth with environmental responsibility. These agencies provide research, technical assistance, and capacity-building programs that help countries implement trade policies aligned with sustainability objectives. The UN also fosters dialogue among nations, enabling international cooperation on issues such as climate change, resource management, and trade equity.

The Role of the World Trade Organization in Global Trade Governance

The World Trade Organization (WTO) is a central body responsible for overseeing international trade rules and resolving trade disputes among nations. It ensures that global trade flows smoothly, predictably, and fairly by establishing agreements that prevent unfair trade practices such as excessive tariffs and subsidies. The WTO also promotes open markets, encouraging economic growth through international trade while seeking to balance commercial interests with social and environmental considerations. In recent years, the organization has increasingly focused on integrating sustainability into trade policies, encouraging member states to adopt green trade initiatives, circular economy principles, and low-carbon supply chains.

International Trade Agreements and Economic Cooperation

Trade agreements play a vital role in shaping global economic relationships, and international trade bodies help facilitate negotiations and enforcement. Organizations such as the World Bank, the International Monetary Fund (IMF), and regional trade bodies like the European Union (EU) and the Association of Southeast Asian Nations (ASEAN) establish trade agreements that regulate tariffs, investment policies, and environmental standards. These agreements help create fairer trade systems, reducing trade barriers while ensuring that environmental and labor standards are maintained. Sustainable trade agreements also encourage responsible production and consumption practices, ensuring that economic growth does not come at the expense of ecological degradation.

Supporting Circular Economy and Sustainable Trade Practices

The UN and international trade bodies actively promote circular economy principles by encouraging sustainable production, reducing waste, and improving resource efficiency. Through policies such as the Basel Convention, which regulates the transboundary movement of hazardous waste, and initiatives that support sustainable supply chains, these organizations help nations transition towards environmentally responsible trade models. The integration of sustainability into trade policies ensures that industries adopt eco-friendly practices, such as using recycled materials, reducing carbon emissions, and implementing extended producer responsibility (EPR) frameworks. By aligning trade regulations with circular economy goals, international organizations contribute to a more resource-efficient global economy.

Challenges and Future Prospects

Despite their significant role in shaping global economic policies, the UN and international trade bodies face challenges such as trade disputes, geopolitical tensions, and resistance from industries that rely on traditional economic models. Ensuring that trade policies support both economic development and environmental sustainability requires strong international cooperation and policy alignment. Moving forward, these organizations must continue working towards fairer, more transparent, and environmentally sustainable trade practices. Strengthening global partnerships, integrating circular economy principles into trade agreements, and fostering innovation will be essential in achieving a balanced and resilient global economy.

6.3 CREATING CIRCULAR ECONOMY ROADMAPS

6.3.1 Local and Regional Circular Economy Initiatives

Local and regional circular economy initiatives are essential for driving sustainable development and reducing environmental impact. By implementing strategies that focus on urban planning, rural sustainability, business collaboration, community engagement, and policy support, regions can create more resilient and resource-efficient economies. These initiatives not only contribute to global circular economy goals but also provide economic and environmental benefits tailored to local needs. As more cities and regions adopt circular principles, they will play a crucial role in shaping a sustainable future for generations to come.

Urban Circular Economy Strategies

Cities are at the forefront of circular economy implementation due to their high resource consumption and waste generation. Many urban areas have adopted strategies to promote circularity in sectors such as construction, transportation, and waste management. Initiatives such as zero-waste programs, sustainable infrastructure development, and material recovery facilities help cities optimize resource use and reduce environmental impact. For example, cities like Amsterdam and Copenhagen have developed circular economy roadmaps that integrate sustainable building practices, promote sharing economy models, and encourage businesses to adopt circular production methods. These localized strategies contribute to a more efficient use of resources while setting an example for other regions.

Circular Economy in Rural and Regional Areas

While urban initiatives receive significant attention, rural and regional areas also play a key role in the transition to a circular economy. Many rural communities are implementing circular strategies in agriculture, water management, and renewable energy production. Circular farming practices, such as composting, regenerative agriculture, and precision farming, help reduce waste while improving soil health and food production efficiency. Additionally, small and medium-sized enterprises (SMEs) in regional areas are exploring ways to repurpose agricultural and industrial byproducts into new materials, contributing to local circular economies. These efforts help create sustainable livelihoods while reducing dependency on external resources.

Business and Industrial Collaboration

Regional circular economy initiatives often involve collaboration between businesses, industry clusters, and local governments to create closed-loop systems. Industrial symbiosis programs, where businesses exchange byproducts and waste materials as resources for production, are becoming increasingly common in regional economies. For example, the Kalundborg Symbiosis in Denmark is a well-known example of how industries share resources such as heat, water, and materials to minimize waste and reduce costs. Similar initiatives in various regions worldwide help optimize industrial resource use while fostering economic growth through circular business models.

Community Engagement and Circular Consumption

Community participation is essential for the success of local circular economy initiatives. Many cities and regions have launched awareness campaigns and incentive programs to encourage sustainable consumption and waste reduction. Initiatives such as repair cafés, swap markets, and community composting programs empower residents to take an active role in circular practices. Educational programs in schools and public institutions also help instill circular economy values in younger generations. By fostering a culture of sustainability at the local level, these initiatives create long-term behavioral changes that support circular economic development.

Policy Support and Funding Mechanisms

The success of local and regional circular economy initiatives depends on strong policy support and access to funding. Many governments provide grants, tax incentives, and regulatory frameworks to encourage businesses and municipalities to adopt circular practices. European regions, for instance, benefit from funding under the EU's Circular Economy Action Plan, which supports local projects in waste management, sustainable product design, and resource efficiency. In other parts of the world, regional policies are being developed to integrate circular economy principles into urban planning, industrial regulations, and local governance. These financial and policy mechanisms enable sustainable innovation at the local level.

6.3.2 Monitoring, Reporting, and Measuring Circular Progress

Effective monitoring, reporting, and measuring of circular progress are vital for ensuring the success of circular economy initiatives. By establishing standardized metrics, leveraging technology, and addressing existing challenges, governments and businesses can track their sustainability performance more accurately. Transparent reporting frameworks enable informed decision-making and drive continuous improvements in circular practices. As circular economy principles become more widely adopted, robust monitoring and measurement systems will be critical in achieving long-term resource efficiency and environmental sustainability.

Key Metrics for Measuring Circular Economy Progress

A well-defined set of metrics is necessary to measure circular economy performance effectively. Indicators such as material circularity, resource productivity, waste recovery rates, and carbon footprint reduction provide insights into how efficiently resources are being used and reused. The Material Circularity Indicator (MCI), developed by the Ellen MacArthur Foundation, assesses how well a product or system keeps materials in circulation. Other metrics, such as recycling rates, landfill diversion rates, and the share of secondary raw materials in production, help measure progress toward reducing waste and promoting sustainable resource use. These quantitative indicators provide a clear picture of circular economy implementation at national, regional, and corporate levels.

Reporting Frameworks and International Standards

To ensure consistency and transparency in circular economy reporting, several international frameworks and standards have been developed. The European Commission's Circular Economy Monitoring Framework provides guidelines for tracking circularity at the EU level, covering aspects such as production, consumption, waste management, and secondary raw material use. The Global Reporting Initiative (GRI) and the Sustainability Accounting Standards Board (SASB) also offer sustainability reporting guidelines that integrate circular economy indicators. These frameworks enable businesses and governments to systematically report their progress and align their strategies with global sustainability goals.

The Role of Technology in Circular Economy Monitoring

Advancements in digital technologies have improved the ability to track and measure circular progress in real time. Blockchain technology enhances transparency by providing secure and verifiable records of material flows across supply chains. Artificial intelligence and big data analytics help analyze circular economy performance by identifying inefficiencies and optimizing resource use. The Internet of Things (IoT) enables smart monitoring of product lifecycles, facilitating predictive maintenance and extending the usability of goods. These technological innovations enhance data accuracy and efficiency, making circular economy monitoring more reliable and actionable.

Challenges in Circular Economy Measurement

Despite the progress in developing circular economy indicators and reporting frameworks, several challenges remain. One major issue is the lack of standardized global metrics, as different countries and industries use varying methodologies for assessing circularity. Additionally, collecting accurate data on resource flows and material recovery remains complex due to fragmented supply chains and limited tracking mechanisms. Businesses and policymakers often face difficulties in integrating circular economy data into existing financial and sustainability reporting systems. Overcoming these challenges requires international cooperation, data-sharing mechanisms, and further refinement of measurement frameworks.

The Future of Circular Economy Monitoring and Reporting

As the circular economy continues to gain global momentum, the need for improved monitoring and reporting systems will grow. Policymakers and industry leaders are working toward the harmonization of circular economy metrics to enable more effective comparisons across sectors and regions. The integration of digital tools and artificial intelligence will further enhance data collection and analysis, making circular progress measurement more efficient and accurate. Moving forward, a strong emphasis on accountability, transparency, and continuous improvement will be essential in ensuring that circular economy initiatives deliver meaningful environmental and economic benefits.

6.4 CORPORATE RESPONSIBILITY AND CIRCULAR ECONOMY

6.4.1 Corporate Sustainability Goals and Circular Strategies

Corporate sustainability goals are increasingly dependent on circular strategies to ensure long-term environmental and economic resilience. By adopting circular business models, setting measurable sustainability targets, and leveraging innovation, companies can contribute to a more resource-efficient and low-carbon economy. While challenges exist, the benefits of circular economy adoption—including cost savings, regulatory compliance, and enhanced brand value—make it a crucial component of corporate sustainability. As businesses continue to integrate circularity into their operations, they play a key role in driving global sustainability efforts and shaping a more sustainable future.

The Role of Circular Strategies in Corporate Sustainability

Circular strategies help businesses achieve sustainability goals by closing material loops, extending product lifecycles, and reducing dependence on virgin resources. These strategies include product redesign for durability, the adoption of reusable and recyclable materials, and the implementation of take-back and remanufacturing programs. Many companies are shifting towards business models such as product-as-a-service, where consumers lease rather than purchase products, ensuring materials remain in circulation. By embracing circularity, corporations not only minimize environmental harm but also create new revenue streams and cost-saving opportunities.

Corporate Commitments to Circularity

Many multinational corporations have set ambitious sustainability targets that incorporate circular economy principles. Companies in the fashion, electronics, and consumer goods industries are committing to reducing waste, using recycled content, and designing products for longevity. Initiatives such as the Ellen MacArthur Foundation's Global Commitment on plastics have encouraged businesses to eliminate single-use plastics and invest in alternative materials. Similarly, the automotive and technology sectors are increasing efforts to recover and repurpose raw materials from end-of-life products, reducing resource extraction and environmental impact. These commitments reflect a growing recognition that sustainability and circularity are essential for long-term corporate resilience.

Measuring Circular Progress in Business Operations

To ensure accountability and transparency, businesses are adopting key performance indicators (KPIs) and reporting frameworks to track their circular economy progress. Metrics such as material circularity, waste diversion rates, and the proportion of recycled content in products help companies assess their sustainability performance. Reporting standards such as the Global Reporting Initiative (GRI), the Carbon Disclosure Project (CDP), and the Sustainability Accounting Standards Board (SASB) provide guidelines for businesses to disclose their circular economy initiatives. Companies that prioritize data-driven decision-making can identify opportunities for improvement and demonstrate their commitment to sustainability to stakeholders.

Challenges and Opportunities in Corporate Circularity

Despite the benefits of circular economy adoption, businesses face challenges in implementing circular strategies. High initial investment costs, supply chain complexities, and regulatory uncertainties can hinder the transition. Additionally, consumer behavior and market demand play a crucial role in the success of circular business models, requiring companies to educate and engage customers on sustainable consumption. However, businesses that overcome these challenges can gain a competitive advantage by fostering innovation, enhancing operational efficiency, and responding proactively to evolving environmental regulations. Collaboration with policymakers, industry peers, and research institutions can further accelerate circular transformation.

6.4.2 Reporting and Transparency in Circular Economy Practices

Reporting and transparency are critical components of circular economy practices, ensuring that businesses and organizations remain accountable for their sustainability commitments. By adopting standardized reporting frameworks, measuring key circular performance indicators, and addressing transparency challenges, companies can enhance credibility and drive meaningful progress in the transition to a circular economy. As demand for sustainability reporting grows, advancements in data tracking and regulatory support will play a vital role in shaping the future of circular economy transparency, ultimately contributing to a more resilient and responsible global economy.

The Importance of Transparency in Circular Practices

Transparency in circular economy initiatives helps build credibility and ensures that sustainability claims are backed by verifiable data. Companies that adopt circular business models must demonstrate how their operations reduce waste, improve resource efficiency, and contribute to environmental sustainability. Without transparency, there is a risk of greenwashing, where businesses make misleading claims about their environmental impact. Open and honest communication about circular economy progress allows stakeholders to hold companies accountable and drives continuous improvement in sustainable practices.

Key Reporting Frameworks for Circular Economy

Several international frameworks guide businesses and organizations in reporting their circular economy progress. The Global Reporting Initiative (GRI) includes sustainability disclosure standards that cover material use, waste management, and resource efficiency. The European Union's Circular Economy Monitoring Framework provides indicators for assessing circular progress at a regional and corporate level. Additionally, the Sustainability Accounting Standards Board (SASB) and the Task Force on Climate-related Financial Disclosures (TCFD) offer guidelines for integrating circular economy metrics into financial and sustainability reports. These frameworks help establish consistency and comparability in circular economy reporting.

Measuring Circular Performance

To ensure meaningful reporting, organizations use key performance indicators (KPIs) to assess circularity. Metrics such as recycling rates, waste reduction percentages, material recovery efficiency, and the share of secondary raw materials in production provide insights into circular economy performance. Businesses also track carbon emissions associated with resource use and evaluate product lifecycle impacts. Companies that adopt science-based targets and data-driven measurement approaches can better align their circular economy strategies with environmental and financial sustainability goals.

Challenges in Circular Economy Reporting

Despite the growing emphasis on transparency, several challenges remain in circular economy reporting. One of the main difficulties is the lack of standardized global metrics, which makes it challenging to compare circular performance across industries and regions. Data collection and tracking can also be complex, especially for businesses with extended supply chains. Additionally, some companies may face resistance in disclosing their full environmental impact due to competitive concerns or lack of regulatory enforcement. Addressing these challenges requires collaboration among industry stakeholders, governments, and standard-setting bodies to develop clear and consistent reporting guidelines.

The Future of Circular Economy Transparency

As circular economy principles become more integrated into global sustainability strategies, the demand for improved reporting and transparency will continue to grow. Digital technologies such as blockchain, artificial intelligence, and real-time data analytics are expected to enhance tracking and verification processes. Governments and regulatory bodies may introduce stricter disclosure requirements to ensure that businesses remain accountable for their circular economy commitments. Moving forward, organizations that prioritize transparent and accurate reporting will gain a competitive advantage, strengthen stakeholder trust, and contribute to a more sustainable and resource-efficient economy.

6.4.3 Consumer Engagement and Behavior Change for Circular Economy

Consumer engagement and behavior change are critical to the success of circular economy initiatives. Through awareness campaigns, incentives, community-driven efforts, and policy support, consumers can transition to more sustainable consumption patterns. Overcoming barriers such as cost, convenience, and social norms requires collaboration between businesses, governments, and civil society. As technology and consumer expectations evolve, circular economy practices will become more mainstream, ultimately leading to a more resource-efficient and environmentally responsible society.

The Role of Awareness and Education

Raising awareness about the circular economy is a key step in changing consumer behavior. Many consumers remain unfamiliar with circular principles such as product reuse, repair, remanufacturing, and recycling. Educational campaigns, public awareness programs, and school curricula can help individuals understand the benefits of circular practices and their impact on the environment. Businesses and governments can use digital platforms, social media, and community events to share information on sustainable consumption and responsible waste management. Clear labeling and certifications on products can also help consumers make informed choices about their purchases.

Encouraging Sustainable Consumption Habits

Shifting consumer behavior requires making circular products and services more accessible and attractive. Companies can promote sustainable consumption by designing durable, repairable, and recyclable products. Business models such as product-as-a-service, renting, and subscription-based services encourage consumers to prioritize usage over ownership, reducing material waste. Incentives such as discounts for returning used products, repair vouchers, and rewards for responsible disposal can further motivate consumers to adopt circular habits. Additionally, digital tools and apps that track environmental impact and suggest sustainable alternatives can influence purchasing decisions.

Community Engagement and Social Influence

Consumer behavior is often influenced by social norms and community engagement. Grassroots initiatives, such as repair cafés, clothing swap events, and zero-waste communities, provide consumers with opportunities to participate in circular practices. Engaging influencers, celebrities, and environmental advocates in promoting circular behaviors can amplify the message and encourage wider adoption. Collaborative efforts between local governments, businesses, and civil society organizations can create a supportive ecosystem for circular consumption. Peer-to-peer sharing models, such as carpooling, tool libraries, and second-hand marketplaces, can also drive behavioral change by making circular solutions more convenient and socially accepted.

Overcoming Barriers to Behavior Change

Despite growing awareness, several barriers prevent consumers from fully embracing circular economy principles. High costs of sustainable products, limited access to repair services, and lack of convenient recycling infrastructure can discourage participation. Additionally, many consumers still associate newness with quality and are hesitant to buy refurbished or second-hand items. Addressing these challenges requires stronger policy interventions, improved product design, and increased investment in circular infrastructure. Governments can implement tax incentives for sustainable products, while businesses can focus on making circular options more affordable and desirable.

The Future of Consumer Engagement in Circular Economy

As circular economy initiatives continue to expand, consumer engagement strategies will evolve to leverage new technologies and behavioral insights. Digital platforms powered by artificial intelligence and big data can personalize sustainability recommendations and track individual progress toward circular consumption. Brands that integrate transparency and circular values into their marketing strategies will likely gain consumer trust and loyalty. With growing environmental consciousness and regulatory support, consumers will play an increasingly active role in shaping a circular economy.

CHAPTER 7

Technology and Innovation in Circular Economy

7.1 ADVANCED MANUFACTURING TECHNOLOGIES FOR CIRCULAR ECONOMY

7.1.1 Additive Manufacturing (3D Printing) for Circular Production

Additive manufacturing is a transformative technology that aligns with circular economy principles by reducing waste, enhancing resource efficiency, and enabling localized production. By facilitating product repair, using sustainable materials, and preventing overproduction, 3D printing offers a viable solution for businesses seeking to transition toward circular production models. While challenges remain, continued innovation and investment in this field will further unlock its potential, making it an integral part of a sustainable and resource-efficient future.

Reducing Waste and Enhancing Material Efficiency

One of the most significant advantages of additive manufacturing is its ability to minimize material waste. Traditional manufacturing methods, such as machining and casting, often result in excess material that is discarded. In contrast, 3D printing uses only the necessary amount of material to create a product, reducing scrap and improving resource efficiency. Additionally, many 3D printing processes allow for the use of recycled and biodegradable materials, further contributing to sustainability. By designing products with minimal material input, industries can significantly lower their environmental footprint.

Enabling Product Repair and Longevity

3D printing plays a crucial role in extending the lifespan of products by making repairs and component replacements more accessible. Instead of discarding entire products due to minor damage or missing parts, consumers and businesses can print replacement components on demand. This reduces dependence on mass production and long supply chains, making repairs more cost-effective and environmentally friendly. Companies in industries such as automotive, aerospace, and consumer goods are increasingly adopting additive manufacturing to produce spare parts and extend product usability, promoting a circular approach to consumption.

Localized and On-Demand Manufacturing

By decentralizing production, 3D printing supports localized manufacturing, reducing transportation-related emissions and supply chain dependencies. Instead of mass-producing and shipping goods across long distances, businesses can manufacture products closer to the point of consumption, reducing carbon footprints and lead times.

This approach is particularly beneficial in remote areas or disaster-stricken regions where access to replacement parts and essential goods is limited. On-demand production also prevents overproduction, reducing excess inventory and waste, which aligns with circular economy goals.

The Role of Recycled and Sustainable Materials

The development of sustainable and recycled materials for 3D printing is further enhancing its circular economy potential. Many industries are exploring the use of bio-based plastics, recycled metals, and composite materials to create eco-friendly products. Innovations in material science have led to the development of filaments made from ocean plastics, industrial waste, and plant-based resins, reducing dependence on virgin resources. As material technology advances, additive manufacturing will continue to offer more environmentally friendly solutions, making circular production more viable across multiple sectors.

Challenges and Future Prospects

Despite its numerous advantages, additive manufacturing still faces challenges in achieving full circularity. The energy consumption of certain 3D printing processes, material limitations, and concerns about the recyclability of printed objects need to be addressed. Additionally, widespread adoption requires further investment in research, infrastructure, and regulatory frameworks to ensure the safe and sustainable use of 3D printing technologies. However, as advancements in technology, material science, and process efficiency continue, additive manufacturing is expected to play a pivotal role in the future of circular production.

7.1.2 Robotics and Automation in Circular Manufacturing

Robotics and automation are key enablers of circular manufacturing, enhancing efficiency, reducing waste, and improving resource recovery. From precision manufacturing and remanufacturing to automated waste sorting and supply chain optimization, these technologies support the transition toward a more sustainable industrial ecosystem. While challenges remain, continued technological advancements and increased adoption of automation will further strengthen the circular economy, making manufacturing more resource-efficient and environmentally responsible.

Enhancing Resource Efficiency and Waste Reduction

Automation in manufacturing improves resource efficiency by precisely controlling material usage and minimizing production errors. Robotic systems equipped with artificial intelligence (AI) and machine learning can optimize production processes by identifying ways to use materials more effectively, reducing excess waste. Automated systems also enable lean manufacturing practices, ensuring that raw materials are utilized efficiently and reducing the environmental footprint of production. By eliminating inefficiencies in the supply chain, robotics supports the shift toward a circular economy where materials are continuously reused and repurposed.

Facilitating Remanufacturing and Product Life Extension

Robotics plays a critical role in remanufacturing, which is a key aspect of circular manufacturing. Automated disassembly systems enable manufacturers to recover valuable components from end-of-life products, refurbish them, and reintegrate them into new products. This reduces the need for virgin materials and lowers energy consumption compared to producing new items from scratch. Advanced robotic systems are also capable of identifying defects and performing high-precision repairs, allowing companies to extend the lifespan of products and reduce electronic and mechanical waste.

Automated Waste Sorting and Recycling

One of the major challenges in achieving circular manufacturing is efficient waste sorting and recycling. Robotics and AI-driven automation are revolutionizing waste management by improving the speed and accuracy of sorting recyclable materials. Automated sorting systems use computer vision, machine learning, and robotic arms to separate different types of materials, such as plastics, metals, and glass, with higher precision than traditional manual sorting. This leads to higher recycling rates, improved material recovery, and reduced contamination in recycling streams, making circular manufacturing more feasible.

Supply Chain Optimization and Circular Logistics

Robotics and automation also contribute to circular manufacturing by optimizing supply chain logistics. Automated warehouses, smart inventory management systems, and robotic delivery solutions help streamline the movement of goods while reducing waste and energy consumption. By using predictive analytics and AI-driven forecasting, businesses can prevent overproduction, reduce excess inventory, and ensure that materials are efficiently circulated within the economy.

This leads to a more resilient and sustainable supply chain that aligns with circular economy principles.

Challenges and Future Prospects

Despite its potential, the integration of robotics and automation in circular manufacturing faces challenges such as high initial investment costs, technological complexity, and the need for specialized skills. Additionally, ensuring that robotic systems themselves are designed for longevity and recyclability is crucial in maintaining a truly circular approach. However, advancements in AI, sensor technology, and machine learning continue to drive innovation in this field. As automation becomes more accessible and cost-effective, its role in circular manufacturing will expand, leading to smarter, more sustainable production systems.

7.2 THE ROLE OF DIGITAL TECHNOLOGIES IN ENABLING CIRCULARITY

7.2.1 Digital Twins and Blockchain for Material Tracking

Digital twins and blockchain technology are revolutionizing material tracking by providing real-time insights, improving transparency, and enabling circular supply chains. By integrating these technologies, businesses can optimize material flows, reduce waste, and ensure that products remain in circulation longer. While challenges exist, continued innovation and collaboration will enhance the effectiveness of these solutions, supporting the global transition toward a more sustainable and resource-efficient economy.

The Role of Digital Twins in Material Tracking

Digital twins provide real-time insights into the lifecycle of materials by replicating physical assets in a virtual environment. These digital models collect and analyze data from sensors embedded in products, machinery, and supply chains. By simulating performance, wear, and resource consumption, digital twins help manufacturers optimize product design, predict maintenance needs, and extend the lifespan of materials. This technology allows businesses to track materials from production to end-of-life, facilitating recycling, remanufacturing, and responsible disposal. Digital twins also enhance supply chain visibility, reducing inefficiencies and enabling better decision-making for sustainable resource use.

Blockchain for Transparency and Traceability

Blockchain technology enhances material tracking by providing a secure and immutable record of transactions throughout a product's lifecycle. Each material movement—whether it is sourcing, processing, or recycling—is logged in a decentralized ledger, ensuring full traceability. This transparency helps prevent fraud, greenwashing, and unethical sourcing practices, as all stakeholders can verify the origin and journey of materials. Blockchain also facilitates efficient reverse logistics, allowing businesses to retrieve and repurpose materials more effectively. By integrating blockchain with digital twins, organizations can create a comprehensive system for monitoring material flows with accuracy and trust.

Enabling a Circular Supply Chain

The combination of digital twins and blockchain fosters a circular supply chain by ensuring that materials are continuously monitored and managed. Companies can track the quality and condition of recycled materials, ensuring that they meet industry standards for reuse. Smart contracts on blockchain can automate sustainable procurement practices, incentivizing suppliers to comply with circular economy principles. With better visibility into material movements, businesses can optimize resource use, minimize waste, and create closed-loop systems where products are designed for multiple life cycles. This integration enhances accountability, making it easier for industries to transition from linear to circular production models.

Challenges and Future Prospects

Despite their benefits, digital twins and blockchain face challenges in widespread adoption. High implementation costs, data integration complexities, and interoperability issues between different systems can slow progress. Additionally, blockchain networks require energy-intensive computing power, raising concerns about sustainability. However, ongoing advancements in artificial intelligence, edge computing, and energy-efficient blockchain solutions are addressing these challenges. As industries increasingly prioritize sustainability, the adoption of digital twins and blockchain is expected to grow, providing a scalable and reliable approach to circular material tracking.

7.2.2 Artificial Intelligence for Optimizing Circular Supply Chains

AI is revolutionizing circular supply chains by improving resource efficiency, optimizing reverse logistics, and enhancing transparency. Through predictive analytics, intelligent automation, and data-driven decision-making, AI enables businesses to transition toward sustainable and closed-loop supply chains. While challenges remain, continued innovation and investment in AI technologies will further unlock their potential, driving the global shift toward a more resilient and circular economy.

Enhancing Resource Efficiency with AI

AI plays a crucial role in improving resource efficiency by analyzing vast amounts of data to identify patterns and inefficiencies in supply chains. Machine learning algorithms can optimize material usage, ensuring that raw materials are used more effectively and reducing excess waste. AI-powered design tools assist manufacturers in creating products with longer lifespans, improved recyclability, and minimal material consumption. Additionally, AI helps companies implement circular production strategies by recommending alternative materials, suggesting ways to repurpose byproducts, and predicting optimal recycling processes.

Predictive Analytics for Demand and Inventory Management

Effective circular supply chains require precise demand forecasting and inventory management to prevent overproduction and material waste. AI-driven predictive analytics enable businesses to anticipate consumer demand, adjust production levels accordingly, and manage inventory more efficiently. By analyzing historical sales data, market trends, and external factors such as economic shifts, AI helps companies align supply with actual demand, reducing surplus stock and minimizing waste. Additionally, AI-powered inventory tracking systems improve material circulation by ensuring that reused and remanufactured components are efficiently reintegrated into production cycles.

AI-Driven Automation in Reverse Logistics

Reverse logistics is a critical component of circular supply chains, involving the collection, sorting, and reintegration of used products and materials. AI enhances reverse logistics by automating sorting systems, identifying reusable components, and streamlining transportation networks for returned goods. Computer vision and robotics powered by AI improve the accuracy of waste sorting, separating materials with higher efficiency and reducing contamination in recycling streams. AI-powered logistics platforms also optimize transportation routes, reducing carbon emissions and lowering costs associated with product returns and recycling operations.

Improving Transparency and Traceability

AI enhances transparency in circular supply chains by tracking materials from production to end-of-life. By integrating AI with blockchain technology and digital twins, companies can create detailed records of material flows, ensuring accountability at every stage. AI-powered data analysis helps detect supply chain inefficiencies, monitor environmental impact, and verify the authenticity of recycled materials. This transparency builds consumer trust and supports compliance with regulatory frameworks for sustainable sourcing and waste reduction.

Challenges and Future Prospects

Despite its potential, AI adoption in circular supply chains faces challenges such as high implementation costs, data privacy concerns, and the need for specialized expertise. Ensuring interoperability between AI systems and existing supply chain infrastructure can also be complex. However, advancements in AI, cloud computing, and IoT (Internet of Things) are making these technologies more accessible and scalable. As businesses prioritize sustainability and governments introduce stricter regulations on waste management, AI-driven circular supply chains will become an essential component of future industrial ecosystems.

7.3 INNOVATIONS IN RECYCLING TECHNOLOGIES

7.3.1 Chemical Recycling and Advanced Sorting Technologies

Chemical recycling and advanced sorting technologies are transforming the recycling industry by improving material recovery, reducing waste, and enabling circular production systems. Chemical recycling provides a solution for processing difficult-to-recycle plastics, while advanced sorting enhances the accuracy and efficiency of material separation. When integrated, these technologies create a more effective and sustainable waste management system, reducing reliance on virgin resources and minimizing environmental impact. As industries and governments invest in these innovations, they will play a crucial role in advancing the circular economy and promoting a more sustainable future.

Chemical Recycling: A Game Changer in Waste Processing

Chemical recycling, also known as advanced recycling, offers a solution for processing plastic waste that cannot be effectively recycled through mechanical methods. Unlike traditional recycling, which involves melting and reshaping plastics, chemical recycling decomposes polymers into monomers or other chemical feedstocks. These recovered materials can then be used to produce new plastics with properties equivalent to virgin materials. This method is particularly useful for handling complex plastic waste, including multilayer packaging, contaminated plastics, and mixed polymer streams. Chemical recycling reduces reliance on fossil-based raw materials and contributes to a closed-loop production system, extending the life cycle of plastics and other materials.

Advanced Sorting Technologies for Improved Material Recovery

The effectiveness of recycling largely depends on the ability to accurately separate different materials. Advanced sorting technologies are transforming waste management by using artificial intelligence, machine learning, and sensor-based sorting systems to distinguish and categorize materials with high precision. Near-infrared (NIR) spectroscopy, X-ray fluorescence, and AI-driven optical recognition systems enable the rapid identification and separation of plastics, metals, and paper, reducing contamination in recycling streams. Robotic sorting systems equipped with high-speed sensors improve the efficiency and accuracy of waste separation, reducing the amount of recyclable material lost to landfills. These technologies help industries and municipalities optimize recycling processes and recover valuable resources more effectively.

Integrating Chemical Recycling with Smart Sorting

The combination of chemical recycling and advanced sorting technologies creates a more efficient and sustainable waste management system. By ensuring that high-quality materials are separated before processing, advanced sorting enhances the effectiveness of chemical recycling. Smart sorting systems can direct materials to the most suitable recycling method, improving overall recovery rates and reducing energy consumption. AI-driven waste management platforms can track material flows, predict recycling efficiency, and provide real-time data to optimize recycling infrastructure. This integration supports the development of circular production models, where waste is continuously reused rather than discarded.

Challenges and Future Prospects

Despite its potential, chemical recycling faces challenges such as high energy consumption, technological scalability, and economic viability. Some chemical recycling processes require significant investment and infrastructure development to become commercially competitive with mechanical recycling. Additionally, ensuring that chemical recycling facilities operate with minimal environmental impact remains a priority. Advanced sorting technologies also require investment in AI systems, robotics, and data management to achieve widespread adoption. However, ongoing research, policy incentives, and private sector investments are driving advancements in these areas. As technology evolves and regulations promote circular economy initiatives, chemical recycling and smart sorting will play an increasingly vital role in global waste management strategies.

7.3.2 Closed-Loop Recycling of Metals, Plastics, and Textiles

Closed-loop recycling of metals, plastics, and textiles is essential for reducing waste, conserving resources, and achieving circular economy goals. Metals offer the highest efficiency due to their infinite recyclability, while plastics and textiles require advanced processing techniques to maintain quality. Overcoming challenges such as contamination and economic viability will require continued innovation, policy support, and industry collaboration. As closed-loop recycling technologies evolve, they will play a key role in creating a more sustainable and resource-efficient global economy.

Closed-Loop Recycling of Metals

Metals are among the most suitable materials for closed-loop recycling because they do not degrade during the recycling process. Aluminum, steel, and copper can be continuously melted and reformed without losing their structural integrity, making them valuable for sustainable production. Efficient collection systems, such as scrap metal recovery and urban mining, ensure that discarded metals are reprocessed and reintegrated into manufacturing. The energy savings from recycling metals are significant, with aluminum recycling using up to 95% less energy than producing new aluminum from raw materials. Investing in better sorting and refining techniques further enhances the efficiency of closed-loop metal recycling, reducing dependency on mining and minimizing environmental harm.

Closed-Loop Recycling of Plastics

Plastics present greater challenges for closed-loop recycling due to degradation and contamination issues, but advancements in chemical and mechanical recycling are improving material recovery. Mechanical recycling, the most common method, involves melting and reshaping plastics, but repeated cycles can weaken the material. Chemical recycling, on the other hand, breaks down plastics into their original monomers, allowing for high-quality reuse. Developing standardized plastic compositions, improving waste collection infrastructure, and increasing consumer awareness are essential for maximizing closed-loop plastic recycling. By integrating artificial intelligence and automated sorting technologies, industries can enhance plastic recovery and ensure that materials retain their properties for continuous reuse.

Closed-Loop Recycling of Textiles

Textile waste has become a growing concern, with fast fashion contributing to massive amounts of discarded clothing. Closed-loop textile recycling aims to recover fibers from used garments and reprocess them into new textiles without compromising quality. Mechanical recycling of natural fibers, such as cotton and wool, involves shredding fabrics into fibers that can be spun into new yarns, though fiber length and strength may decrease over time. Chemical recycling offers a more effective solution by breaking down synthetic fabrics like polyester into raw materials that can be re-polymerized into high-quality textiles. Innovations in fiber sorting, sustainable design, and biodegradable materials are further strengthening the closed-loop recycling of textiles, reducing landfill waste and environmental pollution.

Challenges and Future Prospects

Despite its benefits, closed-loop recycling faces challenges such as contamination, inefficient waste collection systems, and technological limitations. The lack of standardized recycling processes and the complexity of mixed-material products make material recovery difficult. Economic barriers, including the cost of advanced recycling technologies, also hinder widespread adoption. However, increased regulatory support, corporate sustainability commitments, and consumer awareness are driving progress in closed-loop recycling. Future innovations in AI-driven sorting, blockchain-based material tracking, and biodegradable materials will further enhance recycling efficiency and material recovery.

7.4 CIRCULAR ECONOMY IN THE ENERGY SECTOR

7.4.1 Renewable Energy Systems in Circular Economy Models

Renewable energy systems are a fundamental component of circular economy models, enabling industries and communities to operate sustainably by reducing carbon emissions and minimizing resource depletion. By leveraging renewable energy for manufacturing, waste management, and supply chain operations, businesses can achieve long-term sustainability while enhancing efficiency and resilience. Although challenges remain in scaling renewable energy integration, ongoing advancements in technology, policy support, and investment in clean energy infrastructure will accelerate the transition to a fully circular and sustainable economy.

The Role of Renewable Energy in Resource Efficiency

One of the key benefits of incorporating renewable energy into circular economy models is improving resource efficiency. Traditional linear economic models rely heavily on nonrenewable energy sources, which contribute to pollution and resource depletion. In contrast, circular economy models prioritize resource conservation by ensuring that energy inputs are renewable and sustainable. Solar and wind energy, for example, provide long-term, low-carbon energy solutions that can power recycling facilities, manufacturing plants, and transportation networks. Additionally, waste-to-energy technologies, such as anaerobic digestion and biomass energy production, convert organic waste into valuable energy sources, creating a closed-loop system that minimizes waste and maximizes resource utilization.

Decentralized Energy Systems and Localized Production

The integration of decentralized renewable energy systems further strengthens circular economy models by reducing transmission losses and promoting localized production. Distributed energy systems, such as microgrids and community-based solar projects, enable industries and households to generate their own renewable power, reducing dependence on centralized fossil fuel-based energy grids. This localized approach enhances energy security, reduces transportation-related emissions, and fosters economic resilience in communities. Moreover, industrial symbiosis, where businesses share energy resources and byproducts, allows excess renewable energy to be repurposed, ensuring that no energy goes to waste within the production cycle.

Renewable Energy in Circular Supply Chains

Renewable energy is essential for transforming supply chains into more sustainable and circular systems. Manufacturing processes, transportation, and material recovery efforts require substantial energy inputs, and transitioning these processes to renewable energy sources significantly lowers their environmental footprint. Companies that adopt solar- or wind-powered production facilities can achieve carbon-neutral operations while enhancing long-term cost savings. Additionally, integrating battery storage technologies and smart grid systems ensures a stable energy supply, even when renewable sources fluctuate. By powering circular supply chains with renewable energy, industries can align their operations with sustainable development goals and regulatory frameworks focused on carbon reduction.

Challenges and Opportunities for Integration

Despite its advantages, the widespread adoption of renewable energy in circular economy models faces challenges, including high initial investment costs, infrastructure limitations, and intermittent energy supply. The transition to renewable energy requires significant policy support, financial incentives, and technological advancements to improve storage and grid integration. Additionally, industries must adapt their processes to accommodate renewable energy sources, which may require redesigning production systems and investing in energy-efficient technologies. However, continued innovation in energy storage, smart grid management, and hybrid renewable energy systems presents opportunities to overcome these challenges. Governments and businesses that prioritize renewable energy adoption will benefit from long-term cost reductions, energy independence, and environmental sustainability.

7.4.2 Energy Storage and Circularity: Batteries and Materials Recovery

Energy storage and battery materials recovery are integral to the circular economy, ensuring that the growing demand for batteries does not lead to resource depletion and environmental harm. By prioritizing efficient recycling, second-life applications, and sustainable battery design, industries can create a closed-loop system that maximizes resource use while minimizing waste. Overcoming existing challenges will require collaboration between governments, businesses, and researchers to advance recycling technologies, implement supportive policies, and invest in innovative battery solutions. As the demand for energy storage continues to rise, circular strategies for batteries will play a crucial role in building a sustainable and resilient energy future.

The Role of Batteries in Circular Energy Systems

Batteries enable the integration of renewable energy sources such as solar and wind into the energy grid by storing excess power for later use. This function is essential for overcoming the intermittency of renewables and ensuring a stable energy supply. In addition to grid storage, batteries are vital for electric mobility, reducing reliance on fossil fuels and supporting decarbonization efforts. However, the growing demand for batteries raises concerns about resource scarcity, environmental impact, and end-of-life disposal. Implementing circular economy principles in battery production and usage can help address these challenges by prioritizing reuse, refurbishment, and recycling.

Materials Recovery and Battery Recycling

Battery production relies on critical raw materials such as lithium, cobalt, nickel, and graphite, which are finite and often extracted through environmentally damaging mining practices. Effective materials recovery through battery recycling reduces the need for new mining while ensuring a continuous supply of these essential components. Advanced recycling techniques, such as hydrometallurgical and direct recycling processes, allow for the efficient extraction of valuable materials from used batteries. Establishing closed-loop recycling systems ensures that recovered materials are reintegrated into new battery production, reducing waste and lowering environmental impact. Government regulations, extended producer responsibility (EPR) policies, and industry investments in battery recycling infrastructure are crucial for scaling up these efforts.

Extending Battery Lifespan through Second-Life Applications

One of the most effective ways to enhance battery circularity is through second-life applications, where used batteries from electric vehicles and consumer electronics are repurposed for stationary energy storage. Even after their initial use, batteries often retain a significant portion of their capacity, making them suitable for applications such as backup power, off-grid renewable energy storage, and industrial energy management. By extending battery lifespan through refurbishment and repurposing, industries can delay disposal, maximize resource efficiency, and reduce overall environmental impact. The development of standardized battery designs and improved diagnostic tools can further support second-life applications by ensuring compatibility and safety in reuse processes.

Challenges and Innovations in Circular Battery Management

Despite advancements in battery recycling and reuse, several challenges remain in achieving full circularity. Current recycling rates for lithium-ion batteries are relatively low due to economic constraints, inefficient collection systems, and technological barriers. Many batteries are not designed for easy disassembly, making material recovery more complex. Additionally, the high costs of recycling processes can make it more financially viable for manufacturers to use newly mined materials rather than recycled ones. However, ongoing innovations in battery chemistry, such as solid-state and sodium-ion batteries, offer promising alternatives that are more sustainable and easier to recycle. Digital tracking systems, powered by blockchain and AI, can also improve battery lifecycle management by enhancing traceability and optimizing recycling logistics.

7.5 CIRCULAR ECONOMY IN THE MOBILITY SECTOR

7.5.1 Electric Vehicles and Battery Recycling

As the EV industry continues to grow, sustainable battery management is essential for reducing environmental impact and ensuring resource security. Battery recycling and second-life applications provide critical solutions for mitigating waste, lowering raw material demand, and supporting a circular economy. Overcoming challenges such as high costs, technological limitations, and infrastructure gaps will require coordinated efforts from governments, industries, and researchers. By prioritizing innovation, policy support, and investment in recycling technologies, the EV sector can create a sustainable and circular battery ecosystem that contributes to a cleaner and more efficient transportation future.

The Need for EV Battery Recycling

The widespread adoption of EVs has led to an increasing demand for lithium-ion batteries, placing pressure on the supply chain for essential raw materials. Mining for battery components is energy-intensive and often associated with environmental degradation and human rights concerns. Without proper recycling mechanisms, end-of-life EV batteries contribute to hazardous waste and potential pollution. Battery recycling addresses these issues by recovering valuable materials, reducing the need for new mining, and minimizing the carbon footprint of battery production. Establishing efficient recycling systems ensures that materials can be reused in new battery production, creating a closed-loop system that aligns with circular economy goals.

Battery Recycling Technologies and Processes

Several advanced recycling technologies are being developed to improve the efficiency of EV battery material recovery. Mechanical recycling involves shredding batteries and separating components through physical and chemical processes. Hydrometallurgical recycling uses chemical solutions to dissolve and extract valuable metals, offering high recovery rates with lower energy consumption. Pyrometallurgical recycling, which involves smelting batteries at high temperatures, is another method for extracting metals, though it can result in material loss and higher emissions. Direct recycling, an emerging technique, preserves battery components for reuse with minimal reprocessing, making it a promising solution for enhancing material recovery and reducing costs.

Second-Life Applications for EV Batteries

Before recycling, EV batteries can be repurposed for second-life applications, extending their lifespan and maximizing resource efficiency. Even after their initial use in vehicles, many batteries retain significant capacity, making them suitable for stationary energy storage. Second-life batteries can be used in renewable energy storage, backup power systems, and grid balancing applications, providing cost-effective solutions while delaying waste generation. Developing standardized testing and refurbishment processes is crucial for ensuring the safety and reliability of repurposed batteries. By integrating second-life applications into battery lifecycle management, industries can reduce environmental impact while supporting energy sustainability.

Challenges and Opportunities in Battery Recycling

Despite the benefits of battery recycling, several challenges must be addressed to achieve widespread adoption. The lack of standardized battery designs complicates disassembly and material recovery. Current recycling infrastructure is limited, with many used EV batteries not reaching proper recycling facilities due to inadequate collection systems. The cost of recycling can also be high compared to the extraction of new materials, making economic viability a key concern. However, increasing government regulations, extended producer responsibility (EPR) policies, and advancements in recycling technology are driving progress in this field. Investments in automation, AI-driven sorting systems, and blockchain-based tracking can further enhance efficiency and transparency in battery recycling.

7.5.2 Shared Mobility Systems: Car Sharing, Bike Sharing, and Beyond

Shared mobility systems, including car sharing, bike sharing, and micromobility solutions, are reshaping urban transportation by offering sustainable and efficient alternatives to private vehicle ownership. By reducing traffic congestion, lowering emissions, and promoting multimodal transport integration, these systems contribute to more livable and environmentally friendly cities. While challenges remain in terms of regulation, infrastructure, and technology adoption, continued innovation and policy support will play a crucial role in expanding shared mobility networks. As cities embrace digital transformation and sustainable urban planning, shared mobility will continue to evolve, creating a more connected and accessible transportation ecosystem.

The Role of Car Sharing in Sustainable Transportation

Car sharing services provide individuals with access to vehicles without the burden of ownership, offering a flexible and cost-effective alternative to private cars. Users can rent vehicles on an hourly or per-minute basis through app-based platforms, reducing the overall number of vehicles on the road. This model helps decrease carbon emissions, lower fuel consumption, and optimize parking space utilization. Additionally, shared electric vehicles (EVs) further enhance environmental benefits by reducing reliance on fossil fuels. Companies and municipalities are increasingly investing in car-sharing networks to promote sustainable transportation and reduce traffic congestion in urban areas.

Bike Sharing and Micromobility Solutions

Bike sharing has become an essential component of urban transportation, offering an eco-friendly and health-conscious alternative for short-distance travel. Public bike-sharing programs and dockless bike systems allow users to rent bicycles for one-way trips, reducing dependency on motorized transport. The rise of micromobility solutions, such as e-scooters and electric bikes, has further expanded the scope of shared transportation, providing convenient last-mile connectivity options. These systems contribute to lower emissions, reduced traffic congestion, and improved air quality. However, proper infrastructure, such as bike lanes and docking stations, is necessary to ensure the safety and efficiency of micromobility solutions.

The Integration of Shared Mobility with Public Transport

One of the key advantages of shared mobility is its ability to complement and enhance public transportation networks. Car sharing, bike sharing, and ride-hailing services can serve as first-mile and last-mile solutions, bridging gaps in transit accessibility.

By integrating shared mobility with buses, trains, and metro systems, cities can create seamless and efficient transportation networks. Mobility-as-a-Service (MaaS) platforms, which combine various transport options into a single digital interface, allow users to plan multimodal trips efficiently. This integrated approach improves public transport usage while reducing reliance on private vehicles, leading to more sustainable urban mobility.

Challenges and Opportunities in Shared Mobility

Despite its benefits, shared mobility systems face challenges related to regulation, infrastructure, and user adoption. Issues such as fleet management, vehicle maintenance, and equitable access must be addressed to ensure long-term success. Additionally, the expansion of shared mobility raises concerns about data privacy and cybersecurity, as digital platforms collect large amounts of user information. However, technological advancements, including AI-driven demand prediction and smart traffic management, present opportunities to improve efficiency and user experience. Government policies that support shared mobility, such as incentives for EV-based car-sharing fleets and investment in bike-friendly infrastructure, can further accelerate the transition to sustainable transportation.

CHAPTER

8

Social and Cultural Dimensions of Circular Economy

8.1 CONSUMER BEHAVIOR AND CIRCULAR ECONOMY

8.1.1 Shifting from Ownership to Access-Based Models

The shift from ownership to access-based models is redefining consumption patterns, offering financial flexibility, sustainability benefits, and enhanced convenience. By leveraging digital technologies and innovative business strategies, industries can create efficient and resource-conscious economies that reduce waste and optimize asset utilization. While challenges remain in adoption and regulation, continued advancements in technology and policy frameworks will help drive the widespread acceptance of access-based consumption. As consumers increasingly prioritize convenience and sustainability, businesses that embrace this transition will be well-positioned to thrive in the evolving marketplace.

The Rise of Access-Based Consumption

The concept of access-based consumption has gained popularity in sectors such as transportation, housing, fashion, and entertainment. Ride-hailing services, car-sharing programs, and bike-sharing systems enable consumers to access mobility solutions without owning a vehicle, reducing congestion and emissions. Similarly, platforms like Airbnb facilitate short-term property rentals, offering flexible accommodation alternatives. In the fashion industry, clothing rental services provide access to high-end apparel without long-term ownership, promoting circular economy principles. The entertainment sector has also embraced this shift, with streaming services replacing physical media ownership, allowing users to access vast digital libraries through subscription models.

Economic and Environmental Benefits

Access-based models offer financial advantages by lowering upfront costs and providing consumers with greater flexibility. Instead of making large investments in assets that may depreciate or require maintenance, users can pay for temporary access, aligning expenses with actual usage. This approach is particularly beneficial in urban areas where space constraints make ownership impractical. Additionally, access-based consumption reduces waste and resource depletion by extending the lifecycle of products. Shared assets, such as vehicles, tools, and electronics, are utilized more efficiently, decreasing the demand for new production and minimizing environmental impact. As a result, these models contribute to a more sustainable and resource-efficient economy.

The Role of Digital Platforms and Technology

Advancements in digital technology have played a crucial role in the expansion of access-based models. Mobile applications, artificial intelligence, and blockchain solutions enable seamless transactions, secure payments, and real-time tracking of shared assets. Peer-to-peer platforms connect users with service providers, facilitating trust and convenience in access-based exchanges. Subscription-based business models leverage data analytics to personalize offerings and enhance customer experiences. As technology continues to evolve, businesses can further optimize asset utilization, reduce inefficiencies, and expand the reach of access-based services across diverse industries.

Challenges and Considerations

Despite its advantages, the transition from ownership to access-based models presents challenges related to consumer adoption, regulatory frameworks, and business viability. Some consumers may still prefer the security and control associated with ownership, requiring businesses to emphasize the convenience and affordability of access-based alternatives. Regulatory concerns, such as taxation, liability, and consumer protection, must also be addressed to ensure fair market practices. Additionally, businesses must develop sustainable revenue models that balance affordability for consumers with profitability for service providers. Overcoming these challenges requires collaboration between policymakers, businesses, and consumers to create a supportive ecosystem for access-based consumption.

8.1.2 The Role of Education and Awareness in Circularity

Education and awareness are fundamental to the successful implementation of circular economy principles. By integrating circularity into formal education, raising public awareness, engaging businesses in sustainability education, and implementing supportive policies, societies can foster a culture of responsible consumption and production. A well-informed population is better equipped to embrace circular practices, reduce environmental impact, and drive long-term systemic change. As the world transitions toward a more sustainable future, investing in education and awareness will be crucial in building resilient and resource-efficient economies.

Integrating Circular Economy Concepts into Education

Embedding circular economy principles in educational curricula is key to developing a new generation of sustainability-conscious individuals. Schools and universities can incorporate topics such as resource management, sustainable design, and waste reduction into science, economics, and business courses. Hands-on learning experiences, such as circular economy projects, repair workshops, and recycling initiatives, can help students apply theoretical knowledge to real-world challenges. Vocational training programs can also equip workers with the technical skills needed for circular industries, such as refurbishing electronics, sustainable packaging design, and material recovery processes. By integrating circularity into education, institutions can prepare future professionals to drive innovation in sustainable business models and environmental stewardship.

Raising Public Awareness and Behavioral Change

Public awareness campaigns are instrumental in encouraging individuals to adopt circular practices in their daily lives. Governments, businesses, and nonprofit organizations can use social media, community events, and informational campaigns to educate people on reducing waste, choosing sustainable products, and participating in recycling programs. Clear labeling on products regarding recyclability and environmental impact can further empower consumers to make informed purchasing decisions. Behavioral change initiatives, such as incentives for returning used items, discounts for sustainable purchases, and deposit-refund schemes, can motivate individuals to actively engage in circular practices. A well-informed public is more likely to support policies and businesses that prioritize sustainability, driving systemic change at a broader level.

The Role of Businesses in Circular Economy Education

Companies have a responsibility to educate employees, customers, and stakeholders about circularity. Employee training programs can help integrate sustainable practices within business operations, from waste management to product lifecycle design. Businesses that communicate their circular economy strategies effectively can also influence consumer behavior, fostering loyalty among environmentally conscious customers. Corporate social responsibility (CSR) initiatives, such as sustainability workshops, partnerships with environmental organizations, and funding for educational programs, can further enhance circular economy literacy. By prioritizing education, businesses not only contribute to environmental goals but also strengthen their brand reputation and market competitiveness.

Policy and Government Initiatives for Circular Education

Governments play a critical role in promoting circular economy education through policies, funding, and collaboration with educational institutions and industry leaders. Implementing national strategies for circularity education can ensure that sustainability principles are embedded in school curricula, workforce development programs, and public outreach efforts. Incentives for businesses to adopt and promote circular economy training can accelerate industry-wide adoption. International organizations and governments can also collaborate on knowledge-sharing platforms, research initiatives, and policy frameworks to advance circular economy education on a global scale.

8.2 SOCIAL EQUITY AND INCLUSIVE CIRCULAR ECONOMY

8.2.1 Ensuring Access to Circular Economy Opportunities for All

A truly effective circular economy must be inclusive, ensuring that all individuals, businesses, and communities have equal access to its benefits. By addressing economic disparities, investing in education and skill development, making circular products and services more affordable, and implementing supportive policies, societies can create a fair and just transition. Collaboration between governments, businesses, and civil society is essential to overcoming barriers and ensuring that circular economy opportunities contribute to social equity, environmental sustainability, and long-term economic resilience.

Bridging the Economic and Social Gap

The transition to a circular economy should not only benefit large corporations and wealthy consumers but also create opportunities for low-income communities, small enterprises, and informal workers. Many developing economies rely on informal waste collection and recycling sectors, which play a vital role in resource recovery. Providing fair wages, improved working conditions, and legal recognition for these workers can enhance their contribution to circular systems while improving livelihoods. Additionally, financial support such as microloans, grants, and tax incentives can help small businesses adopt circular business models, making sustainability more accessible across all economic levels.

Enhancing Education and Skill Development

Expanding education and vocational training programs is critical for ensuring that individuals from diverse backgrounds can participate in the circular economy. Many circular industries, such as renewable energy, recycling, and remanufacturing, require specialized skills that may not be widely available in underserved communities. Governments and businesses can invest in skill-building initiatives, such as training centers, apprenticeship programs, and online courses, to prepare workers for circular jobs. By equipping individuals with the necessary expertise, societies can create employment opportunities while fostering innovation and economic resilience in circular industries.

Inclusive Access to Circular Products and Services

For circular economy solutions to be effective, they must be accessible to all consumers, not just those who can afford premium sustainable products. Many eco-friendly goods, such as recycled materials, sustainably produced textiles, and circular-designed electronics, often come at a higher price due to production costs and limited supply. Governments and businesses can work to make circular products more affordable through subsidies, incentives, and large-scale production that reduces costs. Expanding circular services, such as repair workshops, rental programs, and sharing platforms, can also provide low-cost alternatives to ownership while promoting resource efficiency.

Policy and Infrastructure for Equitable Participation

Public policies and infrastructure development play a vital role in ensuring widespread access to circular economy opportunities. Governments can implement regulations that promote inclusive circular practices, such as extended producer responsibility (EPR), which holds companies accountable for product lifecycle management. Investments in waste management infrastructure, recycling facilities, and circular supply chains can enhance accessibility for communities lacking the necessary resources. Additionally, policies that encourage social enterprises and cooperatives focused on circularity can empower local communities to participate in the transition toward sustainable production and consumption.

8.2.2 Circular Economy and Job Creation in Vulnerable Communities

The circular economy has the potential to create meaningful employment opportunities in vulnerable communities by fostering sustainable industries, promoting skills development, and supporting small enterprises. By investing in education, formalizing informal work, and implementing policies that encourage circular practices, societies can ensure that the transition to sustainability is inclusive and beneficial to all. A well-designed circular economy not only addresses environmental challenges but also provides economic empowerment, offering a pathway toward greater social and economic resilience.

Expanding Employment Opportunities

The transition to a circular economy creates diverse job opportunities across multiple industries. Waste collection, recycling, and material recovery provide employment in both the formal and informal sectors, offering livelihoods to workers who might otherwise struggle to find stable jobs. Additionally, remanufacturing and repair services generate skilled positions in refurbishing electronics, textiles, and machinery, extending product life cycles while reducing environmental impact. The rise of sustainable agriculture, composting initiatives, and bio-based industries also creates jobs related to organic waste management and regenerative farming practices. These sectors provide long-term employment prospects, particularly in regions where traditional industries are declining.

Skills Development and Training

For vulnerable communities to fully participate in the circular economy, access to education and vocational training is crucial. Many circular jobs require technical skills in repair, recycling, eco-design, and sustainable supply chain management. Training programs tailored to local needs can equip individuals with the expertise needed to work in these industries. Governments, businesses, and NGOs can collaborate to offer workshops, apprenticeships, and certification programs that enhance employability. Investing in skill development ensures that workers are prepared to meet the growing demand for sustainable practices, making the circular economy a viable and long-term solution for economic inclusion.

Supporting Informal Workers and Small Enterprises

In many developing regions, informal waste pickers and recyclers play a crucial role in resource recovery but often face poor working conditions, low wages, and lack of legal recognition. Formalizing the informal sector through cooperatives, social enterprises, and government-supported programs can improve job security and provide better economic opportunities. Small and medium-sized enterprises (SMEs) are also key players in the circular economy, driving innovation in sustainable product design, repair services, and local recycling initiatives. Offering financial incentives, microloans, and business development support can empower these enterprises to scale their operations while creating employment in underserved communities.

Policy and Infrastructure for Job Creation

Governments play a vital role in fostering circular job growth through supportive policies and investment in infrastructure. Implementing policies such as extended producer responsibility (EPR), tax incentives for circular businesses, and public procurement of sustainable products can create demand for circular services and stimulate job creation. Developing infrastructure for waste collection, recycling facilities, and repair centers ensures that circular jobs are accessible in both urban and rural areas. Additionally, promoting social inclusion in circular economy policies can help address unemployment and economic inequality by prioritizing job opportunities for marginalized groups.

8.3 THE ROLE OF COLLABORATION AND PARTNERSHIPS IN ADVANCING CIRCULAR ECONOMY

8.3.1 Multi-Stakeholder Engagement: Government, Business, and NGOs

A successful circular economy depends on the collective efforts of governments, businesses, and NGOs. Each stakeholder contributes unique strengths, whether through policymaking, innovation, or advocacy. By working together, they can create a regulatory and economic environment that supports sustainable production and consumption. Strengthening multi-stakeholder engagement ensures that circular economy initiatives are well-coordinated, inclusive, and impactful, ultimately leading to long-term environmental and economic benefits.

The Role of Government in Circular Economy Governance

Governments are central to enabling a circular economy through policy development, regulatory enforcement, and financial incentives. By implementing extended producer responsibility (EPR) laws, waste management regulations, and eco-design standards, governments can create an environment where circular practices become the norm. Public procurement policies that prioritize sustainable products and services can also drive demand for circular solutions. Additionally, investment in infrastructure, such as recycling facilities and repair centers, ensures that businesses and consumers have the necessary resources to participate in circular systems. Governments also play a key role in fostering multi-stakeholder dialogue by facilitating partnerships, funding research, and ensuring that circular economy policies are aligned with national and global sustainability goals.

Business Leadership in Circular Innovation and Implementation

Businesses are crucial drivers of the circular economy, as they have the capacity to innovate, invest, and integrate sustainable practices into their operations. By adopting circular business models such as product-as-a-service, remanufacturing, and material recovery, companies can reduce waste and extend product lifecycles. Collaboration with suppliers, customers, and policymakers helps create closed-loop supply chains that minimize resource depletion. Many corporations are also investing in digital technologies such as blockchain and artificial intelligence to enhance material tracking and waste reduction. However, businesses must balance profitability with sustainability, which is why regulatory support and financial incentives from governments are necessary to ensure that circular models are economically viable.

NGOs as Catalysts for Advocacy, Research, and Community Engagement

Non-governmental organizations (NGOs) play a vital role in raising awareness, conducting research, and mobilizing communities to support circular economy initiatives. Many NGOs focus on policy advocacy, urging governments to implement stronger environmental regulations and corporate accountability measures. Others work directly with businesses to develop sustainability strategies, providing expertise on waste reduction, ethical sourcing, and resource efficiency. Additionally, NGOs are instrumental in engaging the public through educational campaigns, repair workshops, and grassroots initiatives that promote responsible consumption and waste reduction. By acting as a bridge between governments, businesses, and communities, NGOs help ensure that circular economy efforts are both socially and environmentally responsible.

Building Effective Multi-Stakeholder Partnerships

For a circular economy to succeed, strong collaboration between governments, businesses, and NGOs is essential. Public-private partnerships (PPPs) can drive large-scale investments in circular infrastructure, while industry coalitions and multi-stakeholder forums can facilitate knowledge-sharing and best practices. Governments can work with businesses to create incentives for sustainable innovation, while NGOs can provide independent monitoring and impact assessment. Transparency and accountability are key to successful engagement, as trust between stakeholders ensures long-term commitment and effectiveness. By fostering inclusive dialogue and aligning objectives, multi-stakeholder partnerships can accelerate the transition toward a more resilient and sustainable economy.

8.3.2 Collaborative Business Models and Partnerships for Circularity

Collaborative business models and partnerships are essential for accelerating the circular economy. By working together, companies can create more efficient and resilient supply chains, optimize resource use, and drive sustainable innovation. Industry-wide cooperation, public-private partnerships, and engagement with NGOs and research institutions help businesses overcome barriers to circularity and create shared value.

A well-coordinated approach to collaboration ensures that circular economy principles are effectively integrated into mainstream business practices, contributing to long-term economic and environmental sustainability.

The Importance of Collaborative Business Models

Collaborative business models are essential for achieving circularity because they allow companies to pool resources, knowledge, and technologies to develop innovative solutions. Models such as product-as-a-service, sharing platforms, and industrial symbiosis demonstrate how businesses can shift from ownership-based consumption to access-based systems that minimize waste.

For example, companies offering leasing or subscription-based services extend the utility of products while maintaining control over materials for reuse and refurbishment. Similarly, businesses in different sectors can engage in industrial symbiosis by exchanging by-products and waste materials, turning one company's waste into another's resource. These models create financial and environmental benefits, ensuring sustainability while maintaining profitability.

Partnerships across Industries and Supply Chains

Strong partnerships across industries and supply chains are fundamental to circular success. Manufacturers, suppliers, and retailers must work together to design products with sustainability in mind, using recyclable materials and modular components that facilitate repair and reuse. Companies can also collaborate with waste management firms and recycling organizations to develop efficient collection and processing systems for end-of-life products. Additionally, businesses that rely on raw materials can form partnerships with secondary material providers to integrate recycled content into their production processes, reducing dependence on virgin resources. Such collaborations create resilient supply chains that are less vulnerable to resource scarcity and price fluctuations.

The Role of Public-Private Partnerships

Public-private partnerships (PPPs) play a crucial role in advancing circular business models by bringing together government support and private-sector innovation. Governments can incentivize businesses to adopt circular practices through grants, subsidies, and regulatory frameworks, while companies can contribute technical expertise and investment. PPPs can be particularly effective in scaling circular infrastructure, such as advanced recycling facilities, remanufacturing hubs, and digital platforms for material tracking. By working together, governments and businesses can accelerate the development of circular markets and create a more sustainable economic system.

Collaboration with NGOs and Research Institutions

Non-governmental organizations (NGOs) and research institutions are valuable partners in the circular economy, providing expertise, advocacy, and data-driven insights. NGOs help businesses align their strategies with sustainability goals, ensuring that circular initiatives have positive social and environmental impacts. Research institutions contribute to innovation by developing new materials, waste-processing technologies, and circular design methodologies. Collaborative projects between businesses, universities, and NGOs enable the testing and scaling of circular solutions, driving continuous improvement and long-term sustainability.

CHAPTER 9

Measuring and Evaluating Circular Economy

9.1 CIRCULAR ECONOMY INDICATORS AND METRICS

9.1.1 Key Performance Indicators (KPIs) for Circularity

Establishing and monitoring KPIs for circularity is essential for ensuring the effectiveness of circular economy strategies. By measuring resource efficiency, waste reduction, product longevity, environmental impact, and economic benefits, businesses and policymakers can track progress and make data-driven decisions. A robust framework of KPIs helps organizations identify gaps, optimize circular initiatives, and contribute to a sustainable future. Through continuous evaluation and improvement, circular economy principles can be successfully integrated into mainstream economic systems, delivering long-term environmental and financial value.

Resource Efficiency and Material Use

One of the primary KPIs for circularity focuses on resource efficiency, measuring how effectively materials are used within a system. Metrics such as material productivity, resource consumption per unit of production, and the proportion of recycled or renewable materials in products provide insights into how well companies minimize raw material dependency. Tracking resource efficiency helps businesses and governments assess whether their policies and processes contribute to reducing material extraction and waste generation while maintaining economic growth.

Waste Reduction and Recycling Rates

Waste reduction is a crucial indicator of circular economy success, as it reflects the ability to minimize material disposal through reuse, recycling, and remanufacturing. KPIs such as waste diversion rates, landfill reduction percentages, and the share of products designed for end-of-life recovery help evaluate progress in closing material loops. Additionally, recycling rates of key materials like plastics, metals, and textiles indicate how effectively resources are reintegrated into production cycles. These metrics are essential for companies aiming to meet sustainability commitments and regulatory requirements.

Product Lifecycle and Circular Design

Extending product lifecycles through repair, refurbishment, and remanufacturing is a key principle of circularity. KPIs in this area assess the durability, reparability, and modularity of products, measuring the percentage of goods that can be repaired or upgraded rather than discarded. The average lifespan of products, the availability of spare parts, and the adoption of circular design principles are also important indicators. Companies that incorporate these KPIs into their product development processes can improve sustainability while offering long-term value to customers.

Carbon Footprint and Environmental Impact

A shift toward circularity also requires measuring its impact on carbon emissions and environmental sustainability. KPIs such as carbon footprint reduction, energy efficiency improvements, and water usage in circular processes help evaluate the environmental benefits of circular strategies. Businesses and policymakers track these indicators to ensure that circular economy initiatives contribute to global climate goals, such as reducing greenhouse gas emissions and promoting renewable energy integration. Lowering the carbon footprint of products and supply chains is a critical step toward achieving net-zero targets.

Economic and Social Impact of Circularity

Beyond environmental benefits, circular KPIs also measure economic and social impacts. Job creation in circular industries, revenue generated from circular business models, and cost savings from resource efficiency indicate the economic viability of circular strategies. Additionally, tracking consumer engagement in circular behaviors, such as participation in take-back programs and sustainable purchasing choices, provides insights into societal shifts toward circular consumption patterns. These indicators help assess whether circular economy initiatives are inclusive, financially sustainable, and beneficial to communities.

9.1.2 Environmental and Economic Metrics for Circular Business Models

Effective circular business models rely on measuring both environmental and economic metrics to track sustainability progress and business success. Environmental indicators such as material footprint, waste reduction, carbon emissions, and water usage assess the ecological impact of circular strategies, while economic metrics like revenue from circular initiatives, cost savings, and job creation ensure financial viability. Lifecycle assessment plays a critical role in integrating these metrics into decision-making, helping businesses refine their circular economy approaches. By continuously monitoring and improving circular performance, companies can drive sustainable growth while contributing to a resilient and resource-efficient economy.

Environmental Metrics: Measuring Sustainability Impact

Environmental metrics in circular business models focus on assessing the reduction of negative environmental impacts while maximizing resource efficiency. One of the primary indicators is material footprint, which measures the total amount of raw materials used in production and consumption. A lower material footprint indicates a shift toward sustainable sourcing and resource conservation. Waste diversion rates, which track the percentage of materials kept out of landfills through recycling, reuse, and composting, are also essential for evaluating circularity.

Additionally, carbon footprint reduction is a key metric, as circular business models aim to lower greenhouse gas emissions by optimizing energy use, reducing waste, and incorporating renewable energy sources. Water footprint, which measures water consumption in production and supply chains, is another critical indicator, especially for industries with high water usage. Monitoring these metrics enables businesses to align with sustainability goals and reduce their overall environmental impact.

Economic Metrics: Assessing Business Viability

For circular business models to be successful, they must also demonstrate financial viability and economic benefits. Revenue generated from circular products and services is a crucial metric, reflecting the profitability of business models such as product-as-a-service, remanufacturing, and material recovery. Cost savings from resource efficiency provide insights into how well a company minimizes raw material expenses and waste disposal costs through circular strategies. Another key metric is return on investment (ROI) in circular initiatives, which evaluates the long-term financial gains from adopting sustainable practices.

Job creation in circular industries is also an important economic indicator, as circular business models contribute to employment growth in sectors such as recycling, repair, and sustainable manufacturing. Companies that track these metrics can demonstrate the financial benefits of circularity and attract investment in sustainable innovation.

The Role of Lifecycle Assessment in Circular Metrics

Lifecycle assessment (LCA) is a comprehensive tool used to measure both environmental and economic impacts across the entire life cycle of a product or service. By analyzing resource extraction, production, use, and end-of-life management, LCA provides a holistic view of circular business models' effectiveness.

This approach helps businesses identify opportunities to improve sustainability while optimizing costs and efficiency. Metrics derived from LCA, such as energy consumption, emissions per product lifecycle, and cost savings from extended product use, guide decision-making and innovation in circular economy strategies.

Balancing Environmental and Economic Performance

Achieving circularity requires balancing environmental benefits with economic performance. While reducing resource consumption and waste is essential for sustainability, businesses must also ensure that circular strategies remain financially viable and scalable. Companies that successfully integrate circular economy principles into their business models can create competitive advantages, enhance brand reputation, and meet regulatory compliance while contributing to global sustainability efforts. Transparent reporting on environmental and economic metrics strengthens stakeholder trust and encourages further investment in circular innovation.

9.2 SUSTAINABILITY METRICS AND CIRCULAR ECONOMY ASSESSMENT

9.2.1 Tools for Measuring Environmental Impact and Efficiency

Measuring environmental impact and efficiency is crucial for achieving sustainability and circular economy objectives. Tools such as lifecycle assessment, carbon footprint calculators, material flow analysis, and energy auditing provide valuable insights for optimizing resource use and minimizing environmental harm. Environmental product declarations and circularity reporting frameworks enhance transparency and enable informed decision-making. By leveraging these tools, businesses and policymakers can drive meaningful environmental improvements while ensuring economic resilience in a sustainable future.

Lifecycle Assessment (LCA)

Lifecycle assessment (LCA) is one of the most comprehensive tools for measuring environmental impact across the entire lifecycle of a product or service. It evaluates resource use, energy consumption, emissions, and waste generation from raw material extraction to end-of-life disposal or recycling. LCA provides a holistic view of sustainability performance, helping companies design eco-friendly products, optimize supply chains, and reduce carbon footprints. By quantifying environmental impact at each stage, businesses can identify opportunities for circularity, such as material substitution, energy efficiency improvements, and waste reduction strategies.

Carbon Footprint Calculators

Carbon footprint calculators measure the amount of greenhouse gas emissions associated with activities, products, or entire organizations. These tools help companies and individuals assess their direct and indirect carbon emissions, guiding efforts to reduce energy consumption and transition to renewable energy sources. Many businesses use carbon footprint assessments to comply with climate regulations, develop carbon offset strategies, and communicate their sustainability progress to stakeholders. Advanced carbon tracking software integrates real-time data, providing insights into emissions hotspots and helping organizations set science-based reduction targets.

Material Flow Analysis (MFA)

Material flow analysis (MFA) is a tool used to track the movement of materials and resources within a system, such as an industry, city, or supply chain. It quantifies the input, output, and recycling potential of materials, helping organizations identify inefficiencies and reduce waste. MFA supports the development of circular economy strategies by optimizing material loops, improving resource recovery, and minimizing reliance on virgin raw materials. By mapping resource flows, businesses can enhance material efficiency, reduce environmental impact, and improve supply chain sustainability.

Environmental Product Declarations (EPD)

Environmental product declarations (EPD) provide standardized environmental impact data for products and materials, based on LCA principles. These declarations offer transparent information about a product's carbon footprint, energy use, water consumption, and waste generation, allowing consumers and businesses to make informed purchasing decisions. EPDs are particularly valuable in industries such as construction, manufacturing, and packaging, where sustainable material choices can significantly reduce environmental impact. By adopting EPDs, companies demonstrate their commitment to sustainability while meeting regulatory and market demands for eco-friendly products.

Energy and Water Auditing Tools

Energy and water auditing tools assess consumption patterns, efficiency levels, and areas for conservation. These audits help businesses identify energy-intensive processes, detect leaks, and implement efficiency measures such as renewable energy adoption and water recycling systems. Smart meters and digital monitoring platforms provide real-time insights, enabling organizations to optimize energy and water use while reducing operational costs. These tools are essential for industries with high resource consumption, ensuring compliance with environmental regulations and sustainability goals.

Circularity Metrics and Reporting Platforms

Several digital platforms and sustainability reporting tools enable businesses to track and report circular economy performance. Metrics such as waste diversion rates, recycling efficiency, product lifespan, and secondary material usage are crucial for assessing circularity. Tools like the Circular Transition Indicators (CTI) framework and Global Reporting Initiative (GRI) standards provide structured methodologies for evaluating and disclosing circular economy progress. By integrating circularity metrics into business strategies, companies can improve resource efficiency, reduce environmental footprint, and enhance stakeholder transparency.

9.2.2 Circular Economy and Climate Change Mitigation

The circular economy is a powerful tool for mitigating climate change by promoting resource efficiency, sustainable consumption, waste reduction, and renewable energy integration. By shifting away from linear economic models and embracing circular principles, businesses, policymakers, and communities can significantly reduce greenhouse gas emissions while fostering long-term environmental and economic resilience. As climate challenges intensify, circular economy strategies provide a viable path toward a low-carbon, sustainable future, demonstrating that economic growth and environmental stewardship can go hand in hand.

Reducing Carbon Emissions through Resource Efficiency

One of the primary ways the circular economy mitigates climate change is by improving resource efficiency. Extracting, processing, and transporting raw materials account for a large share of global energy use and carbon emissions. Circular approaches such as material recovery, product life extension, and waste-to-resource initiatives significantly reduce the demand for virgin materials, thereby lowering emissions associated with mining, deforestation, and industrial production. For example, using recycled aluminum requires up to 95% less energy than producing new aluminum from raw ore, demonstrating the carbon-saving potential of circular strategies.

Sustainable Production and Consumption Models

Transitioning to circular production and consumption models can further decrease climate impacts. Eco-design principles, which emphasize durability, reparability, and recyclability, ensure that products last longer and require fewer resources over their lifecycle. Additionally, sharing and leasing models, such as car-sharing and furniture rental services, optimize resource use and reduce the carbon footprint of manufacturing new goods. Businesses that adopt circular supply chains prioritize renewable materials, minimize waste, and incorporate low-carbon logistics, contributing to reduced greenhouse gas emissions across industries.

Waste Reduction and Carbon Sequestration

The circular economy helps mitigate climate change by preventing waste accumulation and promoting carbon sequestration. Organic waste, when landfilled, generates methane—a potent greenhouse gas significantly more harmful than carbon dioxide. Composting, anaerobic digestion, and bio-based material recovery transform organic waste into valuable resources, preventing methane emissions and enhancing soil carbon storage. Similarly, innovative carbon capture and utilization (CCU) technologies integrate circular principles by repurposing industrial carbon emissions into new materials, such as synthetic fuels and construction components, reducing overall atmospheric carbon levels.

Renewable Energy Integration in Circular Systems

A shift toward circular economy models also supports the transition to renewable energy, further mitigating climate change. Circular strategies enhance the efficiency of renewable energy systems by promoting closed-loop material cycles for solar panels, wind turbines, and battery storage solutions.

Advanced recycling processes recover critical materials from electronic waste and decommissioned energy infrastructure, reducing the environmental footprint of renewable energy production. By coupling circular economy initiatives with decarbonized energy systems, businesses and governments can accelerate climate action while securing sustainable energy solutions.

Policy and Business Initiatives for Climate Action

Governments and businesses play a vital role in aligning circular economy policies with climate goals. Regulations such as extended producer responsibility (EPR), carbon pricing mechanisms, and circular economy action plans encourage industries to adopt low-carbon, resource-efficient practices.

Businesses investing in circular innovation, such as biodegradable materials, modular design, and reverse logistics, gain a competitive edge while reducing climate risks. Collaborative efforts between public and private sectors are essential to scaling circular solutions and ensuring their integration into global climate policies and sustainability frameworks.

9.3 MONITORING AND REPORTING PROGRESS IN CIRCULAR ECONOMY INITIATIVES

9.3.1 Reporting Standards: GRI, ISO, and Other Frameworks

GRI, ISO, and other sustainability reporting frameworks provide essential guidelines for organizations to measure, report, and improve their environmental and social impacts. These standards enhance transparency, ensure regulatory compliance, and support the transition to a circular economy. As businesses and policymakers increasingly prioritize sustainability, adopting and aligning with global reporting frameworks will be crucial for driving meaningful progress toward a more resource-efficient and resilient economy.

The Global Reporting Initiative (GRI)

The Global Reporting Initiative (GRI) is one of the most widely used sustainability reporting frameworks, providing comprehensive guidelines for organizations to disclose their environmental, social, and economic performance. The GRI Standards emphasize materiality, ensuring that companies report on sustainability issues that are most relevant to their business and stakeholders. The framework covers various aspects, including energy consumption, carbon emissions, waste management, labor practices, and corporate governance. By adopting GRI Standards, businesses enhance their credibility, align with global sustainability goals, and improve decision-making processes related to resource efficiency and circular economy implementation.

ISO Standards for Sustainability and Circular Economy

The International Organization for Standardization (ISO) has developed various standards that support sustainability and circular economy practices. ISO 14001 focuses on environmental management systems, helping organizations systematically reduce their environmental impact through improved resource efficiency and waste reduction. ISO 20400 provides guidance on sustainable procurement, ensuring that organizations integrate sustainability considerations into their supply chains. ISO 50001 focuses on energy management, enabling companies to improve energy performance and reduce greenhouse gas emissions. Additionally, ISO is developing new standards, such as ISO 59000, specifically tailored for circular economy principles, providing structured methodologies for businesses to implement circular strategies effectively.

Other Frameworks for Sustainability and Circularity

In addition to GRI and ISO, several other reporting frameworks help organizations track and communicate their sustainability performance. The Sustainability Accounting Standards Board (SASB) provides industry-specific guidelines that help businesses disclose financially material sustainability information to investors. The Task Force on Climate-related Financial Disclosures (TCFD) focuses on climate risk reporting, ensuring that businesses assess and disclose the financial impact of climate change on their operations. The Carbon Disclosure Project (CDP) enables organizations to measure and report carbon emissions, water usage, and deforestation risks, helping stakeholders understand their environmental footprint.

The Role of Reporting Standards in Circular Economy

Effective reporting frameworks are essential for monitoring circular economy progress and ensuring accountability. These standards provide businesses with structured methodologies to measure key circularity metrics, such as waste reduction, material recovery rates, and resource efficiency. By integrating reporting standards into their sustainability strategies, companies can improve transparency, attract responsible investors, and align with global regulatory requirements. Standardized reporting also enhances industry collaboration, enabling businesses to benchmark performance and share best practices for accelerating circular economy adoption.

9.3.2 The Role of Data Transparency in Circular Economy

Data transparency is a fundamental pillar of the circular economy, enabling supply chain visibility, informed consumer choices, regulatory compliance, and business collaboration. By adopting open data principles, leveraging digital tracking technologies, and standardizing sustainability reporting, stakeholders can drive the transition to a more resource-efficient and regenerative economic system. As transparency improves, businesses and governments will be better equipped to make data-driven decisions that support circular economy objectives, ultimately leading to a more sustainable and resilient global economy.

Enhancing Supply Chain Visibility

One of the key benefits of data transparency in the circular economy is improved supply chain visibility. Many industries face challenges in tracking the origin, usage, and disposal of materials due to fragmented supply chains and inconsistent reporting practices. Transparent data systems, enabled by blockchain, digital twins, and material passports, allow companies to monitor product lifecycles, verify sustainable sourcing, and ensure compliance with circular economy principles. This level of visibility not only reduces the risk of greenwashing but also helps organizations optimize material recovery, extend product life cycles, and improve reverse logistics.

Enabling Informed Consumer Choices

Consumers play a vital role in the circular economy, and data transparency empowers them to make more sustainable purchasing decisions. Access to clear and verifiable information on product durability, recyclability, and environmental impact allows consumers to choose circular products over linear alternatives. Labels such as Environmental Product Declarations (EPDs) and digital product passports provide valuable insights into a product's lifecycle, helping consumers identify options that align with sustainability goals. Increased transparency also fosters trust between businesses and consumers, reinforcing corporate responsibility and encouraging circular consumption patterns.

Supporting Policy and Regulatory Compliance

Governments and regulatory bodies rely on transparent data to enforce circular economy policies and ensure compliance with sustainability standards. Mandatory reporting frameworks, such as the Global Reporting Initiative (GRI) and the EU's Corporate Sustainability Reporting Directive (CSRD), require companies to disclose environmental performance metrics, including resource efficiency, waste reduction, and carbon footprint. By making this information publicly accessible, policymakers can assess progress toward circular economy targets, design more effective regulations, and incentivize businesses to adopt circular practices.

Driving Innovation and Business Collaboration

Data transparency fosters innovation by enabling businesses to share knowledge, exchange best practices, and collaborate on circular initiatives. Open-access data platforms allow companies to explore material reuse opportunities, identify secondary raw material markets, and develop new business models based on circular principles. For example, digital marketplaces for industrial by-products help businesses repurpose waste materials as valuable inputs, reducing reliance on virgin resources. Collaboration between industries, facilitated by transparent data sharing, accelerates the transition to a circular economy by creating synergies across sectors.

Overcoming Challenges in Data Transparency

Despite its benefits, achieving full data transparency in the circular economy presents several challenges. Data fragmentation, lack of standardization, and concerns over intellectual property can limit the sharing of critical sustainability information. Additionally, companies may be reluctant to disclose environmental impact data due to reputational risks or competitive concerns. Addressing these challenges requires the development of standardized reporting systems, stronger regulatory frameworks, and incentives for businesses to share sustainability data. Advancements in digital technologies, such as AI-driven analytics and blockchain verification, can further enhance data accuracy and accessibility.

CHAPTER

The Future of Circular Economy

10

10.1 EMERGING TRENDS AND INNOVATIONS IN CIRCULAR ECONOMY

10.1.1 Circular Economy in Space and Technology Sectors

The circular economy is emerging as a transformative approach in the space and technology sectors, promoting resource efficiency, waste reduction, and long-term sustainability. From space missions that recycle vital resources to technology companies designing products for reuse and repair, circular strategies are reshaping how industries operate. By integrating advanced recycling techniques, sustainable design, and digital technologies, businesses and space agencies can create a more resilient and environmentally responsible future. As challenges are addressed through innovation and policy support, the adoption of circular economy principles in these sectors will continue to expand, contributing to a more sustainable global economy.

Circular Economy in Space Exploration

Space missions rely on limited resources, making circular strategies essential for long-term sustainability. One of the key challenges in space exploration is managing waste and ensuring resource efficiency in environments where resupply is costly and logistically complex. NASA, the European Space Agency (ESA), and private companies like SpaceX are developing technologies to recycle water, oxygen, and materials on spacecraft and space stations. Advanced recycling systems can convert waste into usable resources, reducing dependence on Earth-based supply chains. Additionally, in-situ resource utilization (ISRU) techniques, such as extracting water from lunar or Martian regolith and repurposing spacecraft components, demonstrate circular economy principles in action.

Sustainable Design in the Technology Sector

The technology industry is a major contributor to electronic waste (e-waste), with millions of devices discarded each year. Circular economy principles in the sector emphasize sustainable design, repairability, and modular components to extend product lifespans. Tech companies are increasingly adopting closed-loop production systems, where materials from old electronics are recovered and reused in new devices. Initiatives such as Apple's Daisy robot, which disassembles iPhones for material recovery, and Google's commitment to using recycled materials in its hardware highlight how the industry is integrating circular strategies. Additionally, advancements in biodegradable and recyclable electronic components offer promising solutions for reducing technology-related waste.

Recycling and Resource Efficiency in Space and Technology

Both the space and technology sectors require critical raw materials, many of which are scarce and environmentally damaging to extract. Circular economy strategies aim to recover and recycle these materials to reduce dependence on virgin resources. In the technology sector, rare earth metals used in batteries, semiconductors, and electronic circuits can be reclaimed through advanced recycling techniques. In space, the concept of orbital debris recycling is gaining traction, with researchers exploring ways to repurpose defunct satellites and space junk into new components or fuel. These approaches not only support sustainability but also enhance resource security for future missions and technological advancements.

Role of Digital Technologies in Enabling Circularity

Digital technologies such as artificial intelligence (AI), blockchain, and digital twins are playing a crucial role in advancing circular economy practices in space and technology. AI-powered analytics optimize resource use by predicting material needs and improving product lifecycle management. Blockchain technology enhances supply chain transparency by tracking material origins, ensuring ethical sourcing, and facilitating responsible recycling practices. Digital twin simulations, which create virtual models of physical systems, allow companies to test circular strategies before implementing them, reducing waste and improving efficiency. These digital innovations enable the integration of circular economy principles at every stage of product development and resource management.

Challenges and Future Prospects

While the adoption of circular economy principles in the space and technology sectors presents significant opportunities, several challenges remain. Technical barriers, economic feasibility, and regulatory constraints can hinder the widespread implementation of circular strategies. In space exploration, ensuring that recycling and resource recovery systems function reliably in extreme environments requires ongoing research and innovation. In the technology sector, overcoming planned obsolescence and encouraging manufacturers to design for longevity and repairability remain critical hurdles. However, as sustainability becomes a global priority, investments in circular economy initiatives are expected to increase, driving innovation and regulatory support for circular practices.

10.1.2 The Impact of Automation and AI on Circular Models

Automation and AI are driving the transformation of circular economy models by improving resource efficiency, optimizing recycling processes, and enabling sustainable product design. These technologies enhance the scalability and feasibility of circular strategies, making it easier for businesses and industries to transition away from linear economic models. While challenges such as energy use, data security, and workforce shifts must be addressed, the potential of AI and automation to accelerate circularity is immense. By leveraging these innovations responsibly, businesses and governments can create a more sustainable, efficient, and resilient global economy.

Enhancing Resource Optimization and Efficiency

AI-powered analytics and automation technologies are transforming how businesses manage resources within circular models. Machine learning algorithms analyze large datasets to identify inefficiencies in material use, allowing companies to design products with longer lifespans and higher recyclability. Automated manufacturing systems incorporate predictive maintenance, reducing downtime and minimizing waste. Additionally, AI-driven demand forecasting helps optimize supply chains, preventing overproduction and reducing surplus materials. These capabilities improve resource efficiency and contribute to a more resilient and sustainable economy.

AI in Recycling and Waste Management

One of the biggest challenges in circular economy models is managing waste effectively, and AI is playing a vital role in improving recycling processes. Smart sorting systems use AI-powered image recognition and robotics to accurately identify and separate different types of waste, increasing recycling rates and reducing contamination. Automated waste collection systems optimize routes, reducing fuel consumption and emissions. AI also enhances material recovery by identifying valuable components in discarded electronics, plastics, and textiles, ensuring that they can be reintegrated into production cycles. These innovations make recycling more cost-effective and sustainable.

Automating Reverse Logistics and Remanufacturing

Reverse logistics—the process of returning products and materials for reuse, refurbishment, or recycling—is critical to circular economy success. AI-powered logistics systems optimize transportation routes, reducing emissions and improving the efficiency of material recovery. Automated disassembly lines enable the efficient breakdown of products for remanufacturing, making it easier to recover valuable components and materials. Robotics are increasingly used in remanufacturing processes, ensuring precision in refurbishing electronic devices, automotive parts, and industrial equipment. These advancements create economic incentives for businesses to adopt circular practices while reducing their environmental footprint.

AI-Driven Product Design for Circularity

AI is transforming product design by enabling businesses to create sustainable, modular, and repairable products from the outset. Generative design algorithms help engineers explore circular solutions by testing different material compositions, product structures, and manufacturing processes. AI also facilitates life cycle assessments, evaluating the environmental impact of products from raw material extraction to disposal. By using AI-driven simulations, companies can ensure that their products are designed for longevity, disassembly, and recyclability, reducing waste and supporting circular business models.

Challenges and Ethical Considerations

Despite the many benefits of AI and automation in circular economy models, there are challenges and ethical considerations to address. The high energy consumption of AI systems and automated processes must be managed to ensure that sustainability gains are not offset by increased carbon footprints. Data privacy and cybersecurity risks associated with AI-driven tracking systems also require robust regulations and safeguards. Additionally, automation may lead to job displacement in traditional manufacturing and recycling industries, necessitating workforce reskilling programs to prepare employees for AI-integrated circular economy roles. Addressing these challenges is essential to maximizing the benefits of AI while ensuring inclusive and responsible adoption.

10.2 CHALLENGES AND BARRIERS TO SCALING CIRCULAR ECONOMY

10.2.1 Policy, Economic, and Technological Obstacles

While policy, economic, and technological obstacles pose significant challenges to circular economy implementation, they are not insurmountable. By addressing regulatory gaps, providing financial incentives, and investing in technological advancements, societies can accelerate the shift towards circularity. Collaboration between public and private sectors, along with strong consumer engagement, will be essential in overcoming these barriers and ensuring a more sustainable and resource-efficient future.

Policy Barriers and Regulatory Gaps

Inconsistent regulations and lack of standardized policies create significant barriers to circular economy implementation. Many countries lack comprehensive legal frameworks that support circular initiatives such as extended producer responsibility (EPR), waste reduction mandates, and recycling incentives. In cases where policies exist, they often vary across regions, leading to fragmented markets and inefficiencies in material recovery and reuse. Additionally, outdated regulations designed for linear economic models can discourage circular innovations by imposing bureaucratic hurdles on businesses seeking to adopt sustainable practices. The absence of strong enforcement mechanisms further limits compliance, making it difficult to achieve circular economy goals.

Economic Challenges and Financial Constraints

Shifting from a linear to a circular economy requires substantial financial investment, which poses a challenge for businesses and governments. Circular business models often demand higher upfront costs for product redesign, infrastructure development, and advanced recycling technologies. Many companies, especially small and medium-sized enterprises (SMEs), struggle to secure funding for circular initiatives due to the perceived financial risks and long return-on-investment periods. Additionally, the economic viability of circular solutions is frequently undermined by the continued affordability of virgin raw materials, which are often cheaper than recycled alternatives due to subsidies and economies of scale in traditional supply chains. Without strong financial incentives such as tax benefits, grants, and subsidies for circular practices, businesses may lack the motivation to transition away from the linear economy.

Technological Limitations and Infrastructure Gaps

Despite advancements in circular technologies, several technical challenges prevent widespread adoption. Many recycling and material recovery processes remain inefficient, with high costs and limited scalability. The lack of advanced sorting and processing facilities results in low recycling rates, particularly for complex materials such as e-waste, multi-layer plastics, and composite materials. In addition, many existing manufacturing systems are designed for linear production, making it difficult to integrate circular principles such as remanufacturing and material reuse. The absence of digital tracking systems for materials further complicates circular supply chain management, as businesses struggle to trace and recover valuable resources. Addressing these limitations requires investment in research, development, and infrastructure to improve circular technologies and enhance resource efficiency.

The Role of Collaboration and Systemic Change

Overcoming these obstacles requires a multi-stakeholder approach involving governments, businesses, researchers, and consumers. Policy reforms must create a favorable regulatory environment that incentivizes circular economy practices while ensuring standardization and compliance across regions. Economic incentives such as green financing, tax credits, and investment in circular infrastructure can help businesses adopt sustainable models without financial disadvantages. Technological innovation should focus on improving material recovery, optimizing circular supply chains, and leveraging digital tools like artificial intelligence and blockchain to enhance transparency and efficiency.

Additionally, consumer awareness and behavioral change are crucial in driving demand for circular products and services, reinforcing the transition to a sustainable economy.

10.2.2 Overcoming Consumer Resistance and Behavioral Barriers

Overcoming consumer resistance and behavioral barriers is essential for the success of the circular economy. By addressing awareness gaps, making circular options more convenient, offering financial incentives, leveraging social influences, and building trust, businesses and policymakers can drive widespread consumer adoption. A holistic approach that integrates education, accessibility, and cultural change will help create a future where circular consumption becomes the norm rather than the exception.

Addressing Lack of Awareness and Misconceptions

One of the primary barriers to consumer adoption of circular economy practices is a lack of understanding. Many consumers are unfamiliar with circular principles such as reuse, repair, and product-as-a-service models. Additionally, misconceptions about the quality and reliability of refurbished or recycled products can discourage people from making sustainable choices. To address these issues, businesses and policymakers must invest in educational campaigns that highlight the benefits of circular consumption. Clear labeling, certifications, and transparency about product quality can also help build trust and encourage consumers to shift toward sustainable alternatives.

Making Circular Choices Convenient and Accessible

Consumers are more likely to adopt circular behaviors if they are convenient and do not require significant effort or lifestyle changes. Many circular practices, such as recycling, renting, or repairing products, can be perceived as time-consuming or inconvenient compared to simply purchasing new items. Businesses can overcome this barrier by integrating circular options seamlessly into existing consumer habits. For example, take-back programs, product leasing, and easy-to-access repair services can help normalize circular behaviors. Digital platforms and apps that simplify participation in circular systems—such as second-hand marketplaces or sharing economy services—can further encourage adoption by making sustainability effortless.

Financial Incentives and Affordability

Cost considerations play a significant role in consumer decision-making. While circular products and services can offer long-term financial benefits, the initial costs of sustainable alternatives can sometimes be higher than their traditional counterparts. Governments and businesses can encourage circular consumption by providing financial incentives such as discounts, subsidies, or tax breaks for sustainable purchases. Subscription-based or pay-per-use models can also make circular products more affordable by reducing upfront costs. Additionally, showcasing the durability and cost savings of circular products compared to disposable alternatives can help shift consumer perceptions.

Social and Cultural Influences

Consumer behavior is heavily influenced by societal norms and peer pressure. Many purchasing decisions are driven by brand loyalty, trends, and social status, which can create resistance to circular options, especially if they are perceived as inferior or unfashionable. To counter this, businesses should position circular products as trendy, high-quality, and desirable. Engaging influencers, celebrities, and social media campaigns can help normalize sustainable consumption. Additionally, fostering community engagement and participation—such as clothing swaps, repair cafés, and sustainability challenges—can create a cultural shift toward circular behaviors.

Building Trust through Transparency and Accountability

Trust is a key factor in encouraging consumers to embrace circular models. Some consumers are skeptical about whether recycled or refurbished products are as good as new ones or whether companies genuinely follow sustainable practices. Businesses must prioritize transparency by clearly communicating their sustainability efforts, product lifecycle information, and environmental impact. Third-party certifications, circular economy standards, and public reporting can enhance consumer confidence and reinforce the credibility of circular brands. Ensuring that circular services—such as repair programs or rental models—are reliable and user-friendly can further strengthen trust.

10.3 THE ROAD AHEAD: VISION FOR A CIRCULAR FUTURE

10.3.1 The Role of Global Collaboration in Scaling Circular Economy

Global collaboration is fundamental to scaling the circular economy and achieving a sustainable future. By harmonizing policies, fostering knowledge exchange, enhancing circular supply chains, securing financial investments, and ensuring social equity, the world can transition toward a more resource-efficient and regenerative economic system. Strong partnerships between governments, businesses, and international institutions will drive innovation and accelerate the adoption of circular practices, creating long-term economic and environmental benefits for all.

Harmonizing Policies and Regulatory Frameworks

One of the key challenges in scaling the circular economy is the lack of standardized regulations across countries. Different nations have varying policies on waste management, recycling, and product design, creating inconsistencies that hinder global circular trade and investment. International cooperation can help harmonize regulations, ensuring that businesses can operate within a unified framework that supports circularity. Organizations such as the United Nations (UN), the European Union (EU), and the World Trade Organization (WTO) play a crucial role in developing global guidelines, agreements, and incentives that encourage sustainable production and responsible resource management. By aligning policies, countries can facilitate the cross-border movement of secondary materials, promote responsible consumption, and support businesses transitioning to circular models.

Knowledge Sharing and Technological Innovation

Global collaboration allows countries and industries to exchange knowledge and best practices, accelerating technological innovation in circular economy solutions. Advanced recycling technologies, digital tracking systems, and material recovery methods can be shared among nations to improve efficiency and reduce waste. Research institutions, multinational corporations, and startups must work together to develop scalable circular innovations, such as closed-loop manufacturing, bio-based materials, and artificial intelligence-driven supply chain optimization. International forums, conferences, and cross-sector partnerships serve as platforms for sharing expertise and fostering the development of new circular technologies that can be adopted worldwide.

Facilitating Cross-Border Circular Supply Chains

A circular economy relies on efficient supply chains that enable material reuse, remanufacturing, and recycling across industries and regions. However, logistical barriers such as trade restrictions, inconsistent waste classifications, and limited recycling infrastructure in certain regions pose challenges to circular trade. Strengthening international collaboration can help overcome these obstacles by improving waste collection systems, investing in sustainable logistics, and removing trade barriers for secondary raw materials. The development of digital platforms and blockchain technology for material tracking can further enhance transparency and efficiency in global circular supply chains, ensuring that resources are reused and redistributed effectively.

Financial Investments and Market Incentives

Scaling the circular economy requires significant financial investments in infrastructure, technology, and circular business models. International financial institutions, such as the World Bank and the International Monetary Fund (IMF), can support the transition by providing funding for circular economy initiatives, particularly in developing countries. Additionally, global corporations and investors must play an active role in financing circular startups, sustainable production systems, and innovative waste management solutions. Governments can also collaborate to establish incentives such as tax benefits, green bonds, and subsidies that encourage businesses to adopt circular practices. A globally coordinated approach to financing circular initiatives will drive economic growth while reducing environmental impact.

Addressing Social and Environmental Equity

A truly sustainable circular economy must consider social and environmental equity, ensuring that all countries and communities benefit from circularity. Many developing nations face challenges in waste management, resource scarcity, and economic disparities, making it essential to provide support through global partnerships. Wealthier nations and international organizations can assist in capacity-building efforts, such as training programs, infrastructure development, and access to circular technologies. Ensuring fair and inclusive participation in the circular economy will create job opportunities, improve resource security, and reduce environmental degradation worldwide.

10.3.2 Long-Term Sustainability and Systems Transformation

Long-term sustainability and systems transformation require a collective effort from governments, businesses, and individuals to reimagine economic, technological, and social structures. A shift toward circular and regenerative systems is necessary to address environmental challenges, ensure economic resilience, and create a more equitable society. By advancing innovative business models, investing in infrastructure, implementing strong policies, fostering behavior change, and prioritizing inclusivity, the world can move toward a future that balances growth with ecological and social well-being.

Redefining Economic and Business Models

A key aspect of long-term sustainability is the transition from a linear to a circular economy, where products, materials, and resources remain in use for as long as possible. Businesses must adopt models that prioritize durability, reuse, remanufacturing, and recycling, reducing their reliance on virgin resources. Innovations such as product-as-a-service, extended producer responsibility (EPR), and industrial symbiosis play a crucial role in minimizing waste and promoting resource efficiency. Governments must support this shift by implementing policies that incentivize sustainable business practices, such as tax benefits for circular enterprises, eco-design regulations, and green financing mechanisms that encourage investment in circular solutions.

Advancing Technological and Infrastructure Development

Long-term sustainability depends on technological advancements that enhance resource efficiency, renewable energy integration, and waste reduction. The adoption of digital technologies such as artificial intelligence, blockchain, and digital twins can optimize supply chains, improve material tracking, and support sustainable decision-making. Investment in infrastructure is equally critical, particularly in waste management, renewable energy systems, and sustainable urban planning. Governments and businesses must collaborate to develop resilient infrastructure that supports circular economies, such as advanced recycling facilities, decentralized energy grids, and smart transportation systems that reduce emissions and waste.

Policy and Governance for Systemic Change

Transforming economic and environmental systems requires strong governance and regulatory frameworks that encourage sustainable practices. Policymakers play a critical role in setting long-term sustainability goals, enforcing environmental standards, and ensuring accountability among industries. International cooperation is also necessary to align policies, reduce regulatory barriers, and promote global sustainability initiatives. The adoption of international sustainability standards, such as the United Nations Sustainable Development Goals (SDGs), the Global Reporting Initiative (GRI), and circular economy roadmaps, helps create a cohesive and effective approach to long-term sustainability.

Shaping Consumer Behavior and Cultural Change

Sustainability is not solely driven by businesses and governments; it requires widespread participation from consumers. Behavior change is essential to shift purchasing habits, encourage waste reduction, and promote the adoption of circular practices such as sharing, repairing, and reusing. Education, awareness campaigns, and incentives can help drive this transformation, making sustainable choices more accessible and appealing. Businesses must also play a role by designing products and services that align with sustainability principles while maintaining affordability and convenience. Encouraging social norms that value sustainability over disposability is crucial for long-term systems change.

CHAPTER

Appendices 11

11.1 GLOSSARY OF CIRCULAR ECONOMY TERMS

Bioeconomy: An economic system that uses renewable biological resources, such as plants and organic waste, to produce food, materials, and energy.

Biodegradable: A material capable of breaking down naturally into non-toxic components through biological processes.

Bioplastics: Plastics made from renewable sources such as corn starch, sugarcane, or algae, rather than fossil fuels.

Carbon Footprint: The total amount of greenhouse gas emissions produced directly and indirectly by an individual, organization, or product.

Circular Business Model: A business approach that prioritizes resource efficiency, waste reduction, and product longevity by incorporating principles such as reuse, remanufacturing, and recycling.

Circular Economy: An economic system aimed at eliminating waste and maximizing resource efficiency by keeping products, materials, and resources in continuous use.

Closed-Loop System: A production and consumption model where materials and products are continuously recycled, remanufactured, or reused without generating waste.

Cradle-to-Cradle (C2C): A sustainable design philosophy that ensures products are designed to be fully recyclable or biodegradable at the end of their lifecycle.

Downcycling: The process of recycling a material into a lower-quality product, often with reduced functionality or lifespan.

Eco-Design: The practice of designing products with sustainability in mind, focusing on reducing environmental impact throughout their lifecycle.

Extended Producer Responsibility (EPR): A policy approach where manufacturers are responsible for the entire lifecycle of their products, including end-of-life management.

Greenwashing: A deceptive marketing practice where a company falsely claims or exaggerates its environmental efforts to appear more sustainable.

Industrial Symbiosis: A collaborative approach where businesses in different industries share waste, byproducts, or resources to improve efficiency and reduce environmental impact.

Life Cycle Assessment (LCA): A method for evaluating the environmental impact of a product, process, or service throughout its entire life cycle.

Material Recovery: The process of extracting and reusing materials from waste products instead of discarding them.

Product-as-a-Service (PaaS): A business model where customers lease or rent a product instead of owning it, ensuring that companies retain responsibility for maintenance, repair, and recycling.

Remanufacturing: The process of refurbishing used products or components to restore them to their original functionality and quality.

Renewable Energy: Energy generated from naturally replenishing sources such as solar, wind, hydro, and geothermal power.

Reverse Logistics: A supply chain process where products and materials are returned for reuse, refurbishment, recycling, or proper disposal.

Sharing Economy: An economic model based on peer-to-peer sharing of goods and services to maximize resource efficiency, such as car-sharing or tool rental services.

Take-Back Scheme: A program where manufacturers or retailers collect used products from consumers for recycling, refurbishment, or safe disposal.

Upcycling: The process of creatively repurposing waste materials or discarded products into items of equal or higher value.

Waste-to-Energy (WTE): A process that converts waste materials into usable energy, such as electricity or heat, through combustion or other technologies.

11.2 RECOMMENDED RESOURCES FOR CIRCULAR ECONOMY PRACTICES

- **Circulytics by Ellen MacArthur Foundation** A digital tool that measures circularity performance in businesses.
- **Coursera – Circular Economy: Introduction & Principles** Free and paid courses from institutions like Delft University of Technology on circular design and business models.

- **Cradle to Cradle: Remaking the Way We Make Things – William McDonough & Michael Braungart** A foundational book on circular design, advocating for regenerative systems that eliminate waste.
- **Doughnut Economics: Seven Ways to Think Like a 21st-Century Economist – Kate Raworth** Challenges traditional economic thinking and proposes a framework balancing economic growth with planetary boundaries.
- **edX – Circular Economy for a Sustainable Future** Courses from top universities on sustainable design, material recovery, and circular supply chains.
- **Ellen MacArthur Foundation** A leading nonprofit driving circular economy innovation and business adoption.
- **Ellen MacArthur Foundation Learning Hub** Online courses, case studies, and interactive tools for understanding circular economy principles.
- **Ellen MacArthur Foundation Reports** Completing the Picture: How the Circular Economy Tackles Climate Change Circular Economy in Cities The New Plastics Economy
- **European Union Circular Economy Action Plan** A policy roadmap detailing how the EU is transitioning to a circular economy through regulation, innovation, and incentives.
- **Global Reporting Initiative (GRI) Standards** Provides sustainability reporting frameworks, including circular economy indicators.
- **ICLEI – Local Governments for Sustainability** Focuses on circular economy initiatives at local and regional levels.
- **Life Cycle Assessment (LCA) Software SimaPro GaBi OpenLCA**
- **LinkedIn Learning – Sustainable Business Strategy & Circular Economy** Short courses for professionals looking to integrate circular economy practices into business strategies.
- **Material Flow Analysis (MFA) Tools** Used for tracking resources, waste streams, and efficiency improvements in circular production.
- **MIT OpenCourseWare – Sustainability & Circular Economy** Free lecture materials from MIT on sustainability, industrial ecology, and circular business strategies.
- **OECD Circular Economy Policy Papers** Analyzes circular economy policies, focusing on economic, social, and environmental impacts.

- **Platform for Accelerating the Circular Economy (PACE)** A collaboration of businesses, governments, and NGOs working on circular economy initiatives.
- **The Blue Economy: 10 Years, 100 Innovations, 100 Million Jobs – Gunter Pauli** Introduces innovative, nature-inspired business models that align with circular economy principles.
- **The Circular Economy Club (CEC)** A global network of professionals working to advance circular economy practices.
- **The Circular Economy: A Wealth of Flows – Ken Webster** Explores the economic and environmental benefits of circular systems, emphasizing system thinking and innovation.
- **United Nations Environment Programme (UNEP) Circularity Reports** Insights on global circular economy trends, waste management strategies, and policy recommendations.
- **Waste to Wealth: The Circular Economy Advantage – Peter Lacy & Jakob Rutqvist** Provides case studies and strategies showing how businesses can transition to circular models for financial and environmental gains.
- **World Business Council for Sustainable Development (WBCSD)** Helps companies implement sustainability and circular business models.
- **World Economic Forum Circular Economy Reports** Covers industry-specific circular strategies, including sustainable fashion, e-waste, and closed-loop production.

11.3 KEY ORGANIZATIONS AND RESEARCH INSTITUTES IN CIRCULAR ECONOMY

Global Organizations

- **Ellen MacArthur Foundation (EMF)** : A leading nonprofit dedicated to accelerating the transition to a circular economy. EMF works with businesses, governments, and academia to develop research, frameworks, and initiatives that promote sustainability and circularity.
- **United Nations Environment Programme (UNEP)** : UNEP plays a crucial role in global circular economy policy development, providing reports, guidelines, and initiatives that help nations transition toward sustainable resource use.
- **World Economic Forum (WEF) – Circular Economy Initiative** : The WEF actively promotes circularity through its reports, multi-stakeholder

initiatives, and collaborations with businesses and policymakers to advance sustainable economic models.

- **Organisation for Economic Co-operation and Development (OECD) :** OECD provides research, policy recommendations, and case studies on how circular economy principles can be integrated into economic and industrial policies.
- **World Business Council for Sustainable Development (WBCSD) :** A coalition of global businesses working on sustainability and circularity strategies through collaborative projects, corporate guidelines, and research reports.
- **Platform for Accelerating the Circular Economy (PACE) :** A global initiative that brings together businesses, governments, and research institutions to accelerate circular economy solutions.
- **European Environment Agency (EEA) :** The EEA provides research, policy insights, and environmental data on the implementation of circular economy strategies in the European Union.
- **European Circular Economy Stakeholder Platform (ECESP) :** A joint initiative of the European Commission and the European Economic and Social Committee (EESC), acting as a hub for circular economy knowledge and best practices.
- **The Dutch Circular Economy Program :** The Netherlands is a global leader in circular economy initiatives, with government-supported programs focusing on waste reduction, sustainable innovation, and circular business models.
- **Chatham House – The Royal Institute of International Affairs :** A leading think tank conducting research on international circular economy policies and resource efficiency strategies.

North American Organizations

- **Circular Economy Leadership Canada (CELC) :** A Canadian initiative fostering collaboration among businesses, governments, and research institutions to promote circular practices.
- **National Renewable Energy Laboratory (NREL) :** A U.S. government research center focused on energy efficiency, sustainable materials, and circular economy innovations.
- **The Recycling Partnership :** A U.S.-based nonprofit working with industries and governments to enhance recycling infrastructure and circular material use.

- **The U.S. Chamber of Commerce Foundation – Circular Economy Program** : Focuses on business-driven solutions for waste reduction, sustainable supply chains, and closed-loop production systems.

Asia-Pacific Organizations

- **Asia Pacific Roundtable for Sustainable Consumption and Production (APRSCP)** : A regional platform promoting sustainable consumption, production, and circular economy strategies across Asia-Pacific.
- **China Association of Circular Economy (CACE)** : A leading Chinese organization that supports the implementation of circular economy policies and industrial symbiosis.
- **Japan's Circular Economy Vision 2020** : The Japanese government's strategic framework for resource efficiency, industrial sustainability, and circular manufacturing.
- **The Australian Circular Economy Hub (ACE Hub)** : Australia's leading knowledge-sharing platform on circular economy policies, business innovations, and sustainability research.

Latin America and Africa Organizations

- **Latin American Circular Economy Coalition** : A regional initiative supported by the United Nations Economic Commission for Latin America and the Caribbean (ECLAC) to advance circular policies and business models.
- **African Circular Economy Network (ACEN)** : A platform connecting businesses, governments, and communities to promote circular economy practices in Africa.
- **The African Development Bank (AfDB) Circular Economy Program** : Supports circular economy projects in African countries by financing sustainable infrastructure, energy systems, and industrial innovation.

Leading Research Institutes and Universities

- **Circular Economy Research Center (CERC) – Ecole des Ponts Business School (France)** : A dedicated research institute studying circular business models, sustainable materials, and industrial transformation.
- **Ellen MacArthur Foundation Research Program (UK):** The research arm of the Ellen MacArthur Foundation, working with academic institutions and businesses to advance circular economy knowledge.

- **The University of Exeter – Circular Economy Hub (UK)** : A leading university research center focusing on circular innovation, business models, and resource efficiency.
- **TU Delft – Circular Built Environment (Netherlands)** : Conducts research on sustainable architecture, circular construction, and industrial ecology.
- **MIT–EnvironmentalSolutionsInitiative(USA)**:MIT'sinterdisciplinary research program focusing on circularity in manufacturing, energy systems, and digital technologies.
- **The World Resources Institute (WRI)** : A global research organization that provides data-driven insights and solutions for circular economy transitions.
- **The Stockholm Environment Institute (SEI)** : Conducts research on sustainable resource management, circular economy metrics, and climate-resilient systems.
- **Fraunhofer Institute for Environmental, Safety, and Energy Technology (Germany)** : A major European research institute specializing in sustainable production, materials innovation, and waste reduction.
- **The Indian Institute for Sustainable Development (IISD)**: Focuses on sustainable policies, circular business models, and green technology research in India.

11.4 CASE STUDIES ON SUCCESSFUL CIRCULAR ECONOMY INITIATIVES

These case studies demonstrate how companies, governments, and industries are successfully implementing circular economy principles across various sectors. From remanufacturing and waste-to-energy projects to reusable packaging and industrial symbiosis, these initiatives showcase the economic and environmental benefits of circular business models.

Philips: Circular Lighting Solutions

Philips, a global leader in lighting, has transitioned from a traditional product sales model to a service-based approach known as "Lighting as a Service" (LaaS). Instead of selling lightbulbs, Philips provides lighting solutions where customers pay for light usage while Philips retains ownership of the lighting infrastructure. This model ensures product longevity, efficient maintenance, and the recycling of components at the end of their life cycle. The initiative has been implemented in airports, offices, and municipalities worldwide, reducing material waste and promoting resource efficiency.

Renault: Automotive Remanufacturing

French automobile manufacturer Renault operates a circular economy initiative at its Choisy-le-Roi plant, specializing in remanufacturing used car parts, including engines, transmissions, and fuel injectors. Instead of discarding damaged components, Renault refurbishes them to meet original specifications, reducing waste and raw material consumption. This initiative has resulted in a 70% reduction in energy use and an 80% decrease in raw material consumption compared to producing new parts.

Patagonia: Worn Wear Program

Outdoor apparel brand Patagonia has pioneered a circular economy approach through its Worn Wear Program, which encourages customers to repair, reuse, and recycle their clothing. The company provides free repair services, sells second-hand Patagonia gear, and offers trade-in discounts for used clothing. This model extends the lifespan of products, reduces textile waste, and minimizes the environmental footprint of the fashion industry.

Interface: Closing the Loop in Carpet Manufacturing

Interface, a global carpet tile manufacturer, has embraced a circular business model by developing a closed-loop recycling system. Through its ReEntry® Program, Interface collects old carpet tiles, separates materials, and reprocesses them into new products. The company's Net-Works™ initiative sources discarded fishing nets from coastal communities, converting them into sustainable carpet materials. These efforts significantly reduce waste, conserve natural resources, and provide economic opportunities for communities.

Loop by TerraCycle: Reusable Packaging Model

Loop, an initiative by TerraCycle, partners with major brands such as Unilever, Nestlé, and Procter & Gamble to offer zero-waste packaging solutions. Customers purchase products in durable, reusable containers that are returned, cleaned, and refilled after use. This system eliminates single-use packaging waste and promotes a circular supply chain for household goods, cosmetics, and food products.

Sweden's Recycling Revolution: Waste-to-Energy Success

Sweden has established one of the most efficient waste-to-energy systems globally, with less than 1% of household waste ending up in landfills. The country converts waste into energy through advanced incineration plants, generating heat and electricity for homes and businesses. Additionally, Sweden imports waste from other countries to fuel its energy plants, demonstrating a circular economy model that maximizes waste utilization while reducing reliance on fossil fuels.

Adidas: Parley for the Oceans Initiative

Adidas has collaborated with environmental organization Parley for the Oceans to produce high-performance sportswear made from recycled ocean plastics. The initiative transforms marine plastic waste into eco-friendly shoes and clothing, reducing plastic pollution while demonstrating a successful circular material flow in the fashion industry. Adidas aims to eliminate virgin plastic use in its products by 2024.

Kalundborg Symbiosis: Industrial Circularity in Denmark

Kalundborg, Denmark, is home to one of the world's most successful industrial symbiosis models, where companies from different sectors share resources, energy, and waste materials. The collaboration between power plants, pharmaceutical companies, and other industries ensures that one company's waste becomes another's raw material. This reduces costs, minimizes environmental impact, and optimizes resource efficiency, serving as a global model for circular industrial ecosystems.

Veolia: Circular Water Management

Veolia, a global leader in water and waste management, has implemented circular economy principles in water treatment and resource recovery. In France, Veolia operates recycling plants that recover phosphorus from wastewater, a critical nutrient used in agriculture. This process prevents environmental pollution while ensuring a sustainable supply of essential materials.

IKEA: Furniture Take-Back and Recycling

IKEA has committed to becoming a fully circular business by 2030 through initiatives such as its Furniture Take-Back Program, where customers can return used furniture for resale, refurbishment, or recycling. The company is also investing in designing modular, repairable, and recyclable furniture to extend product lifespans and minimize waste.

References

A Monetary History of the United States, 1867–1960, *Authors:* Milton Friedman and Anna J. Schwartz *Publisher:* Princeton University Press *Publication Year:* 1963

An Inquiry into the Nature and Causes of the Wealth of Nations, *Author:* Adam Smith *Publisher:* W. Strahan and T. Cadell *Publication Year:* 1776

Capitalism and Freedom, *Author:* Milton Friedman *Publisher:* University of Chicago Press *Publication Year:* 1962

Circular Economy and Sustainability: Volume 3: Environmental Engineering, Editors: Jorge Luis García-Alcaraz, Diego Tlapa, and Guillermo Cortes-Robles Publisher: Springer Publication Year: 2020

Circular Economy and Sustainable Development: A Necessary Nexus for a Sustainable Future, Authors: Wolfgang Lehmacher and Johann Bödecker Publisher: Springer Gabler Publication Year: 2024

Circular Economy in Textiles and Apparel, Editor: Subramanian Senthilkannan Muthu Publisher: Woodhead Publishing Publication Year: 2018

Circular Economy in the European Union, Author: Sepp Eisenriegler Publisher: Springer Publication Year: 2020

Circular Economy: 7. Industrielle Revolution: Der Weg zu mehr Nachhaltigkeit durch Kreislaufwirtschaft, Authors: Wolfgang Lehmacher and Johann Bödecker Publisher: Springer Gabler Publication Year: 2023

Circular Economy: Challenges and Opportunities for Ethical and Sustainable Business, Editors: Helen Kopnina and Kim Poldner Publisher: Routledge Publication Year: 2021

Circular Economy: Economic and Policy Implications, Author: Mika Sillanpää Publisher: Elsevier Publication Year: 2019

Circular Economy: Global Perspective, Editor: Rashid M. Hassan Publisher: Springer Publication Year: 2020

Circular Economy: Recent Trends in Global Perspective, Editors: Sadhan Kumar Ghosh, Masuduzzaman Bakaul, and R. M. Bhatt Publisher: Springer Publication Year: 2021

Cradle to Cradle: Remaking the Way We Make Things, Authors: William McDonough and Michael Braungart Publisher: North Point Press Publication Year: 2002

Das Kapital, *Author:* Karl Marx *Publisher:* Verlag von Otto Meisner *Publication Year:* 1867

Designing for the Circular Economy, Editor: Martin Charter Publisher: Routledge Publication Year: 2018

Maritime Decarbonization: Practical Tools, Case Studies and Decarbonization Enablers, Editors: Wolfgang Lehmacher and others Publisher: Springer Gabler Publication Year: 2023

Material Concerns: Pollution, Profit and Quality of Life, Author: Tim Jackson Publisher: Routledge Publication Year: 1996

Principles of Economics, *Author:* Alfred Marshall *Publisher:* Macmillan and Co. *Publication Year:* 1890

Principles of Political Economy and Taxation, *Author:* David Ricardo *Publisher:* John Murray *Publication Year:* 1817

The Affluent Society, *Author:* John Kenneth Galbraith *Publisher:* Houghton Mifflin *Publication Year:* 1958

The Circular Economy and the Global South: Sustainable Lifestyles and Green Industrial Development, Editors: Patrick Schröder, Manisha Anantharaman, Kartika Anggraeni, and Tim Foxon Publisher: Routledge Publication Year: 2019

The Circular Economy Handbook: Realizing the Circular Advantage, Authors: Peter Lacy, Jessica Long, and Wesley Spindler Publisher: Palgrave Macmillan Publication Year: 2019

The Circular Economy in the European Union: An Interim Review, Author: Sepp Eisenriegler Publisher: Springer Publication Year: 2020

The Circular Economy: A Wealth of Flows, Author: Ken Webster Publisher: Ellen MacArthur Foundation Publishing Publication Year: 2015

The Circular Economy: Case Studies about the Transition from the Linear Economy, Editors: Helen Kopnina and Eleanor Shoreman-Ouimet Publisher: Routledge Publication Year: 2018

The General Theory of Employment, Interest, and Money, *Author:* John Maynard Keynes *Publisher:* Palgrave Macmillan *Publication Year:* 1936

The Road to Serfdom, *Author:* Friedrich A. Hayek *Publisher:* University of Chicago Press *Publication Year:* 1944

The Theory of Moral Sentiments, *Author:* Adam Smith *Publisher:* A. Millar *Publication Year:* 1759

The Theory of the Leisure Class, *Author:* Thorstein Veblen *Publisher:* Macmillan *Publication Year:* 1899

The Upcycle: Beyond Sustainability—Designing for Abundance, Authors: William McDonough and Michael Braungart Publisher: North Point Press Publication Year: 2013

The Wealth of Nations, *Author:* Adam Smith *Publisher:* CreateSpace Independent Publishing Platform *Publication Year:* 2014

Waste to Wealth: The Circular Economy Advantage, Authors: Peter Lacy and Jakob Rutqvist Publisher: Palgrave Macmillan Publication Year: 2015

Index

www.ingramcontent.com/pod-product-compliance
Lightning Source LLC
LaVergne TN
LVHW071245210926
848486LV00008B/348